THIRD REALITY:
Crafting a 21st Century Latino Agenda

By Ernesto Nieto

Third Reality Publications, Maxwell, Texas

Copyright © 2014. Ernesto Nieto.

Third Reality: Crafting a 21st Century Latino Agenda

Copyright © 2014 by Ernesto Nieto

All rights reserved. No part of this book may be reproduced or utilized in any form or by any means, electronic or mechanical, including photocopying, recording, or by any information storage and retrieval system without written permission from the Publisher. Inquiries should be addressed to Third Reality Publications, P.O. Box 220, Maxwell, Texas 78656.

First Edition 2001
First Printing 2001
Second Printing 2002
Third Printing 2004
Fourth Printing 2007
Fifth Printing 2011
Sixth Printing 2014

Library of Congress Catalog Card Number: 2001091113

Dedication

It's taken me a long time to write this book. Working sixteen hour days and then coming home every evening to spend several more hours hovered over a computer is not the way a book should be written. Something inside of me, however, saw me through. I had ideas to express and time was the only obstacle between getting my thoughts on paper or forever allowing them to remain permanently sealed in my head.

I cannot adequately thank Gloria de Leon, my wife, for constantly challenging me to not give up, and for making me feel that my thoughts were worth reading, worth the countless hours that many times were required to chain together a simple concept.

To Chris, Roy, Marc, and Nicole, my four children: They have been the joy and inspiration for my work. This book is a collection of stories that started with their grandparents – my father, Santos, and my mother, Esther, - two individuals who gave so much to others though life gave them so little. Their work lives in me. It continues to live in the work of my children and will live on in the lives of my grandchildren to come. And who could ever say enough about "Uncle Louie," Albert Nieto? His example of giving purely to share his gifts with others is what life is all about. I thank him for his support and especially for being my brother.

And to all the 90,000 Latino youth who have allowed me the pleasure of looking at the future through their eyes. I can never express enough gratitude to them for letting me be a small part of their lives. I sincerely hope that this book accurately reflects what together we see in tomorrow.

Contents

	Dedication	3
	Preface	5
	Introduction	7
Chapter 1	Legacy of Family	9
Chapter 2	Winds of Darkness	22
Chapter 3	Loss of Innocence	28
Chapter 4	Conflicts in Identity	42
Chapter 5	Tejano Millionaires	52
Chapter 6	Potomac Fever	60
Chapter 7	Lonely Road Back	66
Chapter 8	Proceed Only on Faith	78
Chapter 9	The Turmoil of Change	85
Chapter 10	The Will to Endure	92
Chapter 11	The House on the Hill	100
Chapter 12	Let the Ship Sink	107
Chapter 13	Conflicts Within	113
Chapter 14	Responsibility for the New	120
Chapter 15	Freeing the Mind	129
	Epilogue	140

Preface

This book had to be written. It's not a scholarly depiction of Latinos in the United States. It's also not based on a study about Latinos that required long hours of research. To the contrary, it's a story that revolves around actual accounts of individuals who lived life the way it was handed to them and attempted to cope in the best ways they knew.

Unlike European immigrants who came into the United States by the millions during the 1900s, Latinos in the nation were not welcomed, embraced, or integrated into the American experience. Their sole purpose was harvesting the fields of large business interests. They were America's low-wage earners, toiling for pennies an hour in the assembly plants of a growing industrial complex. They weren't invited in to be educated, given opportunities to succeed and contribute, or seen as citizens who represented value to our nation's needs and aspirations. If anything, Latinos in the United States were used and exploited, influenced to believe that "bootstrapping" – starting from the bottom – was the "American Way," the means to achieve success in a highly competitive society.

This book depicts those early times, the human suffering experienced by not just a few Latinos in the United States, but by millions. In the 1920s, 1930s, and 1940s, it didn't matter whether a person was Mexican, Mexican American, Puerto Rican, Cuban, or otherwise. Being Latino meant being seen as a foreigner in your own country, ridiculed, excluded, and made to feel unimportant.

Contrary to popular opinion, racial discrimination was not common to all immigrants. Latinos were viewed as threatening the racial stock of the Europeans, as having the potential to "mongrelize" other more attractive ethnic cultures that were being melted into a strong, better American model.

This account touches on those realities and the ways in which Latinos attempted to cope. It also describes how the long-standing tensions of those times eventually erupted into "El Movimiento" (The Chicano Movement) of the 1960s, a period depicted by social unrest that also saw thousands of high school Latino youths start voicing long-overdue concerns regarding equity and social justice. For the first time in U.S. Latino history, the beliefs that had driven Latinos throughout the 1900s began to change as a new generation of leaders started to broaden an opportunity structure that for so many years had its doors open for only the select few.

The question today and in the future is whether or not an activist thinking that was borne out of the Chicano era continues to be valid in a changing twenty-first century world. An equally important issue is whether the training of future Latino leaders should be driven by a continuing need for social reform and advocacy or perhaps should be based on an altogether different outlook and model. These were the ideas that my father, mother, and I used to spend hours discussing in our backyard in Houston. It was these same questions that also confronted Gloria and me when first starting the National Hispanic Institute in 1979. It was the need to create different answers that kept me awake at night searching for new and better ways of working with our future leaders.

This book chronicles a journey. It shares feelings, describes events, pinpoints personal setbacks and disappointments, and draws attention to the challenges that our youths will face in the years ahead. More importantly, it draws comparisons between conditions that compelled past leaders to act and the comforts many of our future twenty-first century spokespersons enjoy that may influence how they feel towards Latinos as a whole.

In the final analysis, the book spends little time complaining about the past or pointing fingers at others. Instead it provides us with a mirror through which we may individually and collectively raise questions about which directions we should consider as we come to particular crossroads in our community's journey.

Should we surrender to the omnipresence of mainstream culture and merely attempt to fit in, whatever the costs to our identity as community and culture? Should we continue the fight for social justice and reform?

Or is there a third choice, a third reality?

These have been lingering questions not only in my mind, but, as I came to find out in my discussions with friends and colleagues, in the private thinking of many others. I can never thank enough those special friends like Mary Helen Gonzales who read my early drafts and gave me critical feedback, and especially Francisco "Paco" Gonzales and his brother, Calistro, for being part of these discussions and editing the early drafts of this book.

To my mentor, Sam Moreno of Dallas, gracias for helping me puzzle together the many influences that shape the individual, especially when it comes to our spiritual beliefs. To Dr. Daniel Garcia and Elizabeth Barraza, I extend thanks for their personal assistance.

The same has to be said to Father Jack Minogue, president of DePaul University in Chicago, for his encouragement and for making me feel that our efforts at the Institute are important breakthroughs in Latino thinking.

Ultimately, however, everything goes back to Gloria de Leon who made me feel special enough to write this book. Gloria represents millions of Latinas out there in the world who continue to hold our culture together, and who make us feel whole and complete in a world of constant challenges and changes. They remind us to be proud of our accomplishments, but never to the extent of forgetting either our past or the directions we must take as we move forward into the future.

Ernesto Nieto
President and Founder
National Hispanic Institute
Maxwell, Texas
June 2001

Introduction

"The unexamined life is not worth living (Socrates)"

Ernesto Nieto's autobiography, <u>Third Reality</u>, is an outstanding reflection of the experiences that influenced the direction he has, thus far, chosen to take during his life's journey. Ernesto does far more than simply describe personal, family, social, political, and cultural events that merely happened to or around him. He also reflects deeply on the personal meaning he attributed to those events and he shares his hopes and fears about how these events influenced his aspirations and dreams. Ernesto analyzes these events with particular attention to their implications for himself, his wife and life partner, Gloria de Leon, his children, his relatives and friends, the national and international communities of Latinos and Latinas, and the National Hispanic Institute.

Indeed, Ernesto has written a model for enhancing his self-reflective awareness through which he enabled himself to make informed decisions about how, where, and with whom he wanted to live his life. Each chapter describes a different phase of Ernesto's life building upon his previous phases and serving as the foundation for the next phase. Each chapter has the emotional and intellectual impact to stimulate similar self-reflection for you, the readers of this unique book.

In great detail, Ernesto describes his process of creating - and recreating - the world in which he wants to live. He experiences and makes some sense out of his early years with the gentle assistance of his loving and caring parents. He experiences profound dissatisfaction with the world, as it currently exists for him. He scans the environment and identifies opportunities that may benefit him. He sets goals, makes plans, and executes those plans to achieve his goals. This requires him to move beyond the familiar, comfortable world in which he grew up and into a new world that challenges his existing knowledge and problem-solving skills. The new world - e.g., college life - has an unfamiliar culture, different values and belief systems, people who do not look or talk like him, and vague pathways to achievement and recognition. In effect, he was like a rat that had to run a maze in a psychological experiment in order to reach the cheese. he has to learn how to run this - and many other - unfamiliar social and organizational mazes that were constructed by people who were quite different than him. His beliefs about the way people should treat him and how he should behave in order to be successful and accepted do not entirely work as well as he expected. He experiences confusion, disappointment, self-doubt, and anger. He challenges himself: "What did I expect?" So, he analyzes his assumption and expectations. He revisits his goals and plans, modifying them on the basis of what he has learned about the new world and about himself - he reflects and gains clarity about what he thinks and how he feels and how his thoughts and feelings influence his actions. He recognizes that he may easily fail to survive in this new world and that he could choose the easier path - that is, he could withdraw from this strange new world and return to the comfort and safety of his familiar world. But, he chooses to take the risks involved in moving forward. He discovers the meaning of courage - that is, to acknowledge his fear and still do what he believes is the right thing to do. He increases his capacity to enhance his effectiveness; he is successful. He moves on to new challenges as a college graduate. He works in various roles in public service and, as measured by status and salary, he is successful and learns a great deal about institutional discrimination. But, when he encounters the predictable surprise of being a political employee who is laid off as a consequence of a change in government administration, once again he experiences the cycle of confusion, disappointment, self-doubt, and anger. He has lost what he thought was an opportunity to fulfill his purpose. He searches inwardly and in his environment. He discovers a great deal of information and insight that he had not known he did not know. He seeks the wisdom of his parents, mentors, and Tejano millionaires. He reassesses his beliefs, his values, his vision, and goals for the future. Once again, he courageously takes risks, starts NHI, makes many sacrifices, and, over time, overcomes considerable difficulties and is successful. But the world kept changing. So he discovers that what got him and NHI where they are will not keep them successful. Once again, he has to reassess, reevaluate, and reinvent himself and his organization.

In effect, Ernesto discovers that his life is a series of temporary realities and that there is no finish line. His life is a never-ending series of reiterative cycles of scanning, reflecting, analyzing, learning, planning, executing, assessing results, and reevaluating.

Ernesto's reflections and analyses stimulated many challenging questions for me. They will, I am sure, challenge you as well. I have composed a number of questions for you to ask yourself after reading each chapter. To derive maximum value from these questions, you will find it useful to buy a notebook to use as a personal journal. I suggest that you write down your responses to these questions, chapter by chapter, in sequence. So, buy a large notebook. I believe your journal will prove to be extremely valuable for you in the present as well as the months and years to come as you make consequential life decisions and, like Ernesto, as you learn your way into the process of creating your future.

Arthur M. Freedman, MBA, PhD

Arthur Freedman is a life-long friend of Ernesto Nieto. In various circles of American psychologists, he is considered an outstanding professional with extensive experience in teaching graduate students at different universities and consulting both national and internationally. Throughout his professional life, Arthur has remained close to both Ernesto and his wife, Gloria de Leon, often involved in long hours of conversation regarding the work and direction of the National Hispanic Institute. More recently he has been consulting with the Institute on board development and has agreed to become a founding member, along with Ernesto and Gloria, in furthering the work and influence of NHI by establishing the Centre for Latino Leadership Development.

In developing a training format to assist students in studying Ernesto Nieto's book entitled, Third Reality: Crafting a 21st Century Latino Agenda, Arthur uses critical questions for self reflection and self awareness.

Chapter One
Legacy of Family

The story of the National Hispanic Institute (NHI) doesn't start on July 20, 1979, the day of its incorporation. It begins sometime between 1903, the year my father was born, and 1940, the year of my birth.

Perhaps the idea for an institute for Latinos started before anyone of us was around. My father used to say that the work we did in the community as a family came from a higher calling. Sometimes he explained our abilities to attract youth as something spiritual, a gift beyond our understanding.

"El saber como trabajar en la comunidad," he would say, *"viene desde allá, antes que tú nacieras.* (Knowing how to work with the community comes from way before you, even before you were born.) *Es algo que traemos en las venas de tiempos pasados, un don que Dios nos dio.* (It's something inside our veins from the past, a special gift from God.) *Lo traigo yo. Lo treas tú y lo trairán tus hijos y tus nietos. Quién sabe como pasó esto, pero no intentes comprenderlo y acéptalo.* (I have it. You have it and so will your grandchildren. Who knows how this came to pass, but don't try to understand. Just accept it.)"

It didn't occur to me back then that those late night talks with my mother and father would eventually shape the perception of my life's work.

Growing up in Houston, Texas, in the 1940s, I didn't view Esther and Santos Nieto as different or a couple with a higher calling. Like most other parents, they made the rules and supervised my two brothers and me. They were our protectors and the two individuals who wielded power over our lives. As we grew older, we thought they seemed old-fashioned and a little out of touch with our youthful realities. When doling out punishments, their dosages always seemed much tougher than the small mistakes we committed.

Each morning, they were up by the crack of dawn. They worked like sharply honed clocks to make sure that Albert and Roy got up in time for school. Albert was the oldest. Tall and skinny with jet-black hair, his complexion was fair in comparison to my middle brother and me. Albert worked hard to make good grades in school and eagerly looked forward to being the student crossing guard at Looscan Elementary School. He enjoyed the authority that came with making cars stop when children on their way to school had to cross the street.

Roy was shorter and darker. He got more of my father's genes. He had a strong resemblance to dad. As a baby, the older cousins who took care of us on weekends called him "Chi Chi Roy." He enjoyed the attention he got from cutting up in front of others. He was the one with the personality and a flair for attracting attention.

I was the youngest of the three boys. Like Albert, I was tall for my age and maybe even thinner. Although we looked more like my mother's side of the family, Dad's sister, Tía Feliz, claimed that I looked like my *abuelito* (grandfather), Donaciano Nieto.

No one in the Nieto family was allowed to sleep late on weekends. Mom and Dad worked as a team. When she cooked, he washed dishes. When she washed clothes, he mopped floors or worked in the yard. Often, he'd spent hours fixing our one family car that always seemed to need one repair or another.

As the little one around the house, I was his assistant mechanic, handing him wrenches and adjusting the outside light so he could get a closer look at a transmission, motor, or brakes. The scent of burnt oil and grease was always present along with Dad's stern voice: *"No mueva la luz. ¡Ponga atención!"* (Don't move the light. Pay attention!) For the most part Dad never used profanity around us, but, sometimes, when a hot engine burned his hand, a "dammit" could be heard blurted from under his breath.

This was a slice of life in deep Northside Houston in the early 1940s. Being part of the Nieto family meant pitching in. Complaints were prohibited. Responsibility was demanded. When Mom left us alone at home to go shopping, she'd call us together to remind us of the house rules.

"*Alberto, tú te encargas de Roy,*" she would say, "*Roy tú ves a Ernesto.* (Albert, you're in charge of Roy. Roy you look after Ernesto.)"

"*¿Y yo mama?* (And what about me, mom?)" I would ask naively, the only one without anyone to supervise.

"*¡Usted mijo,*" she would respond half-smiling, half-serious, "*se encarga de los gatos y los perros!*" (You, my son, you're in charge of the cats and dogs!)"

In our community, people understood the importance of being neighborly. "*Buenos vecinos,*" Mom would say. Borrowing coffee or sugar from other families were common practices.

Weekends were spent helping other married couples with children finish a roof or add a room to their houses. It was a one-step-at-a-time, pay-as-you-go life. These were young Mexican-American families out in rural north Harris County. The neighborhood was nothing more than a scattering of small houses among hundreds of tall pine trees. It was "out in the sticks," as Dad used to say. Some people had horses while others, like our Tía Maria, raised pigs. Hardy Street was the only paved road that cut through the small neighborhood. The rest were dirt roads or grass trails where cars always got stuck after a heavy downpour.

Rey Saldivar, my boyhood friend, and his family lived directly behind us. A large, open vacant area, which also served as our sports field on weekends, separated our two houses. It was there that we learned to play tackle football and ran bases in pickup games of baseball. The Morales family lived a couple blocks away. Mom would describe them as being a *chorro* (unending flood) of kids. Ms. Smith, an elegant Black lady with a ready-made smile and gorgeous gray hair, lived to the front of our house. A ditch, which was used by the neighborhood kids as a community swimming pool after a hard rain, ran between our two houses. Her son, her pride and joy, was a doctor who visited her almost every weekend.

Life was pretty laid back in the Northside. On late Saturday evenings, the Blum family always held choir practice on their front porch for the Black Baptist Church. The melodious sounds of their gospel hymns would at times carry two blocks or more through the stillness of trees. In the cool of the evening, neighbors quietly visited with one another on their backyard porches.

I found listening to older people fascinating. It was interesting to hear them talk about their youth and the hard times they endured. The stories were riveting, almost always about their personal struggles and the setbacks and obstacles they faced.

As a youngster, it was difficult for me to imagine traveling by wagon 100 miles or more from South Texas to pick cotton all summer long in the scorching heat of Seguin, Brookshire, or Hempstead, Texas. It was incomprehensible how it must have felt to my parents or their neighbors going to bed hungry as little children. To these families, having a steady job and a two-bedroom shell was better than sleeping on the floor or in some corner of a crowded boarding house.

This was the way family histories were passed on to the next generation. Books were unnecessary. All that was required was a crowd of wide-eyed, attentive kids listening to stories told by the people who lived them.

Most people walked wherever they went. For us, it was a fourteen-block hike to the nearest bus stop. The only local gathering place was Chonita's Grocery Store that also housed a beer joint in a back room. "*Lugar de viejos borrachos y viejas sin vergüenza,* (A place for drunkards and women without shame,)" Mother would say. Mom had no other way of seeing life. She was born out of wedlock and reared since childhood by a strict and religious grandmother. To her, drinking beer was as immoral as it was for women to be seen in beer joints.

My brothers and I disliked going to Chonita's. The place was dark and menacing, and smelled of old stale beer. After work and on Saturday nights, los conjuntos (Mexican folk music) inside could be heard for blocks around. Cheo, Chonita's husband, ran the place. A tall, burly man who was probably in his late forties, he had a noticeably mean look about him that made us uncomfortable every time Mom sent us to his store for milk or a loaf of bread. We could never leave Chonita's fast enough. Next to him was Smokey, a large German shepherd with a similar stare and disposition. We used to own Smokey, but Dad gave him to Cheo the day he stood up and growled at Mom after she tried to get him off of her freshly made bed. Anyone who got too close to Cheo's chair received a similar growl and snarl.

Chonita's was also a place that caused me to lay awake at night as a child, nervously waiting for Dad to return home. We disliked it when he went there with friends to relax or shoot a game of pool. Barroom fights were frequent. Gunshots could be heard at times. It wasn't unusual to hear squealing tires as cars tore down Hardy Street following a fight. People had been shot or killed there. As a four-year-old, I feared that my father would be arrested or hurt by a faceless drunk. Many times it wouldn't be until after hearing the latch to the backdoor being unlocked and Dad's footsteps that I would finally doze off to sleep. Even Mom getting up to scold him about being out late at dangerous places was music to my ears. To me, Dad was home safe and sound. That was all that mattered. No one had taken him away from us.

Despite being out of the way and lacking the modern conveniences of city life, the Northside was where Dad chose to build our first home. It was a community of young, struggling Mexican-American families where everyone knew one another. Mary Lou Acosta had several girls our age. She was one of Mom's closest neighbors. Her nephew, David Veloz, was in the Navy. He lived right next door to our house. When on furlough, he'd come home with a duffel bag draped over his back. His dress was Navy blue uniform and white cap. David was also our neighborhood hero, someone all of us admired. He taught us baseball, volunteered with the Club Scouts, or spent a Sunday afternoon throwing a football high in the sky to see which one of us was good enough to catch it.

As children, none of us knew war was being waged on the other side of the world against Germany, Italy, and Japan. Mom was close to her nephew, Alfred, and several other older cousins who were serving overseas in the armed forces. She wrote them daily. This was her way of keeping their spirits up. They wanted to know about their moms and dads, their younger brothers and sisters back stateside. They were also hungry for information about their friends, about life in the neighborhood. "Had anything changed at all or was it still the same?" "How was El Juanillo or was La Gloria as good looking as ever?" "Tell everyone I'll be home soon and pray for me." To my cousins, Mom was a beacon of hope, their light at the end of a dark and ominous tunnel.

One day, however, Mother's screaming in the front yard of our house startled us. She stood there, holding a piece of paper in her trembling hands. Something was seriously wrong. Somehow she had gotten a delayed letter from Alfredo Nieto two weeks after we had been notified by the War Department that he had been killed during the invasion in Europe.

World War II was frightening for all of us, an experience constantly filled with human tragedy and sorrow. Thousands of Mexican Americans never came back to their homes and families. Of those who did, many changed for the worse. Being there made them different. It altered life in the United States. While American soldiers were off fighting in distant lands, the war industry back home also stemmed the tide of an economic depression. Warships and tanks had to be built.

Dad was lucky. After several hours of training, he became a welder. Many times, he worked double shifts at the Houston shipyards. For many there was more work than hours in the day. These changes, however, didn't include most Mexican-American families. Most barely made it from one paycheck to the next. Circumstances forced them to live only on the bare essentials, oftentimes eating rice and beans for days. Mom and Dad understood their despair, their needs. As children, they too had been reared in similar desperate conditions, trapped in an economic hole with no bottom.

For Dad, growing up in Laredo in the early 1900s, survival meant having only a tortilla and butter for supper. *"Se pasaban las semanas,* (Entire weeks would go by,)" he'd remember. He revealed stories of he and his sisters going to bed early to avoid the physical pangs of hunger that accompany young empty stomachs. When they could no longer bear not eating, he and his mother picked the fruit from native cactus plants to make jelly. That was all they had.

Those early life experiences taught Dad to be conservative and frugal. He was never one to spend on foolishness. To the contrary, he took particular pride in saving money whenever he bought anything. He also made it his responsibility to pass these life lessons on to us. He didn't want us to become wasteful. Instead he preferred that we value what we had by taking care of our things.

He taught us these lessons around the kitchen table during supper. Some stories were stories were so tragic and filled with despair that he'd break into tears when reliving the suffering he had to endure. Crying was his way of coping. Mostly, however, his accounts were humorous. There were always lessons for us to learn as children.

The Mexican Revolution of 1910 took place right across the Rio Grande River from his home. It was like a "giant drive-in movie" as he described it. A boy of seven years during that time, he saw it as a form of entertainment. *"Yo y mis hermanas nos sentábamos en las barrancas en este lado par aver el tiroteo como si fuera en el cine,"* (My sisters and I would sit on the cliffs of the river on this side to see the shootout as though being at the movies,) he would say.

"Eran los Villistas contra las fuerzas de Carranza. (It was the Pancho Villa soldiers against the military forces of Carranza.) *A veces llegaban soldados a mi casa para comer y descansar los caballos. Allí estaban, con sus carabinas y pistolas, todos llenos de lodo y sudor. Después se iban otra vez a la guerra."* (Sometimes, soldiers would come over to our home to eat and rest their horses. They would sit with their riffles and guns next to them, their clothes covered with mud and smelly sweat. Afterwards, they'd return back to the war.)

In early 1917, family tragedies forced Dad, then thirteen, to leave Laredo to join his older brother in Houston. His oldest sister, Jesusita, died in the Great Influenza Epidemic of 1917. She left a husband and a six-month-old son behind. Dad's mother, Gregoria Medrano-Nieto, passed away two days later from the same illness.

Dad spent the final evening at his mother's bedside reading her the Bible by candlelight. She couldn't read. Dad never forgot the last moments with his mom, watching her take her final breaths. It was just the two of them alone. *"Ya cuando te pegaba la fiebre, no se quitaba,* (Once you got the fever, it wouldn't go away,)" he'd recall. *"A mí me dejó sordo de un oído.* (The fever left me deaf in one ear.)"

After burying his mother, my father sold the family donkey and bought a train ticket to Houston. The clothes on his back, a suitcase with a blanket, and a dime were his only possessions. With no idea where life was taking him, his only concern was finding a way to survive.

Once there, what he found was a world of tough grown men laying railroad ties for a few cents a day in the suffocating Houston heat. Finding work was everyone's concern, young and old. *"Tenías que hacer todo,"* Dad would recall, *"o te llevaba a la fregada.* (You did anything that made money or you wouldn't be able to make it.)"

In a matter of a few months, he became a jack-of-all-trades. He learned *"carpentería* (carpentry), *plomería* (plumbing), *como empapelar* (how to install wall paper), *construcción* (construction), *y también le entraba de mecánico* (and he also learned about fixing cars)." He was proud that he never stood in a soup line nor sought public assistance during the Great Depression. *"Vendía lata, garras, fierro, lo que fuera para hacer dinero,* (I sold tin, old rags, iron, anything to make money,)" he would remember.

"*La Depresión ya se pasó,* (The Depression already is behind us now),*"* he'd remind us while relaxing around the table after supper. *"Ahora no es nada. ¡Qué ahorita! La tenemos hecha. Duro fue entonces. Todos estabámos fregados. Nadie tenía nada, ni una tortilla para comer. Estaban bien duros los tiempos.* (Today is nothing. We have it made. The really hard times were back then. Everyone was down on their luck. No one had anything, not even a tortilla to eat.)"

Mom's life wasn't much different. Born and reared in a small, rural farming community near Seguin, Texas, her early life involved picking endless rows of cotton form sunrise to sundown. This was life for most Mexican Americans in the early 1920s and 1930s.

Shortly following her mother's second marriage, her stepfather died suddenly of a heart attack while working in the blistering Texas heat. Attending school was not an option for Mom. Instead she helped her mother raise three younger brothers and a sister. She never knew what it meant to be a little girl, to play with dolls, or have friends her age. Her daily schedule allowed only enough time to gather wood for the stove and cook for the hungry men coming in from the fields.

Mom never saw the inside of a classroom until she moved to Houston to live with her grandmother, Ana Maria Reyes. By then, she was almost ten years old. Being the oldest and tallest in her first grade class, she felt uncomfortable and distant. Sunsets were something else she didn't enjoy because they were a reminder of the loneliness she experienced growing up, forced to work every day.

"Tu abuelita, (Your grandmother,)" she'd remind us, tears swelling in her eyes, "used to pick more cotton than the men who worked alongside her. She could go as high as 500 pounds a day, pick an entire cotton bale. *Pobrecita, mi mama. Tuvo una vida muy dura. Sufrío mucho, mi madrecita.* (Poor Mom. She had a very tough life. My mom suffered a lot.)"

Tragedy continued following my parents even after their marriage in 1929, at the start of the Depression. Mom was nineteen. Dad was twenty-six years old. Their first child – Santos, Jr. – died of pneumonia shortly after his second birthday. At the time, the disease was incurable. A year later, Ernestina was born premature and lasted only a few hours. Dad's brother, Mike, gave his newborn son to my parents. Tío Mike's wife, Tía Maria, died in childbirth. Sickly from the start, Danny survived less than a month.

Despite these tragedies, their deep religious faith never wavered. They remained close to church, attended regularly, and sang with the choir. They remained active in community cultural events or helped newly arriving Mexican immigrants adjust to the rough-and-tumble life of Houston.

Several years passed, and then my two older brothers and I came along. My folks weren't only grateful; they were ecstatic! Their prayers had been answered. God had blessed them with children. Their bouts with tragedy, however, made them cautious. Mom constantly took us to the well-baby clinic to make sure that we all had the proper vaccinations and nutrition. She boiled our clothes in hot water to prevent childhood diseases. The house was kept spotless and our meals were always balanced and on time.

Mom's top priority was making us get plenty of rest. Until the time we were twelve years old, everyone was required to be in bed by 9:00 P.M. We were allowed to stay up until 11:00 P.M. only on Fridays. Staying up on Saturdays was out because of Sunday morning services.

With all the care we got, Mom was also concerned about teaching us proper behavior. She wanted us to be respectful of others. *"Ser buenos hijos, respetuosus, y obedientes"* (Being good sons, respectful of others, and obedient) was our family code. This meant complying with certain house rules. On Saturday mornings everyone got up early. By six in the morning Dad was out in the yard mowing the grass or fixing the car. He was up before sunrise, sipping down four or five cups of hot coffee, eating breakfast, and spending quality time talking with Mom. We were allowed to sleep a little later. By seven, she would quietly come in our room and tenderly shake us to get up.

"*Ándale,* (Hurry,)" she would gently whisper, pulling our covers, covering our foreheads with kisses, *"Tienen que aprender a granjear mis hijitos. Si quieren algo después, ya lo granjearon antes.* (Learn to earn your way in advance. If you need something afterwards, you've already earned the right to ask.)"

When we finished our chores, there was always something fun to do as a family. We particularly enjoyed going downtown to window shop and buy inexpensive toys. We regularly watched movies at the Ritz Theater. The main attractions were popular Mexican movie stars like Pedro Infante or Jorge Negrete. Mom gave us each a quarter to buy popcorn, a cold drink, or a tasty dill pickle. She was always careful, however, to get us home early to bathe, iron our clothes, and rest up for church. Of course, as young boys, we weren't particularly excited about bathing.

"*¡Muchachos! Báñense, para que estén listos en la mañana.* (Boys! Take a bath now, so that you're ready by the morning.)" Being the youngest, I always got pushed to the head of the line by my older brothers. Bathing was a ritual. Dad would start by pouring cold well water into a large bucket that Mom heated over a wood-burning stove. No families in the neighborhood back then had indoor plumbing, much less, warm, running water. Everything was done the old way. My brothers and I stood in line in our underwear, waiting to be called to the kitchen. Mom took special care in scrubbing our hair, the entire time repeating the importance of personal hygiene. Afterwards, she wrapped us in a towel and called the next. Then it was bedtime.

Sunday mornings at 7:00 A.M., Dad made sure everyone was awake. Attending services was a requirement no one avoided. You had to be on your deathbed to not attend church. Even when a cold or other childhood malady forced us to stay in behind, the rule was to remain in bed the entire day. Somehow, my parents knew how to work this psychology.

El Mesías Methodist Church was a large, woodframe structure that had once served an all-Anglo congregation in the 1920s and 1930s. Time had taken its toll on the building, and it needed repairs. As Mexican immigrants started moving into the community, the Anglos began leaving. El Mesías was close to downtown, on McKee Street, in the middle of the "Bloody Fifth Ward." Gang fights between young Mexicans gave the Fifth Ward an image of being an unsafe place to live. Still, it was in this community where my parents arrived in 1919 and met. Years later, they exchanged vows at the church. It was an attraction for young Mexican families who were eager to become Americans. Joining for many meant leaving their Catholic faith to become Methodists.

Worship for these families carried a special meaning. None came from affluence or wealth. To the contrary, most had stories of struggle and sorrow, and little in the way of material resources to offer. For the majority, El Mesías Church provided these families with a protective sanctuary away from the rest of the world. It gave them the strength to continue living, to confront their hardships, to visualize a better future, and to attempt making sense out of life. Almost everyone was related. If they weren't relatives, it didn't take too long before marriage caused families to become larger.

I never knew if the Nietos were among the larger or smaller families of El Mesías. On Dad's side, twenty relatives or more often sat next to each other when counting all our cousins, uncles, and *"tías"* (aunts). Mom's side of the family was almost twice as large. All I knew was where the Nieto clan sat during Sunday morning services. Left side, third and fourth rows from the front.

Church for my brothers and me was also much more than attending a worship service. For us, it was also a family event. It gave us the opportunity to play with cousins our age, and spend time with aunts and uncles.

During services, many times there wasn't a dry face in the entire congregation listening to the booming voice of El Hermano (Brother) Medellín, the church pastor, belting scriptures from the pulpit. He not only preached about the Bible and the hereafter to the congregation; he interpreted life. When it came to understanding his congregation, Reverend Medellín was a master. He understood the anxiety of finding yourself without alternatives.

The reverend also had a talent for transforming personal dejection into celebration in an instant. He gave people a reason to live, to work harder, to overcome their problems, and to confront the challenges of life. Services offered parishioners the opportunities to re-arm themselves and to fuel their faiths. The vibrant and celebratory hymns re-energized the congregation. Many older church members like my parents sang certain hymns by memory. This was their way of making a religious statement, of affirming their beliefs in God.

In contrast, my brothers and I struggled, especially when faced with having to sing hymns in Spanish. Spanish didn't come easy to us. We grew up speaking mostly English at our house and in school. In a church where only Spanish was used, we were challenged in a different way, especially when it came to the ritual readings and responses to passages in the Bible. Dad would turn away at times to keep from laughing, hearing us stumble across parts in the Bible that were especially hard. The amusement he found in watching his three young sons struggle was more than he could handle.

"Pobrecitos mis hijitos, (My poor children,)" he would sometimes respond. Dad wasn't making fun of us. He was enjoying observing us go through the sometimes difficult, but harmless steps of growing and learning. In church, however, his sense of humor would sometimes get the best of him. It was a kind of thing between a father and his sons. A quick stern look from Mom put an end to it all, at least temporarily. We were there to worship and show reverence, not to horse around. We all knew the rules, Dad included.

After church, we spent the afternoon visiting relatives at the homes of Tía Feliz, Dad's sister, or Mom's cousin, Tía Becky. At the conclusion of a long bus ride back home, Dad would carry me, asleep in his arms, the fourteen-block walk back to our little white frame home in the woods.

Years later, I understood the reasons that church played such a vital role in our lives. It started with Mom. She was not permitted to date or attend dances as a teenager. Only on special occasions was she given permission to go out for a few hours with her cousins, but always under the watchful eyes of her accompanying Tío Esteban. Her life was abiding by the rules of a religious and strict grandmother. El Mesías Methodist Church became her life, and, later, her guide to rearing her family.

Wednesday nights were reserved for *"noches de consejo"* (family guidance night) when we discussed life and read scripture. We learned about values, the importance of respecting adults, and the difference between being good and being bad. Guests to our house were invited to participate. Afterwards, we knelt on the floor, listening to Mom's eloquent and seemingly endless prayers. It wasn't until years later that I learned to value her role in my life. Spirituality meant being humble and thankful to God. Even today, at ninety, she reminds me to thank God for my blessings and to pray for guidance when faced with the difficult challenges that life brings us all.

"Usted ponga su fé en Dios, mijo. Dios es muy grande. Él lo guía en su vida. Pero tienes que tener fé en Él primeramente. (You put your faith in God, son. God is great. He'll guide you in life. But you first have to have faith in him.)"

Like Mom, Dad was also religious, but in a different way. Mom grew up in church under the guidance of missionaries and a highly religious grandmother. Dad learned his life lessons in the streets without the guidance of parents. While Mom grew up under the close supervision of family and church, Dad slept on the floor of his brother's home, with no one holding him accountable except to pay rent at the end of the month. The little he knew about religion came from his childhood in Laredo as a young boy with his mother. It was she who converted from Catholicism and later had her children baptized in the Methodist Church. It was also Gregoria Medrano-Nieto who gave her youngest son a different understanding of religion and a legacy for him to direct his life.

She taught her son the importance of figuring out problems on his own. He stayed up late into the night scribbling notes in search of answers to his schoolwork. He was taught to believe in a God who gave all people the same brains and the same capacities to solve problems and manage their individual lives.

"Todos somos hijos de Dios, (We're all God's children,)" he would say. *"A mí me dio el mismo cerebro que le dio al otro. Entonces de mí tienen que venir las soluciones para vivir y sobrevivir en este mundo, no de otros. Solamente por medio de mi mente, mis acciones, y mis hechos.* (He also gave me the same mental capacities that He gave others. That's why solutions in life must come from me to survive and thrive in this world. Not from anyone else. Only through my mind, my actions, my deeds.)"

It took years and a lot of afterthought before my two brothers and I fully understood and learned to appreciate the importance of these early childhood lessons. Santos and Esther Nieto were much more than the parents in our development. Eventually, they also became our greatest teachers. They didn't teach us about life in the traditional sense. Their messages went deeper. They had a profound and lasting impact on our thinking and development.

There was another message in their words of counsel. They taught us about life, ethics, and fair play. They transformed family truths into practices that taught us to look to each other for help. We learned the importance of working through the family and community to solve difficult challenges.

They instilled a strong work ethic and the importance of being connected to a higher spiritual being for guidance. They taught us to use imagination and creativity in our everyday work, especially in achieving goals that sometimes appeared beyond our grasp.

The idea of Santos and Esther Nieto being deeply involved in the life of the community was never something I thought about. All I knew was that our home was a fun and exciting place to be. There were always kids and adults around as far back as the middle 1940s when Mom organized the first Cub Scout pack in the neighborhood.

One summer evening, when the Scout pack gathered at our home to build a campfire near the woods, my brother Roy and I started crying because we weren't old enough to join. Albert and his friends looked particularly sharp in their neatly pressed blue uniforms and caps. In her always imaginative and caring manner, Mom carefully painted our faces with bright red lipstick. Then she put a couple chicken feathers on a piece of cloth, carefully tied them around our heads, and let us sit around the campfire with the others as "friendly Indians." We boiled eggs with the older kids and listened to Dad talk about camping in the hills of Laredo as a boy. Listening to tales of roaming coyotes yelping and howling at the moon scared the daylights out of the two newly inducted friendly Indians. By midnight, while the older boys slept quietly in the backyard under a brightly-lit moon, Roy and I tiptoed back to the house to the warm security of sleeping next to Mom.

Being active in the community didn't start when my parents got married or started having children. By the time she was twelve years old, Mom was already a volunteer in her church. During the week, after finishing her chores at home, she could be found working with young pre-school children at the Wesley Community House under the guidance of two Methodist missionaries, Ms. Morgan and Ms. Smith.

Dad's approach was different. By age sixteen, the little spare time he had – when he wasn't working sixteen-hour days - was spent running around with barrio friends playing baseball and soccer. There was little else to do on weekends. For the majority of young Mexican boys his age, jobs were as scarce as was money to spend. The economic hardships of the times only served to heighten already agitated race problems for the growing number of Mexican families from towns along the Texas side of the Rio Grande or cities in the interior of Mexico like Monterrey and Saltillo. Other who came from surrounding farming communities in South Texas faced the same hostile realities. Whether one was a Mexican national or a U.S.-born Mexican American didn't matter. Boys, in particular, took the brunt of the racial hatred. They constantly had to be on the lookout for marauding gangs of German and Italian youth who beat them.

"Hey Mezkin, you wanna fight?" Those were the words Dad used to describe the situations he and his friends faced daily. Young arrogant thugs knew the police wouldn't do much to stop them. They waited on street corners for the chance to jump on unsuspecting young Mexican boys on their way home from work or looking for jobs.

"You know what made it worse," he used to recall, "was la policia. They did nothing to protect us. They too didn't like us either. *No había justicia para los mexicanos.* (There was no justice for Mexicans). Either you got beat up by *Los bolillos o la policía. No importaba sí éramos muchachos o hombres ya casados. Ya sabíamos que no podíamos andar solos después de que bajaba el sol.* (It didn't matter if we were mere children, or adults, even married men. All of us knew not to be caught out alone after sunset.)"

For Dad, playing for baseball or soccer teams became more than athletic competitions. It provided a certain amount of protection. As racial problems mounted, he got involved in organizing boxing club of tough barrio youth. *"Nos cansamos de las freguizas,* (We got tired of the beatings,)" he used to tell me. *"Nos teníamos que defender. Ya era mucho.* (We had to defend ourselves. It was too much for us to endure.)"

As their confidence grew, Dad and his Fifth Ward friends started venturing out to nearby towns like Pasadena, Baytown, and Galveston, places with anti-Mexican reputations. They purposely crossed boundaries looking for fights, wanting the chance to retaliate. Tensions worsened. A look or an off-color word was all it took for fists, clubs, and baseball bats to start flying. Most of the time, my father and his buddies came out on top. If the police ever caught them, they already knew they didn't stand a chance of being heard. Their only out was to run and hide.

It wouldn't be until 1929 that life for my father would change for the better when he exchanged wedding vows with Mom at the church where they first met. Now it was time to settle down, raise a family and become a good husband and father. In 1951, life took another turn for my parents. Mom was asked by a local civic club to consider becoming the director of a newly constructed city recreation center in a community called Magnolia, the largest immigrant community in Houston. It was named DeZavala Park, after a Texas war hero during the state's fight for independence in 1836. "El Parque" (the park) was built only a few blocks from the Houston Ship Channel, between Canal and Navigation streets. Two years later, Dad was recruited for the same job, but at Hennessey Park in the Fifth Ward where he spent his teenage years.

Neither one of my parents had a high school diploma as preferred by the city. Their formal education didn't go much farther than elementary school. Influential Houston leaders, however, respected them for their work as community volunteers with youth, especially in Scouting. In their view, communities like Magnolia and the Fifth Ward needed strong, determined leaders with vision. Mom and Dad fit the description perfectly.

At thirteen years of age, I used to sit at the table or in the living room intently listening to my parents talk about their work at the parks. As a young boy I was taught never to interrupt, only to pay close attention. The discussions fascinated me. They planned girls' fast-pitch softball tournaments, Ping-Pong contests for the younger ones, and amateur wrestling events. They organized softball leagues for boys to keep them from joining gangs and getting into fights that often took place between families and neighborhoods. Park dances were used mostly as fundraising events to buy uniforms for the teams. Mom even drew lines on the dance floors of the teenage dances at DeZavala to keep the younger ones from being excluded. She recruited tough, barrio boys for the much-coveted security guard roles. In planning their monthly menu of park events, discussions between Mom and Dad sometimes turned into squabbles. Working together was always their goal and they knew never to take disagreements too far.

Sometimes Dad would turn and ask me, *"¿Y qué piensas tu mijo?* (And what do you think son?)"

I never knew what he meant or expected me to answer. It was the look in his eyes that made me uncomfortable. It was a kind of stare that went through you. All I could do was smile back sheepishly and shrug my shoulders to indicate having little to say or offer. Dad knew, however, that I enjoyed being at the table with them, and that someday I might want to do the same work. I could have easily been outside with my brothers or friends running around in the neighborhood. Instead, I stuck around, sometimes for hours.

On occasion, my only role was to give them a glass of ice water, pour another cup of coffee, or run down the street to buy them some *"pan mexicano"* (Mexican sweet bread) to eat along with their coffee. Always, I remained glued to their talks. It was fun going with them downtown for meetings at City Hall or attending special functions in the community. Listening and helping were the price of learning, and both mom and dad were tough teachers.

Sometimes when Dad demanded more of me from their discussions, Mom would come to my defense. *"¡Déjalo Santos!* (Leave him alone, Santos!)" she would argue back, putting her arm around my shoulders to console and protect me. *"Esta muy chiquito mijo ahorita.* (My son is much too young right now.) *Pero vas a ver, un día de estos.* (But you will see one of these days.)"

Through park activities, barrios that were once known as places where even the police were scared to enter soon were transformed into places where young people of all ages started to mature and gain recognition. No matter how strong the competition was elsewhere, boys and girls teams from Magnolia and the Fifth Ward always seemed to end up in the finals of most citywide basketball or fast-pitch softball tournaments. Trophies lined the walls of Hennessey Park and DeZavala Park offices. There were teams and activities for all ages and skill levels. Barrio youth competed in Ping-Pong tournaments on Saturday mornings, participated in teenage talent shows, or played roles in the widely recognized Park cultural shows. With literally hundreds of youth involved each year; there were also strict rules to follow. Cussing and fighting were grounds for immediate expulsion.

Many times, young boys expelled from the park could be seen sitting on park benches by a clump of trees where most of the *"vatos locos"* (crazy guys) hung out. They talked with Dad for hours. Most of them wanted back in, to be part of the park's community life. His compassion always gave them an out. He never alienated them. He understood these young boys only too well, no matter how mean they looked at times or if they had serious police records. He grew up in the same environment. Sometimes they took long walks around the park grounds, always ending up at the front door of the park office as though going to an appeals court. Mom was the judge, the final decision-maker who determined the length of their exile. She kept careful, handwritten records on every boy and girl who came to the park. Signing up was a requirement.

She knew everyone who came to the park, their phone numbers, whether or not their parents worked and how many brothers and sisters they had. This is how my parents organized activities at DeZavala and Hennessey and eventually entire communities. They took pride in knowing how people thought and what they did for a living. They especially knew how to reach the hearts of the adults through their children.

Mom and Dad never gave scant attention to the accomplishments of park youth. *"Tenemos que hacerles wato,* (We have to do things for them,)" Dad would insist.

Special dinners were held to honor teams that won city titles. Some of the best Mexican restaurants in Houston were picked for these occasions. Each year formal Valentine's dances were sponsored at Magnolia in the local union hall on Avenue D. Young women participated in queen contests. At the coronation event, they were escorted by their dates for everyone to admire while the soft melodic sounds of well-known Mexican orchestras like Alonzo y sus Rancheros played in the background. Teenage boys, who rarely had more than two or three pairs of pants for school, wore suits and ties, most for the first time in their lives.

The annual queen coronation was only one of many events. On Friday evenings, free shows were sponsored for elementary and pre-school age children. Hundreds showed up with their parents eagerly anticipating cartoon films or old cowboy movies. Always, however, Mom first made sure that before the movies got started, everyone there also got a good dosage of special films on health, especially on tuberculosis prevention and polio. And before anything else got going, Mom was there, microphone in hand, for a moment of prayer. Thanking God was deeply embedded in her beliefs. She saw it as her role, her responsibility, *"su deber"* (her duty).

"Hay andaba la señora de la Biblia, (There she was, the Bible lady,)" Dad would say, poking fun at her once back home.

"Tu callete Santos, porque Dios te castiga, (You shut up Santos, because God will punish you,)" she would argue back. *"Yo se lo qué hago.* (I know what I'm doing.)"

DeZavala Park and later Hennessey Park, not only established strong programs; teenagers were also given duties in the community. During evenings and weekends, it wasn't unusual to see twenty or thirty high school boys and girls going door-to-door soliciting signatures to pave streets or install streetlights. Sometimes they passed out special Thanksgiving baskets to needy families. Whether we liked it or not, my two brothers and I were also expected to volunteer and go along.

On the streets, close buddies would poke fun. *"Hay vienen las tres señoritas Nieto,* (Here come the three Nieto girls,)" they would say. We either ignored the jabbing or went along with the joke. There was no use being angry with friends who never backed out of a fight. To us, it was a matter of either weathering the *"piquetes"* (jabs) or dealing with Mom's disappointment. The choice was easy, but it didn't necessarily make life in the barrio easier or more comfortable.

The standards we had to observe seemed a bit tougher than those our contemporaries had to follow. *"¿Si ustedes no se portan bien y ponen el ejemplo,"* Mom would point out in private, *"¿cómo esperan que podemos enseñar a los demás?* (If you boys don't behave right and set the example, how do you expect us to teach the others?)"

Life in Magnolia, the Fifth Ward, and the Northside was filled with fun and excitement. We had heroes to look up to, role models to follow, families to pattern our lives after. Our neighborhoods were not like the accounts in the newspapers. In fact, there were two realities in place: one in which we lived our daily lives, bound together by a common culture and life experience that gave us an identity and a sense of belonging; the other, a place of nightly shootings, drugs, and gang wars that were reported daily in the newspaper accounts.

We preferred our own version of life in Houston. For my parents, it was exciting, even exhilarating, seeing life change for young men and women who came to the park. They enjoyed reading about their young charges in the sports columns or the neighborhood sections of the Houston Press or Houston Chronicle. Their roles were to provide the means for community youth to gain positive exposure. Watching them transform themselves made all their efforts worth the sweat, the tears, and the hours. Their excitement running high, many times they stayed up until the early morning organizing another project, getting ready for the next event. There was never a dull moment at the Nieto home.

Sometimes Grandma Alfaro would get a little anxious with all the activity. With her bedroom being immediately next to the dining room where my parents frequently met, she found it hard to sleep with the lights on at all hours. *"Ustedes hablan, duermen, y sueñan pelota,* (You talk, sleep, and dream baseball,)" she would kiddingly complain the next morning. *"¡Santos y Esther! Ustedes tienen que descansar.* (You have to rest.)"

While my parents could have afforded nicer homes in other parts of town, they never left the communities where they worked. Northside, Fifth Ward, Magnolia, and Denver Harbor were communities where they felt comfortable. Grocery shopping at local stores turned into long conversations. Park youth and their parents often stopped by our house. Dad enjoyed having them over. He would spend hours with other dads remembering times working together at the Houston Compress or shipyards years before. These were people he deeply valued and respected. A few had served time in prison. Others had reputations for being outstanding athletes or just outright mean. Given the circumstances they faced growing up in Houston, they survived the times. Mostly they wanted something more, higher paying jobs, and better educations for their children. My parents had *"respeto"* (respect) for all of them. They had ingrained in us that we never look down on any family. Dad, especially, was vocal about his sentiments.

"A nadie le gusta ser pobre, no tener que darle a sus hijos, (No one enjoys being poor, not having anything to give their children,)" he would remind me. *"Todos nosotros deseamos mejores vidas, desde el más pobre hasta el más educado.* (All of us desire better lives, from the poorest to the most educated.)"

Neither of my parents ever forgot the poverty they endured as youngsters, the human suffering their brothers, sisters, and parents had to endure. The most important lesson they wanted for us, however, was to never turn our backs on the Mexican community – not for anyone, not for any price. This was the one legacy they most wanted us to embrace as a family and eventually pass on to the rest of the children to come.

Chapter One: Legacy of Family

1. What three major life lessons did Ernesto learn from his family as he grew up?
2. What three major, enduring life lessons did you learn as you grew up?
3. How have your enduring life lessons influenced:
   a. How you have made sense out of your life experiences?
   b. How you felt about significant events and people in your life?
   c. The choices you made in dealing with the challenges you have encountered?
4. Write a brief story about a time when you used one of your life lessons to make a decision about how to deal with an important, challenging situation.
   a. What was the situation? What made it significant and challenging?
   b. What was the life lesson that you used?
   c. What did you choose to do about the situation?
   d. What were the results of your choice? Did you get the results you wanted or

expected?
- e. What did you learn about the way you addressed challenging situations?
- f. What did you learn about the value of your life lesson?

Chapter 2
Winds of Darkness

For young people, life seems endless. We get caught up in going to school, getting started on our careers, marrying, and rearing children. Years pass almost without notice and formerly close relationships change or take on a different meaning.

Between the time that I left Austin in 1968 and 1978, my parents and I enjoyed a close relationship, but mostly involving my children. They wanted to be right next to their grandchildren, to put them in bed at night, tell them stories, and laugh at their *"tonterías"* (youthful pranks). Dad enjoyed his oldest grandson Roy, teaching him how to curve a baseball the way he did in the 1920s. Nicole was the daughter Mom never had. And both were completely ecstatic about their *"cuatitos"* (twins), Marc and Chris. It wasn't unusual at all for the twins or Roy and Nicole to spend several weeks with them in Houston during the summer vacation months.

It also wasn't until 1979 that I also started to appreciate the vast wealth of knowledge both of my parents could offer me in my efforts to start the institute. We always talked about eventually creating a special place for Latino youth, a school that could offer them the latest and best in leadership training. After 1979, a relationship that primarily revolved around grandchildren became one in which they became my most trusted mentors. Hours were spent in their living room, going over ideas and concepts, arguing over differences of opinion, and discussing the Latino community. Dad and Mom understood my vision; however, they wanted me to proceed cautiously. We continued talking for the next several years.

One Saturday morning in the spring of 1993, Dad called me at my home in Austin. It was generally Mom who called, not Dad. For the most part, it was me who called them to visit with "la jefa o el general" (the boss or the general). Dad rarely asked for anything. This time, the tone of his voice was serious. He wanted me to drive that morning over to Houston to go over some private business. After arriving at his house, we rode around old neighborhoods for several hours. My teenage twin sons, Marc and Chris, accompanied us. We ended up in Galveston, alongside a fishing area.

Age had taken its toll on my father. Despite having a small stroke and other health problems, his spirit remained strong. Dad rarely complained about anything. He was eighty-nine. I was fifty-three. We sat silently next to each other for one of our last times together, until he fell asleep.

How I love this old man, I thought to myself, my eyes fixed on his face for several long minutes. Flashbacks of our lives together ran wild in my mind. I visualized memories of Dad teaching me baseball and of him carrying me into the house late at night as a young boy. Many times we'd harmonize together, singing old ranchero songs. Rarely did we complete a song without bursting out with laughter. While there had been many serious and even tragic moments in our lives together, we mostly enjoyed good times, plenty of *"abrazos"* (hugs), endless hours talking and sharing. Dad was my life guide, teacher, and companion.

A fishing pole that Chris and Marc had given him rested in his hands as the wind gently moved through his white, wavy hair. The crashing waves against the sand were the only sound that broke the silence. Dad had lived a wonderful and happy life. He and Mom had done it all. From nothing, they had put together a sixty-three-year marriage. They raised a family, and served the public as well. They had influenced entire communities, changed the lives of thousands of young people.

This time, however, he wanted to talk. There was something different in the air, something dreadful I didn't want to hear. *"¡No me voy a morir ahorita, mijo!* (I'm not going to die this moment!)" he said, almost in a whisper when he woke up. *"¡Pero ya me llega el tiempo! No te me pongas triste. Quiero que cuides mucho a tus hijos, tu hermano, especialmente a tu mamá. Ella se va sentir sóla.* (But the time is nearing, son! Don't be sad. I want you to take care of your children, your brother, and especially your mom. She's going to feel particularly lonely.)"

Dad was accepting the inevitable. As a child, I had come to understand his life tragedies, his victories, his dream, and the passion he had for living. We were now facing his final days, his final moments. Why had he chosen me to tell? Why not someone else?

We hugged and cried quietly until we no longer had tears to shed. Gently patting each other's shoulders, kissing each other's eyes over and over, all we could do was stare at one another amid a million fleeting thoughts and memories only we could share together. For a long time, there had been an uneasiness in of me, something that made me feel distant, unvalued in his eyes. I felt that maybe I wasn't his favorite. That was Roy, the middle son, the one who looked exactly like him.

The memories suddenly came running back like a hard pounding rain. It was August 1961. Roy, my brother, and I had talked for over an hour the previous night. He wanted to go to Ciudad Juárez, Mexico, across the river from El Paso, where he was stationed at Fort Bliss. Only two months remained before serving out his enlistment. He joined the Army right after graduating from high school to get his military duty behind him.

I never trusted my brother's judgment. He was too much like Dad, always angry inside and ready to pick a fight. I begged him not to go. It was already almost midnight. The next morning, mom called the swimming pool at DeZavala where I was a lifeguard during the summer. Coach Henry Goméz who supervised the pool looked concerned as he approached me.

"There's an emergency at your home. You better call your house immediately," he said in a low, rough, but concerned voice. Mom answered my worried call and immediately started screaming. "Roy's dying," she let out. "Roy's dying. Someone stabbed him in Juárez early this morning. Come home mijito (my son), come home."

Once home, I walked into my parent's bedroom, shut the door behind me, and started praying out loud, asking God to take me. Why take away the strongest son, my Dad's favorite? Why not me? No one would ever really miss me, not me.

I couldn't bring myself to go with my parents to El Paso. I couldn't bear to see my brother gasping for air, dying in front of me. Instead I shut myself inside my grandmother's house. My parents and my older brother Albert left on an early afternoon flight. Seven days later, in the early morning hours, Roy took his final breath.

It was storming in Houston the evening before. Lightening lit up the skies while thunder made the night appear endless. At about the time Roy was dying, I sensed a voice inside of me. I woke up and silently walked outside. The torrential rain beat hard against my face as I looked around listening closely to a whisper.

"I'm leaving. Take care of the parents. I'm leaving. Take care of the parents."

Grandma found me kneeling under a tree, screaming uncontrollably. "Roy just died abuelita," I kept mumbling between gasps. "Roy just died."

Grandma, who was well into her seventies, did everything she could to console me. Somehow, I made it back to the porch and inside her small living room. I must have passed out with exhaustion on the living room couch, because early the next morning, there was a gentle tap on the front door that eventually woke me up. It was the Reverend P.F. Valdez, our minister. The look on his face relayed the bad news.

Roy's body was brought back to Houston a few days later. Hundreds of high school friends, family members, and parishioners from El Mesías were at the funeral.

I didn't attend. I couldn't come to terms with the permanent absence of my brother. He was my protector and my confidant. We were the ones who promised each other that we would always protect

Albert, our oldest brother. It was Roy and I who would eventually go into business together. We planned on buying Mom her dream house and Dad a new pickup. From one moment to another, the dreams we talked about in private were in flames. The realization that we would never see each other again, laugh together, or hang around as brothers was beyond my comprehension.

It took seventeen years for me to gather the courage to visit his grave. Soon after NHI was started, my wife Gloria left with me one day for Houston. It was something that had to be done. I needed my brother's forgiveness for having run away, for hiding behind my fears, and for lacking the courage when my family most needed me.

Once at the cemetery, it took several minutes before I found his grave marker. Dad and Mom had buried Roy in the military section alongside other veterans. There he was, Private Roy Santos Nieto. Born 1939. Died 1961. His name was written in stone almost too small to recognize. How I savagely loved him still after all these years. Roy—the short one of the family with the dark skin, straight black hair, and contagious smile. I would give my life for one moment to touch his face, hug him if only for a brief moment, to just sit and talk and laugh, and remember, and cry together, and throw footballs back and forth, and dream, and dream.

The years since Roy's passing had been an emotional roller coaster. I often awoke exhausted from nightmares. The thought and fear of death consumed me. I was deeply afraid of dying, not the act of dying, but leaving my parents and brother Albert alone. Who would take care of them? Who would love them like Roy and I did? Who would protect them from harm? Mom couldn't withstand the death of another son. She became terribly ill when Roy died. She lost weight, couldn't eat. She stopped working for a while, even stayed away from church for a few months. Religion no longer had the same meaning.

Visiting the grave site after all the years was a terribly frightening experience. The emotions began to choke my insides. For a few moments, I did everything possible to control my breathing. I could hear my heart pounding inside my head. Tears streamed down my cheeks. The long awaited encounter was finally taking place.

There was a deep, howling sound to my screams and trembling body as Gloria knelt next to me, gently stroking my forehead, encouraging me to cry as much as I wanted. Time had taken its toll on me and this was the beginning of a long-awaited healing process. A weight was being taken off my soul. I was finally there again, next to my brother, captured in the privacy of racing thoughts that took me back to all the times we shared and laughed together. For once, the sky was blue again. The clouds slid by silently to the melodies of singing birds. Roy's soul was there next to me, consoling my pain as he did when we were little boys. It was all right to go on. He would still be there with me, in my work, through my children.

The thirty-two years after Roy's death took its toll on my father. Another crisis was about to take place in our family, like the swirling winds of an impending hurricane gathering strength in the Gulf.

A few yards down the seashore, my sons' laughter broke the silence as they ran along the bay. They were dad's pride and joy, his *cuates chiquitos* (young twins). Words weren't needed between two people who had spent a lifetime being son and father. We understood only too well what was to come. Holding me closely, he whispered a message that will remain with me the rest of my days. No greater gift of confidence could ever be given from a parent to a child. His words instantly healed a lifetime of doubt.

"*Aprendiste bien mijo,* (You learned well, son,)" he said, staring at my eyes with the same intensity that convinced every youth he touched to change their lives. "*Más no te puedo enseñar.* (More, I cannot teach you.)"

A week later, Dad took his last breath. At the hospital, I stood by his bed watching him, until the doctors and nurses asked my brother Albert and me to step outside. Moments later, I was allowed to come in the room and spend a few private moments at his bedside. He lay there motionless. It was hard to imagine my father gone. In between the millions of thoughts that were unleashed in my mind, in between gasping for air in my feeble attempts to be strong amid the flow of uncontrollable tears, all I could do at that instant was raise my hand to my head to give *"mi General"* a final salute.

At the cemetery, Mom looked at me to convey our gratitude to everyone who attended the funeral. The night before, the chapel was filled with relatives, old friends, and people from the neighborhoods where we had lived that I had not seen in years. They came from all backgrounds. Several gathered enough courage to speak in front of everyone, recalling personal experiences that only they had individually shared with my father. Some broke down and openly wept, revealing conversations with Dad that changed their lives forever. Now it was time for our last good-byes.

For an instant, I could almost hear my father saying, *"Esto es mucho. ¡Ya mijo! ¡Dile a la gente que sigan las veredas en sus vidas!* (This is too much. Enough, son! Tell the people who are gathered here to go on and follow the pathways that life has placed before them!)

This was truly Dad in his understanding of life. You live it and despair when tragedies occur. But then you get up off your knees and continue moving forward. These were the lessons that life threw at him when he lost his mother as a young boy, his father as a young adult, and later his son when everything in his life appeared perfect.

Turning to the scores of people huddled around the gravesite, I said, "My father would want to thank you for your kindness and the respect you show toward all of us as a family, especially my mother. But he would also want me to tell you to now go on with your lives. But as his son, I do have something to say for you to think about. The lesson of my father's journey is that he loved his community with all his heart and did so much for so many people despite the little that life gave him in the beginning. Let his gift be how we remember him and a lesson in life that will continue to inspire and guide us in the future."

Today, an iron fence out back at the National Hispanic Institute in Maxwell, Texas, surrounds five live oak trees. It symbolizes our journey together as a family. Two of the larger oaks are intertwined, symbolizing Mom and Dad and their work. The remaining three represent my two brothers and me. The roots of all five trees are intertwined with each other deep down into the earth. Albert is a retired police officer. I remain behind to further the work of my parents and continue our family vision. And behind me stand my four children, Roy II, Nicole, Marc, and Chris. At first it didn't seem possible, but they too have that special attraction to the community, that special energy that comes from being involved. It shows in their work. They get a particular enjoyment from helping others. Dad was right. Maybe the gift doesn't have to be understood, only accepted.

Years went by before I finally understood the struggles of my parents. It took me just as long to appreciate and value the struggles of others like them. Their experiences are representative of thousands, possibly millions of other Latinos who came to the Unites States during the twentieth century searching for better lives for themselves and their children. Instead, they found hostile environments who exploited their vulnerabilities for personal gain. The National Hispanic Institute has long understood this history and its impact on the thinking of Latinos. Towards the end, before his death, Dad started to express concern regarding the impact he saw these social forces having on Latinos as a community.

"Una gente dominada que no tiene dirección," he would say. *"Pierde la capacidad a depender en ellos mismos. No podemos dejar que les pase eso o se nos apaga el mundo.* (A dominated people have no direction. They lose the capacity to rely on themselves. We can't let this happen or the sun of hope will fade on our world.)

In his view, Latinos were starting to show signs of losing faith. They were beginning to look outside themselves for answers to problems and challenges. In the old days, when government didn't play a visible role in Latino community life, people created their own homespun systems to help out neighbors. Common need forced families to connect with one another, help each other out in times of stress and despair. Barrios were not just places to live. They were also care-giving systems of interconnected people who trusted each other, who worked together to solve problems. It was this life Dad wanted me to understand and appreciate.

"*Hay bien en toda gente mijo,*" he used to say, "*desde el más matón hasta aquel que se cree la gran cosa. Tienes que hallar el bien en la persona.* (There is good in all people, son, from the one who sees himself as being a mean person to the one who thinks of himself as being important to the world. You have to find the good in each person.)"

In my haste to get started, however, Dad also advised me to take one step at a time. He wanted me to study the community and avoid making erroneous assumptions about people. He wanted me to understand that not all Mexicans were alike, that they didn't all think the same way, that they didn't approach life with the same beliefs and values.

"*Con calma mijo,* (Be calm, son,)" he would remind me. "*Tú tienes que aprender como llevarte con toda clase de personas. No puedes hacer diferencias entre gente porque uno tiene más que el otro, porque un individuo tiene más educación, más posición en la comunidad y el otro no tiene nada. Tienes que tocarle el alma a la persona. Ellos responden. A nadie le gusta ser pobre, no tener que comer, estar paralizados en sus vidas. Todo humano quiere ser lo posible, llevar nueva dirección, tener éxito. Nunca le creas a gentes que te hacen creer que no podemos, que nos faltan las capacidades intelectuales.* (You have to learn to get along with all classes of people first. You can't favor one kind of people over others because one group of people has resources and the other has nothing, because one individual is educated, enjoys greater social status in the community, while the other has nothing to offer. You have to touch the soul of the person. They'll respond. No one likes being poor, not having enough to eat, being paralyzed in their lives. Every human being wants to do everything possible for himself, have a new beginning, and enjoy success. Don't fall for people who want us to believe that we lack the intellectual capacities to do for ourselves.)"

Dad wanted me to have every advantage in my knowledge of my community and in my mental and spiritual readiness. "*El Mexicano tiene mucha resistencia* (The Mexican has enormous capacities to endure,), he would say with pride. "*Ya venimos enceñados por añales como gente que sabe sufrir. También no puedes estar enojado con el mundo, mijo, por lo pasado, por la discriminación. En esta pelea, no uses tus manos. Usa tu mente. Pero primeramente, pon tu fé en Dios. Él te guía. Crea tu escuela para desarollar un nuevo pensameinto. Y no hagas esta obra por la atención que te viene a ti. Si es que te va bien, que sea por el beneficio que le viene a la comunidad.* (We come trained through the ages as a people able to endure suffering. You can't be mad at the world, son, for what happened in our past, for the discrimination. This fight is not about using your fists to get back at others. Instead use your mind. But first, place your faith in God. He'll guide you. Create your school to give rise to a new thinking. And don't do this work for the attention it may bring you. If things go well for you, let it be to benefit others in the community.)"

More than twenty years after the founding of the National Hispanic Institute, the lessons crafted by my parents are part of the training curriculum for working with Latino students. We find ourselves transmitting many of the same lessons, beliefs, and messages used by my parents in their work with young Latinos in Houston decades earlier. The lives they led and the lessons they shared with me are part of our foundation. Mom and Dad taught me to manage my life, share with others, believe in myself, take pride in my work, and not put myself above others. They provided me with the cultural pathways to return home, to be among those who care and love me, and to put life into proper perspective. They guided me to believe in the Latino community, to understand its promise and be forgiving of its faults. However, their greatest gift was in giving me the means to develop a spiritual connection to my community that frees the soul to place no boundaries on the aspirations of people or limits on the possibilities they can achieve.

Despite the many lessons and the time they dedicated in guiding me, it took years to fully grasp what ultimately motivated them in their work. At first, I was too brash and immature to listen. A large part of my early life, my college years and immediately after, was spent chasing career stardom, trying to fit into a different world, another reality. I bit into the American mainstream, hook, line, and sinker. I was out to prove myself, show others that I possessed all of the right ingredients to succeed. Sometimes this meant turning away from the basic values and beliefs Mom and Dad passed on to me. It wouldn't be until after my star crashed and burned that other possibilities entered my mind. Mom and Dad always left the golden gate of retreat slightly open. It was time for a thorough review of my life and to accept responsibility for my actions.

Sometimes, in looking back, I still see Dad standing next to me outside the institute in Maxwell, during one of our final times together. He loved the white, Victorian structure, the steeple tin roof, the white columns on the wraparound porches, and the trees out back. If anyone had a profound understanding for the institute and its place among Latinos, Dad did. Sometimes he gazed for long periods of time at the building. He never failed to remind me to use extra caution with the building and property. *"Este lugar nunca lo pierdas hijo,* (Don't ever lose this place,)" he would say. *"Es de todos.* (It belongs to everyone.)"

"Don't worry *mi General*," I would say while hugging him closely. *"Cómo me decía cuando era niño. Este trabajo viene de Dios. Está en las venas. Primero fue usted y mamá. Después yo y Gloria."*

"Y el día que yo me acabe, seguirán mis hijos y después de ellos, mis nietos. Pero también vamos a ver muchos otros muchachos que serán inspirados por el mismo sueño y deseo. Esto ya no viene nomás de nosotros si no por muchos más. Va a ver. (Like you used to tell me. This work comes from God. It's in our blood, our veins. It started with you and Mom. Then came Gloria and me. And the day I'm no longer around, my children will follow, and then my grandchildren. But we will also see other youth inspired by the same vision. This work is no longer ours alone. Others will join as well. You'll see.)"

Smiling, Dad would look at me with the same penetrating stare that I remembered from my childhood and nod his approval.

Chapter Two: Winds of Darkness
1. Write a brief story about a time in your life when you experienced a profound loss.
    a. What was this loss? Was it a person? An object? A relationship? An idea?
    b. How did you think about this loss?
    c. What did you feel about this loss?
    d. What did you choose to do?
2. In what ways did this loss (and your response to it) influence the way that you make choices?

Chapter Three
Loss of Innocence

Defining moments occur throughout peoples' lives. It is a continuing process. Something happens at any given moment. An incidental word of encouragement from a teacher on the playground becomes a key element of the chemistry that propels a young woman eventually to become a doctor. Reading about a high school football idol in the newspaper serves as the impetus for a young boy to become a professional football player. These experiences happen to each of us. They occur throughout our journeys. They have a profound lasting impact on our worldview. More importantly, they're never constant. Six months, maybe a year pass by before something else happens. These moments are never planned. They leave, however, an indelible mark on our minds. Some are almost invisible, small ingredients that together become notable influences in our development. The process repeats itself, forcing us to constantly review, define and redefine ourselves.

Such was the case for the National Hispanic Institute. The idea of an institute for Latinos in the United State didn't occur as a dream or vision. It didn't come from one moment to another. It started years before my time as the founder.

I remember my parents telling me about the Tijerina family in early Houston in the 1930s; they founded the Little Red Schoolhouse to educate Mexican children who were barred from enrolling in the public school system. In the late 1970s, soon after retiring from their jobs with the city, Dad and Mom became the principal organizers of a community school for undocumented Mexican children. Similar to earlier periods when my parents first moved to Houston, Mexican children were kept from public schools because their parents were undocumented workers. At the same time, Jacinto Treviño College opened in the Texas Rio Grande Valley, followed by Juárez-Lincoln University in Austin.

The idea of these organizers was to make education more culturally relevant to Latinos. Other examples are easily traceable to Latino leaders from different organizations that responded to clear injustices. Their ideas fall father from memory as a new millennium unfolds, but the history is definitely there. Some ideas lived a short time because they only served pressing needs. Others may have laced the capacities to sustain long-term involvement or capture the imagination of people.

Perhaps it's impossible to ever really know the specific experiences that ultimately led particular Latino leaders of the past century to start organizations that became well-known community movements. We may never fully grasp what factors and conditions led individuals like César Chávez to establish the United Farm Workers Union in the 1960s. We may never know what compelled Jose Angel Gutiérrez to become a principal force behind the Raza Unida Party. Most of us are left to only imagine and attempt to understand.

Ideas can lay dormant for years, even decades. Some become confined to family discussions or conversations among friends. At critical junctures, however, these thoughts take on their own identity and direction. Someone assumes the challenge of his or her own identity and direction. Someone assumes the challenge of sharing these thoughts with others, giving them public recognition, and advocating on their behalf. They become visionaries who transform ideas into action, persuading others who might not understand or who might be afraid to take a stand. Alert to the challenges of keeping ideas moving, they maintain interest and enthusiasm among supporters. They fuel organizations, train the managers and make the key decisions that keep the work thriving. In each of these individuals, there were earlier life-defining moments that eventually led them to act, to risk going public with their thoughts, to propose answers, and to create visions compelling enough for others to follow.

The historical journey that culminated in the creation of the National Hispanic Institute followed a similar pattern. The social conditions and early life experiences that ignited my parents to become involved in the Houston Latino community may never be fully understood. The more apparent reasons were the intense poverty Latinos were being forced to live, the blatant discrimination against them, or even a higher calling, as Dad often suggested. Whatever the conditions or forces of those times, they eventually led my mother and father to take their ideas to the communities where we lived. In my case, years later, the concept of an institute for the Latino community was the difference between endless talking and doing something about it. If the motivation behind their work was anything similar to what happened to me, it was in realizing the difference between discussing ideas and gaining the confidence to initiate action.

Gloria and I started talking in earnest about an institute for Latinos during a five-hour drive to the Texas Rio Grande Valley in 1978. Year before, my parents and I had talked about this concept. For me, working for government was no longer an option. My involvement with Latino politicians in Austin was a disenchanting experience. Instead of providing the Latino community with new opportunities, they did little other than replace the old guard and assume the same tired controlling attitudes of their predecessors. It continues today.

On a larger scale, I had also become discouraged with the Chicano movement. Leaders were no longer exhorting people to organize and problem-solve. The Nixon administration had effectively shut down the legacies of Presidents Kennedy and Johnson by dismantling community nonprofit organizations. Federal government had been relegated to the court of last resort.

State and local governments were back in control, doling out favors arranged behind the scenes in boardrooms. "Sweetheart funding" had become the catch phrase of political powerbrokers. Chicano leaders, formerly staunch advocates of community change, abandoned La Raza Unida Movement to join an eagerly awaiting Democratic Party. The death of the Raza Unida Party caused a huge vacuum in leadership. To compound this, a new crop of Latino Republicans emerged. These were individuals who placed personal business issues above social causes, except their own.

The 1967 La Raza Unida Conference at John F. Kennedy High School in San Antonio called for the Latinos to look at themselves for changes in their thinking and self-perceptions as a community. The conference not only motivated the community; it provided us with the means to develop cultural pride and confidence. It caused us to take stock of our enormous human potential. At lease that was what I took away after listening to the eloquent presentations of Dr. Ernesto Galarza and Dr. Jorge Lara-Braud, both highly respected intellectual leaders. My father and my uncle, Miguel Nieto, accompanied me to the conference. Despite our wide age differences, all of us were deeply touched by having gone through the experience.

Only twenty-seven years old at the time, I gained hope and a reason to involve myself in the Mexican-American community. Little did I suspect that just six years later, "El Movimiento" -the social movement that inspired so many young Chicanos to become politically active- would reduce to a philosophical memory.

"Se acabó la unidad, (Our unity movement for our community is over,)" Dad would say in later years. *"Ahora es la época de cada uno pa' su santo. (Now, it's everyone for themselves.)"*

Gloria and I spent the entire trip to McAllen reflecting on these developments. We argued about what could have happened to La Raza Unida as a community experience, what caused its demise, where leaders got caught up between personal and community agendas. My stance was that the most important aspect of the movement was in its appeal to young Chicanos.

"There were few at the conference older than twenty-five years of age the year I went," I told her. "There were a lot of college kids and high school students leading the change. An ideological tug of war was taking place between young Chicanos with radical ideas of where to take the community and older, conservative leaders who were more comfortable being tied to larger established political interests. That was the practice for years. The young trying to change the old; the old hanging on to what they knew best."

I told Gloria that while the older leaders eventually won the political battle of ideologies in the 1970s, the real loss was in the political downturn that followed.

"So what do you plan to do about it?" Gloria responded. "You can't go back. You don't trust the old leadership."

"You see a need to do something new? Do something about it."

Only Gloria could handle me this way. She challenged me to act and stop talking. She was never nice about it. Sometimes she even appeared uncaring, unnecessarily confrontational. The same dynamic that started at the kitchen table of my parents' home years before was now being played back between Gloria and me.

Years before, what might have been community concerns at DeZavala Park or Hennessey Park in the Fifth Ward from my parents was being repeated on a different scale.

"I think we need something more than a movement. Maybe we need a think tank, an institute that teaches young people how to participate in the life of the Latino community, something that teachers them to become leaders in a world of their own making. Maybe that's the difference between then and now."

"And are you the one who wants to do this?" she asked. "You think you have the background, the credentials, the ability?"

"I think I can motivate people, organize them," I responded. "I may not have the academic credentials to establish an institute, but I do have ideas and the connections to at least start the process."

"I know you can do it, honey" she remarked looking at me with a reinforcing smile. "You're probably the only one who can." In retrospect, this conversation was crucial in my decision to move beyond the talking stages. Others had listened to my ideas before, including my parents and friends. This was different. This time someone extremely important in my life was validating my thought, compelling me to act, telling me that my instincts were not only correct, but worth pursuing. Before this exchange, doing something different with my life was only a vague, fleeting thought.

Years before, sports were the center of my identity. The thought of eventually becoming a high school basketball coach was my life's ambition. Seeing myself as a coach became the motivation to attend college. Having claim as a player, even better a starter, was the ultimate prize for a barrio boy who came from the dust playgrounds of DeZavala and Hennessey parks. Like my friends used to say, *"La tienes hecha, vato. (You have it made, dude.)"*

Playing college ball was the way of reaching dreams that were not within our abilities to attain in our barrios. Only once in a while did someone do something significant. Lupe Lopez who played basketball for the University of Houston came from our barrio by the ship channel. The same happened to Robert "Manos" (*Hands*) Vasquez from Houston's East End. It was either going for the big dream or being forced to face the cold realities of life that most Mexican Americans lived. That's what made the offer from University of Houston Coach Guy Lewis so attractive for me when he came by Jeff Davis High School one day to offer me a scholarship. It made me one of the few with the opportunity to get out and succeed in the outside world.

This chance, however, was short lived. The racial intolerance and mistreatment Johnny Mendoza and I experienced at the hands of the coaching staff led to our quick departures. Johnny, who had played with me throughout high school, transferred to St. Thomas University. I moved to Southwestern University in Georgetown, Texas, where life for me became four years of fraternity activities, being popular on campus, and making All-Big State Conference two years in a row.

After graduating in 1964 my life started changing, slowly at first. My first job was with the Red

Shield Boys Club, close to downtown Houston. Several months later, I landed a job as an elementary school special education teacher with the Houston Independent School District. Afterwards, I transferred to a higher paying job with the Deer Park Independent School District while working on my master's degree in school administration at the University of Houston. Two years later, an off-the-wall job offer came from graduate professor who turned me into a community organizer with a Houston nonprofit organization at twice what I made as a teacher.

The crossover from being in the classroom in a Houston suburb to becoming a community worker didn't seem important at first. Soon, after seeing the life of poverty firsthand the reminders of how the poor were ignored and disenfranchised, my thinking was challenged and a drive developed in me to become more community conscious. The job change became an important shift towards a different journey and destination. Similar experiences came along the way. Some were small. Others had much greater impact, sometimes becoming major forces in reshaping my beliefs, my views, and my direction. Not everything that occurred was planned. These surprises taught me neither to assume anything nor to take anything for granted, ignoring their feelings.

One of these occasions came shortly after meeting Sergeant Shriver, director of President Johnson's War on Poverty in June of 1966. He was in Houston touring poor neighborhoods. Scores of reporters scurried alongside taking photographs while he stopped to make speeches in different parts of the city. Hundreds of people, mostly Mexican Americans and African Americas, stood silently under the hot steamy sun in the northeast part of town, carefully absorbing his every word. A new time had come for America's minorities. New leadership was needed from our nation's youth people, a leadership that didn't turn its back on the poor and disenfranchised, the people whose circumstances forced them to operate outside the periphery of America's mainstream.

Shriver reiterated a special challenge to our country's youth that had been used before by his brother-in-law. "Ask not what your country can do for you. Ask what you can do for your country."

Only a few years before, these words described the vision of a fallen American president, John F. Kennedy. The applause that followed was thunderous and long after our speaker from Washington, D.C. finished.

Shriver looked and acted powerful. Graying hair on his temples, the dark pinstriped suit, and the way in which he carefully crafted his words were indicative of a person who came from wealth and good breeding. He was easy in his delivery, yet confidently forceful. This was my first introduction to politics: the Kennedys' championing the cause of the poor and appealing to a nation that had allowed over thirty-three million impoverished people to become "the other America." There was reason to be concerned, angry and dismayed. An entire sector of our nation had virtually been ignored for generations. The evidence of our nation's oversight was all around us. It didn't take a social engineer to recognize the problem, to understand its ramification. A challenge was being thrown at us. A new inclusive national agenda was needed.

Images of my parents raced through my mind. They had it pretty hard growing up. My brothers and I had also grown up in the barrio sharing life with people who weren't making it. Everybody knew them. They were immigrant Mexican families at the bottom rung of society's ladder. They lived in shacks that lacked indoor plumbing and hot running water.

The men of these families faced lives of low-paying, unskilled labor in the burning heat of summer and the numbing cold of winter. Their families were almost invisible. Their wives kept mostly to themselves, only leaving their houses to walk to a nearby store. Once in a while they'd peer out through the torn screen front doors to check on their unsupervised offspring. These families weren't connected to the community. They only lived there. On occasion, their children went to the park, but never really mixed with the others. In a barrio where everyone was working-class Mexican, they knew their place.

Something had to be done to help them and improve their lives.

Throughout Shriver's remarks, Gilbert Campos, a co-worker, and I stood in awe of everyone around us. The mayor was there. So were Congressmen, the county judge, city council members, and labor leaders. Our place was much farther back with the rest of the crowd. The air was filled with political excitement and the possibilities of better days ahead for those of us considered part of our nation's minorities.

Being political novices didn't bother us. We were barely twenty-five years old. There was plenty of time to get involved. Besides, politics was getting hot in Houston. A week before I had picketed for the first time in my life against a merger between two anti-poverty agencies. The Houston Harris County Community Action Agency was considered too militant. The Houston Youth Services Agency was seen as too conservative. An old friend and veteran community activist, Ben Canales, sarcastically used to say "One organization is all mouth and no brains; the other one all brains and no mouth. Merging these two organizations is like witnessing a perfect marriage."

After the entourage from Washington left, Gilbert and I walked over to our cars to leave. We first decided, however, to stop in Bonita Gardens, a small Mexican-American neighborhood on Hirsch Road to have a beer. There was a lot to talk about and accomplish. We were the young Turks being politicized. LULAC (League of United Latin American Citizens), PASSO (Political Association of Spanish Speaking Organizations), and the newly formed United Organization Information Center (UOIC) were the Latino power brokers of Houston. We were concerned that the Black community would get all the top positions during the merger leaving the Mexican-American community out altogether.

The neighborhood bar was typically Mexicano. The parking area was a gravel driveway. The small wooden structure was large enough to fit no more than ten to fifteen people. Inside, neon-lit beer signs adorned the wall behind the cheap, plywood bar painted dark brown. A small, quarter-slot pool table was towards the back end of the place, directly in front of the restrooms. The selection of music in the jukebox included everything from old favorite Mexican standards to the latest sounds around "la frontera" *(the border area)*.

The place was empty. The only occupants were the bartender and a couple sitting quietly drinking beer. Gilbert and I didn't pay attention to them. You learn early to ignore, to look down, or not look around at all. You know enough to mind your own business. Besides, we were on a roll from the afternoon and the excitement of having met a national political figure. The bartender asked us what kind of beer we wanted.

"Danos dos Perlas carnal, (Give us a couple Pearl beers,)" I requested, also motioning that he include the woman and man at the bar. Both of them turned to see who we were. Briefly acknowledging that the complimentary drinks were on me, Gilbert and I continued our discussion.

Out of the corner of my eye, I noticed the woman walk by the pool table, toward the bathroom. She was the usual *"cantinera"* as grandma used to describe them, *"medias pansonas, cabello teñido, mucho lippy-sticky, y zapatos puntados"* (*a bar woman, sort of fat, red painted hair, tons of makeup and pointed high heel shoes*).

The man got up slowly moving his gaze from me to Gilbert. The man had already had one too many as he slightly swayed back and forth, the effects of drinking several beers already telling in his eyes. It didn't change his menacing look. His question wasn't friendly either. He felt offended and wanted the culprit.

"Pues fui yo, guey *(It was me, guy,)"* I responded. "The beer was on me."

At first I couldn't tell what was behind the question. Maybe he wanted to thank us. Maybe not. My instincts told me, however, to go slow and be particularly careful with my words.

Turning and staring at me for a moment, he asked, *"¿Que pasa Ese?" ¿Que crees? ¿Que no puedo comprarle birria a mi chavala? (What's up dude? What's on your mind? You figure I can't buy my woman a beer?)"*

The expression on his face suddenly transformed into look of rage. Reaching in his back pocket, he drew a chrome revolver and pointed it directly at my face.

My eyes kept darting back and forth from his eyes to the gun. Gilbert and I sat there without moving an inch, momentarily frozen.

Roy, my brother, had been killed only four years back in a similar situation. He should not have left the barracks at Fort Bliss in El Paso to defend his friends in Ciudad Juarez across the river. He should have stayed in bed. I should have never come in this bar. We could have easily gone downtown to a private club or even my cousin's place on Wallisville Road in Denver Harbor. Nothing would have happened there. Gilbert remained still, but with his hand on the beer bottle as though ready to use it at any moment. The man and I kept staring at each other for several more seconds. This was not the time for any off-the-wall comments. It was my move, my turn to say something.

"¿Sabes que, carnal? (Want to know something, brother?)" I somehow managed. *"Este guey y yo estabamos hablando aqui de la comunidad y como ayudar. Es todo. Discuplame, ese. Creiamos que todo estaba bien.* (This friend and I were talking about the community and how to help. That's all. Pardon us, but we thought everything was cool.)"

The man kept staring at me. If he was thinking about his next move, he wasn't sharing it with either one of us. He only kept looking, as though caught in a deep, complex thought of deciding his next step.

"¿Pues saben que chavalos? (You know what punks?)" he growled, slightly relaxing his hand, pointing his gun towards the floor, *"Pues lleven sus ideas a otros, porque yo ni mi chavala no queremos su ayuda. ¿Me entienden? (Take your ideas to someone else, 'cause me and my woman don't want your help. Understand me?)"*

By now, the woman had returned from the bathroom. Seeing what was going on, she stopped and, for a brief moment, looked at Gilbert first, then me. *"¡Deja esos vatos Richard! (Leave those dudes alone, Richard!)"* she said without any emotion, never showing concern for what was happening. Lighting a cigarette, she continued watching for a second, completely separated from the drama taking place in front of her.

Richard remained staring as though taunting us to make the next move. We stared back, but not with the same expression. We knew not to attempt anything strange. All we wanted was to exit safely.

Slowly, he put the gun back. Without saying any more, he turned and quietly walked back to the bar stool where had been sitting, giving his back to us, similar to the matador who turns and walks away from the bull in the bull ring. He never turned or said anything else. He and his girlfriend continued drinking the beer we had bought them as if though nothing had happened.

"!Vale más que se vayan! (You two guys better leave!)," the bartender cautioned us. He hadn't said a word during the entire episode. We made our way quietly towards the entrance, working hard to look cool and composed, silent the whole time. The beers on our table remained full. Even after having driven a few blocks down the street, we were still in shock, silenced by what had just gone on. No thoughts were exchanged, now words needed to describe what must have been thinking. We had just dodged a bullet in our young lives. Over thirty-five years have passed since the Sergeant Shriver speech in Houston and the Bonita Gardens incident. Sometimes Gilbert's face races to my mind, and I wonder what he may be doing today. There was an excitement back then about becoming involved with the Mexican-America community as young, emerging professionals. I also recall the intense look of disbelief in his eyes as we both faced a potentially disastrous turn of events.

The lesson was clear. Being motivated or inspired to champion the cause of the Mexican-American community wasn't enough. It never crossed our minds that what we perceived as a neighborly or kind gesture would offend others. Seeing that people needed help was only one part of the equation. Knowing that help was needed and recognized by the community we wanted to serve was something we assumed. Gilbert and I had tough questions to ask ourselves. Maybe we had a greater need for identity in the community rather than serving its interests. Maybe we wanted to feel needed. Maybe we thought of ourselves as being slightly better? Possibly that was the message we were giving at the bar.

Over the next couple of years, my work took place in mostly Black, low-income Houston neighborhoods. Our work was to get roads paved and sewage systems installed. We took steps to ensure that the City of Houston installed water mains in overlooked communities like Trinity Gardens. As I longed to participate with the Mexican-American community, my off-time was spent mostly as a volunteer involved in grassroots organizing, getting people involved in demanding better services and job opportunities. My parents started to notice changes in my views. Anger started to well up in me to fight and criticize people in leadership positions who were not responding to the needs of Mexican-Americans living in Magnolia, Second Ward, Crisol, Northside, and Denver Harbor. I either grew up in those neighborhoods or had family and close personal friends still living there.

When we were teenagers, school and sports had mostly consumed life for my brothers and me. The routine at home was to have a part-time job, usually a paper route or working at a downtown meatpacking plant, help our parents with chores around the house and spend evening with friends playing a basketball or fast-pitch softball at the park. On Sundays, we attended church. Life was simple and predictable. Close-knit families lived near each other and "carnales" (*close neighborhood friends*) hung around at dances on Saturday nights at the Pan-American or Cinderella Nightclub.

Everyone knew each other. Sometimes a fight or two would break out at a party or dance. Nothing really serious or dangerous happened, at least not to us. Working in government programs began to make life appear different. Human problems took on a political air. Influence and power for the poor were measured by which community demonstrated the most anger or spoke the loudest at public meetings. It also hinged on who did the best jobs in dramatizing their despair. Those were the factors that influenced the politicians in the distribution of public resources and jobs. As government programs grew, the manner in which people received assistance also changed. In days past, individual families in Mexican-American communities helped each other with food, childcare, and other family needs. Government programs started to alter these customs and traditions.

Looking to government for help was a new experience for many Mexican-American families. Looking outside themselves, their extended families, or friends in the barrio was not their custom. Mexican-American activist organizations saw their missions as ensuring that these families got their fair share of a seemingly unending source of government help. Late-night meetings were organized to plan strategies. Entire grassroots campaigns were staged to register people to vote, become involved in local elections, and rally behind candidates who seemed to care for the Mexican-American and didn't mind exchanging favors for votes. Ethnic politics became the currency of deal making in the 1960s as Mexican-American leaders and their organizations rushed to awaken the "Sleeping Giant."

For those in the trenches of the community, it didn't dawn on us that the game of politics involved larger, behind-the-scenes interests. We didn't see ourselves directly or indirectly linked to a larger political process. We didn't pause to analyze and figure out what was really happening at other, higher levels of political deal making. It would be later that we would understand the game being played wasn't only about helping out Mexican-Americans. There were larger interests at stake.

The political landscape of our country was being reshaped. A more liberal philosophy of politics had been injected into the stream. It started with the election of John F. Kennedy and continued with

Lyndon Baines Johnson. It made clear distinctions between old ideas and new thinking. Liberal ideology painted conservatives as the people against America's minorities, as those who turned their backs on the poor and disenfranchised. Great Society programs gave us the means and reasons to fight back. A different form of coalition politics was emerging.

Previously, unions, business interests, and people who shared similar ideologies formed the mainstream political organizations of our country. For Latinos, ethnic politics became a force of its own. Mexican-Americans were seen as potentially being able to make a strategic difference in the delicate balance of power among those who controlled public resources, especially when candidates with divergent political beliefs were evenly matched. This realization, and the promise to channel huge amounts of money to our local communities, fueled many Mexican-American organizations and scores of young adults like me to become political activists.

On the public level, the Kennedy-Johnson era meant jobs, better housing, improved health care, and legal services for the poor. Privately, however, most of us were also driven by the acquisition of power and influence in the Mexican-American community. It meant being on center stage, becoming the gatekeepers with the power to make the system more accessible to other Mexican-Americans who wanted in.

By becoming involved in organizing communities and advocating for Latinos, we molded our beliefs into simple demands. The more education a person receives, the higher he goes in the hierarchy. The higher in the hierarchy, the more help can be given to others. The more resources the person controls, the more help is made available to the community. The more power is amassed, the more control the person has over outcomes. It never occurred to us that the Great Society might possibly have been the biggest political "buy out" in the modern day history of America's so-called "minority" leaders. First, you buy the leaders; then they feel compelled to defend the existing policies. You throw money at poor communities and let them become consumed with fighting over who gets the most. You make upward mobility into America's service class more accessible to a few educated individuals, and they in turn defend the status quo against the outcries of the less skilled who get left behind to fend for themselves. You make the new, emerging leadership more economically and socially dependent on the larger system to maintain their status. The prospect of making costly changes in the policy that widen the opportunity structure for others is forever weakened.

These possibilities never crossed the minds of us young warriors. The race for power, position, title, and influence in the larger society was the driving force that blinded all of us.

I first realized this in the mid-1970s when invited to attend a meeting at the Hilton Hotel in Atlanta, Georgia. The conference theme was on small town, rural development. I was part of a Texas project that included private foundations, a few state agencies, and a scattering of major corporations like the Levi Strauss Company. My role in representing the Texas Department of Community Affairs was to give a brief talk on the special needs of small rural communities. Earlier in the year, officials of the Levi Strauss Foundation invited us to Embarcadero Center in San Francisco to meet Walter Haas, St., chairman of the board of the Levis Strauss Company. Rudy Flores, special assistant to Governor Dolph Briscoe, Ben McDonald, Jr., executive director of the Texas Department of Community Affairs, and I flew to California. It was there that we also met a younger Haas family member who was in college at the time. Despite the enormous wealth and influence of the Levi Strauss Company, Wally Hass III didn't seem too different from most college kids. It struck me as interesting that he had long hair down to his shoulders and wore faded blue jeans and sandals. He looked hippy-like.

The second time Wally and I saw each other was a few weeks later at the symposium in Atlanta. He darted in and out of meetings, stopping only for a moment to exchange greetings before going on to another session. During a break, we ended up visiting and conducting small talk for several minutes.

Wally invited me to join him at a special rap session with friends.

Inside the closed-door session, away from the larger conference, a few college-age students sat on the carpet of a large private meeting room. All of them were in a heated a discussion with an older gentleman. He was tall and well-groomed, maybe in his late fifties wearing his tailored pin-striped suit and well-selected accessories. He appeared to be a person of influence, maybe the head of a large firm. By the time we entered, tempers had already started to flare. Edging a little closer to better understand what was happening, I whispered to Wally to explain. Everyone was too involved in the arguments to notice or even acknowledge our presence.

"This is an organization of children who inherit wealth," he whispered back, "We get money from our parents to run community foundations. Money goes to support Third World organizations like Trabajadores de la Raza in San Francisco."

"What kind of money are you talking about?" I said, eagerly wanting more information. "And what do you mean by community foundations?"

"We're talking one or two million per foundation," he responded. "Sometimes several million. It all depends on who it is, what they're doing, or who their parents are. These kids run the foundations. They create the rules and make regulations for community giving."

Wally talked as though there wasn't anything special or important about the meeting. To him, no one ever agreed on anything anyway.

"And who's the guy standing up? Why are they arguing with him?" I asked curiously, while beginning to realize that my participation at the symposium was little more than a small insignificant sideshow. Larger, almost invisible forces were in place that Wally was inadvertently allowing me to witness firsthand.

"Oh that guy?" he continued. "He's our tax attorney and advisor. He's the guy who explains what we can or can't do. He basically keeps the foundations out of trouble. He's not the bad guy. I've never understood why my friends get so mad at him. He's just doing his job."

They were involved in the lives of people and determining outcomes. They were getting hands-on, job training better than any business school they attended could possibly provide in dealing with important social issues while also experimenting with community charity and learning about tax laws.

"An expensive social toy," I angrily thought to myself. "We're their social and business experiments. These college students are learning the real-life business of working with people and organizations through groups like us who go to them for help. This is social engineering at its highest. They make the rules and determine the outcomes. We only comply by following the rules. Wow!"

I never shared my feelings and thoughts with Wally. Nothing would be gained from revealing my rage. The next day, while standing in line waiting for a conference closing speech by newly appointed United Nations Ambassador Andrew Young, a couple of women standing behind me carried on a similar conversation.

"You make the motion," one asked the other. "I'll second it. But do it."

There was no question that they came from wealth. Their clothes, the jewelry, their look – everything about them said it all. The next day, the front page of the *Wall Street Journal* announced the news that corporate America was getting behind the Women's Movement. On the final evening, before returning to Austin, I made a late night call to Arturo Gil, a longtime friend and associate at the state agency where we both worked.

"Hey Tootie," I said, "forget about this stuff called self-determination and self-empowerment. Our future is being shaped as we talk. We're only pawns in an invisible chess game."

"What are you talking about?" he asked, not having the slightest notion of what I could have possibly meant.

"Forget about it," I responded. "We'll talk later."

In 1979, when a new administration came to power in Texas to run state government, everything crashed for me. I was rushed away from my desk and into a side office.

"We need your job, Mr. Nieto," came the request. "Do you mind clearing it out by noon?"

A twenty-seven year old was asking me to vacate my desk, put my life's work on hold.

By now, over twelve years had gone by working in the public sector. Life had been generous to me. Beginning with my first job in Houston in 1964, advancement had been constant and the money that followed reliable. The end, however, was quick and sudden.

After being let go for the first time in my life, I drove back to Houston to be with my parents. Jobless and no longer having a title was weird. For the moment, my most immediate concerns were paying bills and putting food on the table for my four children. Years before, my former boss, Bend McDonald, after losing his bid to be re-elected mayor of Corpus Christi, observed, "I could have called all my friends with a quarter." Strangely, I felt the same way at that moment.

I felt alone as I drove to Houston. It was almost midnight when I finally reached my parent's driveway. Difficult as it was, we always talked openly, *"con confianza"* (with a frankness).

"I was fired, mom," came my sudden announcement sitting at the dinner table where hot coffee and pan mexicano were always available. I couldn't bear to see their eyes, their faces. All I could do at first was drink my coffee and remain staring down at the floor. Mom and Dad were generally cool under fire. It would take them a few moments to gather their thoughts and respond.

"¿Como, hijo? (How, son?)" asked Mom.

Sitting by the dinner table, she walked over and gently cupped her hands around my face. There was nothing else to say or analyze. Several seconds went by in silence with the three of us sitting around the dinner table. Dad was at the other end like always. His elbows rested on the table, his hands were clasped together. His look said everything. Rough as he was, he also had a special kindness when times were difficult. Here I was, his youngest son at thirty-nine, in the process of a divorce, unemployed with no plans for anything.

"Te dije que no metieras en la politica, mijo, (*I told you not to get involved with politics, son,*)" he said.

"¿Pero sabes que, Ernesto? Él sabe por qué, (*But you know what, Ernesto? He knows why,*)" he said, slowly pointing upwards to signify his belief in God.

Looking up to listen, I noticed his eyes welling up with tears. Dad understood my hurt at the time, the embarrassment of being let go, my suddenly unsettled life.

"Vamos pa' fuera, mijo, (*Let's go outside, son,*)" he motioned to me. Whenever we discussed intimate thoughts and feelings, it was always in private. We sat out back the remainder of the night, until the early morning sun broke through an overcast Houston sky. It was time to think, to map out a different future.

The next day, I got in my car with a few dollars in my pocket and left for north New Mexico. I needed the open spaces of mountains and winding roads to think. Towards midnight, I pulled into a gas station in Hobbs. Not having too much money to waste on a motel room, the attendant gave me an estimate on the driving time to Las Vegas, a small town between Santa Fe and Raton.

"About 150 miles," he said pointing northward. "Maybe three or four hours."

After an hour on the road, the flickering light of little village towns along the way slowly turned to darkness. Only the headlights of my car guided me along the narrow and lonely road. Another half-hour later, not even farm lights could be seen off in the distance.

My nerves and mind started playing games. "Have I gone too far already? Maybe I shouldn't continue?" By now, radio stations were out of range. No music or talk shows to occupy my time, nothing but darkness and total silence.

"I shouldn't have come to New Mexico," I thought to myself, "especially in my state of mind."

Two hours later, after imagining the worst that could possibly happen to me or any other human being, I came over a small mountain pass. Right below me were the bright, shining lights of Las Vegas, New Mexico! Only a small, mountain town of less than 14,000, Las Vegas might as well have been New York City. At the moment, that's the way it seemed to me. More importantly, I was safe. I made it after eighteen hours straight on the road, all the way from Houston.

After catching up on my sleep at a small motel, I rode around alone looking at the town and surrounding villages. I ate lunch in Mora, eventually ending up in Peñasco. The people had a particular peace about them. Unlike me, they were settled, unhurried, anchored in the earth.

Staying over a couple of more days wasn't a difficult decision. The time would allow me to drive around the mountain roads, stopping on occasion to watch the streams quietly gushing down the mountains. The Trucha Mountains were like a personal retreat. They gave me time to think about my career and reflect on beliefs that were taking me in different direction. Much had to be evaluated.

There was a lot to consider that went beyond salaries, benefits, and opportunities for promotions. Government was out of my immediate future. Returning to Houston was not a consideration, mainly because my children were in Austin. Nothing could ever cause me to leave them, even lucrative job offers from as far away as Washington. The thought occurred that maybe this was the best time to let go and proceed with the idea of an institute for Latinos. Mom, Dad, and I had discussed this possibility many times before.

Despite my efforts to think otherwise, I felt increasingly abandoned and empty. Service to the community had taken fourteen good years out of my life. In the end, was it all worth it? Was there something compelling about these experiences that could take the edge out of ending my career as a government employee? Maybe I was no more than another in a litany of faceless players who did little more than serve the interests of others.

Questions gushed from my mind. Sometimes the answers jumped out. They were real, obvious, right there in front for me to evaluate. At times I concluded that I had been fooled. The thoughts continued pouring into my head. How do you teach young future Latino leaders to define their own playing fields, determine their own directions, and respond to the self-interests of their own communities? How do you steer them away from the illusions of power and influence held out by others as the payoff for involvement in schemes in which they control neither the process nor the outcomes? How do you make future Latino leaders more rule makers rather than followers?

Answers didn't come easily. All I could do at times was stare off into the distance and sit along a mountain stream absorbed in the silence of open spaces. I remembered Arthur Freedman, a mentor-friend of mine. Our relationship dated back to my days with the War on Poverty in 1968 Houston. He had been a key dealmaker in "keeping Houston cool." Arthur had also worked with the Black Stone Rangers in Chicago and was developing a reputation for himself as a trainer in community organization. I recalled a story he once told me while discussing the prospects of starting an institute in the Latino community.

"Be careful Ernie," he said. "Look around and make sure that you don't get sucked into other agendas that have no relationship to the work you want to do."

Arthur described an incident when a group of nurses in Chicago organized a strike against a local hospital in reaction to low wages and bad working conditions. This was 1968, during the Vietnam Conflict, when protests and public demonstrations were common. A walkout by nurses took place that not only made front-page news in the *Chicago Tribune;* it literally paralyzed the hospital administration. The demands became public news. A committee of nurses and their supporters met with the hospital management to hammer out an agreement.

The list of demands was later reported. The plight of the nurses no longer remained the lead headlines. Instead, the demand that the United States get out of Vietnam occupied top billing.

Understanding the possibilities of something similar happening again, Arthur wanted me to use caution. We talked for hours on problems I could encounter. He was concerned about me falling prey to the private interests of others or becoming entangled in the agendas of those who didn't have my best interests in mind.

Arthur also wanted me to appreciate that not all my former experiences with government had been wasted. Much had been learned working as a community organizer, a supervisor and manager, and as an executive policy advisor. Through the years, these jobs had exposed me to experiences that might have been beyond my reach in other more traditional work settings. State and federal governments gave me an understanding of public policy. I was able to gain firsthand insight into the dynamics of in-house political struggles for dominance. I acquired other skills that would later benefit me, such as knowledge of state and federal regulations on non-profit management, organizational development, budget and finance, and evaluation.

I acquired these skills and capacities through years of on-the-job training. Now it was time to separate myself from the herd, take a different direction, and attempt to go at it alone. Being in northern New Mexico, at that moment of my life, without friends, family, or the security of a job, forced me to take a long and close view at the upcoming journey.

In my state of mind, there was little to show for my life since graduation from college. I lasted only two years as a classroom teacher, two years with a local organization, five years with federal government, and an equal amount of time with the state. By thirty-nine, when most professionals start to emerge, life for me came to an abrupt halt. I was fired from my job. No more paychecks, no retirement program, no investments, nothing to fall back on. On top of these setbacks was a divorce and separation from my children.

"¿Y por que te pones triste, mijo? (And why are you sad, son?)" Mom would ask me during these moments. *"Tienes tu salud, una mente sana, y el resto de tu vida. Estás joven, y te falta mucha vida. No se ponga triste mijo. Sea fuerte y haga su propia vida.* (You have your health, a healthy mind, and the rest of your life. Be strong and go on with your life.)"

At this juncture in my life, questions had to be asked and answers contemplated. What were my mistakes? What were the warning signs that I failed to observe? Had a thinking of social reform and no self-enterprise blinded me? Was I little more than a reflection of prevailing Mexican American thoughts and beliefs?

Maybe it was time to take a step out and start seeing myself as having ownership of my life's plans and solutions, without depending on someone or something else to come save me. The War on Poverty certainly didn't hold the promise I had dreamed about. In the end there was no Sir Lancelot to defend or lead Latinos into the future. May it was little more than an attempt to realign the political structure of American society by private interests more concerned with wielding power than solving poverty in our country. Could that have been the real underlying motive?

The experience in Atlanta made me realize that larger political and economic games are constantly in play. A similar lesson was learned regarding La Raza Unida Party. No matter the hype and the public attention any social or political movement receives, the media play a large and important role in conveying its meaning to the public.

The bar incident in Houston was another lesson in life. You don't assume. You don't place yourself in a higher position of power or authority over others because they seem to have less. You don't go around representing yourself as championing the cause of others unless you spend the time and energy earning that right. And finally, the Arthur Freedman story prepared me to become alert to those who become part of community efforts, but only with the intent of furthering their own private political motives and agendas. Arthur wasn't counseling me to be defensive about forming partnership with other community groups and business interests. He wanted me to be lean in my agenda and careful in selecting those invited to come in.

Literally hundreds of other experiences continued to influence and shape my thinking along the way. Undoubtedly, working in anti-poverty programs, having top positions in state and federal government agencies, and becoming involved in the politics of the Latino community were key factors in my development. The most important outcome of these experiences, however, was in coming to grips with how little control I had come to exercise over my journey as an individual first and also as a Latino.

Life for most of us was spent surviving, reacting to our needs and aspirations. It wasn't up to us to solve the problem. We could only point to the pain. We weren't at a stage in our development where we could enjoy the privilege of thinking, analyzing, and pursuing our lives' interests and ambitions. Life for us was one of comparing what it was we didn't have as a community and organizing to remove what stood in the way of accomplishing what we wanted. The role of our political leaders was to negotiate on our behalf and point us in the right direction. We never stopped to think or evaluate the stakes involved, the price we were expected to pay along the way, and the outcomes we would be asked to accept.

Soon after returning from New Mexico, my thoughts began pointing me in a different way. Where before I would have immediately thought of solutions through government assistance or private philanthropy, the search for answers took me inward, toward the Latino community. Seeing Latinos as problem-solvers, not merely conveyors of needs, was at first a difficult philosophical leap for me. Decades of history, personal experiences, and social conditioning had impacted my views and beliefs. The Latino community was more influenced by its poverty and suffering than by its capacities and abilities. Besides, it was easier to explain the pain than to prescribe the medicine.

After all the years of pursuing the old, thoughts started to occur that offered a different bent. Perhaps it was better to work towards gaining more control over our needs and aspirations as a community rather than rely on government and conventional politics to intervene? Maybe an important first step was to design strategies that changed our ways of thinking and relating to one another? And perhaps there was an urgent need for a different kind of institution in the Latino community, one that would concern itself with changing Latino self-images to those of an intelligent, enterprising, and resourceful people with vast untapped potential.

The need for an organization like the National Hispanic Institute, as we know it today, begun to unfold. And, having Gloria at my side, at this juncture of my development, discussing life in the future on the way to the Rio Grande Valley was perfect timing for a man who was desperately searching for new answers.

Chapter Three: Loss of Innocence

    1. Write one or two brief stories to describe one or two defining moments in your life so far.
    2. How did these defining moments influence your sense of purpose in your life?
    3. In what ways have your defining moments raised questions about how you engage your life experiences and deal with the challenges by which you are confronted?
    4. How have your defining moments challenged your beliefs, opinions, or assumptions about how you deal with your life challenges?
    5. What do you think and feel about these challenges? What have you chosen to do when confronted by challenging life situations?

6. How effective have you been in dealing with challenging life situations?
7. What have you learned about your self- e.g., your beliefs, assumptions, hopes, fears, expectations, and aspirations – as a result of trying to cope with your challenges?
8. What have you learned about other people? Who is helpful (and why)? Who is not helpful (and why)?

Chapter Four
Conflicts in Identity

In the beginning, giving the newly created National Hispanic Institute a public identity and role in the Latino community was a difficult and time-consuming task. We spent countless hours carefully crafting our work and trying to anchor the institute of community.

At times, our talks appeared endless, lasting late into the early morning hours. We needed to provide NHI with an image that was distinct from other Latino groups. The answers had come from our souls. We couldn't just be different. We needed to have a believable reason for existing and accepted public good to serve. We needed core beliefs and values to guide our ideas. Our goal was to become self-supporting instead of dependent on government funding and private charity.

It was difficult to watch other Latino organizations get hundreds of thousands, even millions of dollars, from different government agencies and private foundations. Because of my background in government, it would have been simple to call former colleagues and ask them to intervene in guiding proposals through the funding process.

We knew people in influential circles. In the early 1980's, we still had contact with various government agencies and Latino officials. Several were close friends. We knew that making a few calls and getting their support meant money.

However, obtaining government funding was not the driving force in establishing the institute. Our struggle was emotional. We had to fight off the urge to go after the "easy money." Taking the unconventional route would be difficult. We would take our case before the Latino community. If the National Hispanic Institute was intended to thrive, its capacity to succeed had to come from the people we intended to serve. We weren't there to meet the interests or needs of government programs or the priorities of foundations and corporate interests. Our task was to channel our energies in a different manner to strike a responsive chord in the Latino community.

We understood from the start that this would be a difficult task. We were all stuck on perceptions and ideas built on past experiences. For individuals like me, who were influenced by the 1960's and 1970's, government programs played an enormous role in shaping our social thinking and our understanding of community need. The popular belief was that the "squeaky wheel gets grease."

Through NHI, we were poised to point to particular problems in the Latino community and tell our story. We were ready to run the gamut on a range of community needs, neatly putting a price tag on each. This was not, however, what we wanted for NHI.

We needed authenticity and clear purpose in our work. None of us realized the difficulties we would encounter along the way in becoming innovators and crafters. The process of shaping something new became a difficult and sometimes overwhelming task. This was not a struggle with the community. This was an inner struggle to extend beyond the limits of our realities.

In 1980, NHI's first program wasn't aimed at high school youth. Our agenda was to address the special needs of young professional Latinos entering government employment. During my years as a state and federal employee, I witnessed the enormous encounters of young Latinos who were attempting to make the jump from their hometowns in South Texas, the Rio Grande Valley, and El Paso to the mainstream settings of Dallas, Austin, and Washington D.C. Making the cultural leap to live in new social and cultural arenas was strenuous for these individuals. They were more accustomed to former lives of being around other Latinos. I experienced this firsthand when I left Houston in 1968.

When I moved 160 miles away from Austin, I might as well have been going to the other side of the planet. The change not only involved having to adjust to a different social and cultural climate; it also required making emotional and psychological changes into a new job environment where the performance requirements were much more demanding on my stamina and the time I spent with my family. I went from an eight-hour day spend mostly in neighborhoods close to home in Houston to a new routine that included days, sometimes weeks of policy discussions with difficult supervisors. I left family for extended periods while on business trips. My new work culture involved working sixteen-to-eighteen hour days.

In the late 1960's and 1970's, the number of Latinos working for the government agencies in professional capacities swelled. At that time, the higher paying positions weren't in corporate America. Those doors were shut for Latinos. Conversely, government-funded, nonprofit organizations established to serve low-income minority families offered new career opportunities. For the lucky few who had college degrees, upward mobility was not as difficult as it was for our predecessors prior to the 1960's. We were diamonds in the rough, waiting to be discovered and plucked.

In 1964, right out of college, I worked for a few months in Houston with the Salvation Army's Red Shield Boys Club. My starting salary was slightly less than two dollars an hour. As a first-year teacher, my income jumped to $4, 800 a year. Later, a position with the Deer Park School District took me up to $5,700 a year. With less than twenty-four months of teaching under my belt, my career track changed again. This time, however, a job with an anti-poverty agency started me at $15,000 a year, an unheard-of salary for most people who grew up in the barrio. Other opportunities followed soon after with a federal agency, where I doubled my previous salary.

Years later I discovered that other, more tenured, career federal employees worked entire lifetimes to reach salary schedules that had been offered to me as a first-year person. There was another problem involved: I didn't know what to do with my newfound affluence. My life had been spent struggling to make ends meet. As children, my brothers and I shared pants and shoes. Going out meant being extremely frugal. Every dime we earned as teenagers was turned over to mom. No one had personal ownership over anything. Everything belonged to everyone. In college, Mom sent me ten dollars every two weeks to spend. Owning a car was out of the question. Now there was an abundance of money that was far more than our daily needs required.

In 1968, a two-bedroom house in Austin cost $80 a month for my wife and six-month-old son, Roy. The monthly payment for a brand new 1968 Chevy Sports Coupé was $125. My dilemma was what to do with my money. After years of going to college and struggling to get a degree, I had the means to lead a better quality of life, purchase better things for my family, and even do something special for Mom and Dad.

Having more financial access also placed me at different level of community life, it allowed me the first-time opportunity to buy a new wardrobe at department stores like Sakowitz and Norton Dittos, where most Latinos never shopped. Buying suits cost over $150 back then was a thrilling experience for a young Latino. Being referred to as "Mr. Nieto" by the salesman while walking out with a name brand suit in a plastic garment bag from a well-respected clothing store gave me a different identity, a new sense of importance.

A few extra dollars also made me recall my teenage years when shopping meant only peering through store windows at what we wanted. I was finally able to purchase Stacy Adams wingtips that were beyond my economic means in high school. As a young kid in the Northside, I was fascinated by the sleek, cut down shoes of the "carnales" (neighborhood buddies). You could almost comb your hair with your reflection on the spit shines.

"Cómo te vistes," Dad used to say, *"le dice al mundo quién eres.* (How you dress, tells the world who you are.)" He wanted me to look the role of a young executive on his way up.

It was also during this time that golf was introduced to me. Few Latinos at the time played golf. While in college at the University of Houston, Homero Blancas was constantly in the newspaper for leading the Cougars to repeated number-one ratings. He was a three-time All-American who learned the game playing alone after hours at the River Oaks Country Club, where his father was a greens keeper and gardener. A sensational golfer, he was the first notable Latino on the professional golf tour.

I was part of a new, emerging, professional class of Latinos, mostly in their late twenties to early thirties. A handful of colleagues like me happened to be in the right place at the right moment when history took a different turn and opportunity knocked on our front doors. Political change was rapid. America's opportunity structure widened and became more inclusive. More of us started to get in, although in small number. I was lucky enough to be there, college degree in hand, ready to be embraced.

A strange psychology occurs whenever a person moves from one economic social stratum to another. At least that was the case for many of my young Latino contemporaries and me. We never stopped to grasp that upward mobility also had its pitfalls. Moving up plays games on the mind and often confuses the emotions. There was a certain guilt associated with being able to afford luxuries in life that others close to me couldn't afford. I made it my personal goal to buy Dad a band saw for his workshop. Mom went with me to personally pick out the lamps she felt would give her house a more attractive look. We were out more often and took longer vacations. In 1972, Dad and I flew to Mazatlán, México, for a weeklong summer vacation of relaxation and deep-sea fishing in a charter boat rented only for us.

Mom stayed home to take care of my daughter, Nicole. At six months of age, she was too young to travel. Besides, Nicole was the daughter Mom never had. It was their private time together.

Dad also had a companion, his three-year-old grandson, Roy. They picked seashells, fed the seagulls and roomed together at out hotel by the seashore. Each morning, we were up by five to run over to Mazatlan's Copa de Leche con Café for breakfast and coffee. Barely peaking over the horizon, the sun's rays painted a deep, blue sky as we quietly ferried out to the sea amidst giant, ragged rocks that broke the surface of calm-day waves and clear waters of the Pacific. The sounds of engines working and hungry seagulls with outstretched wings far off in the sky created a certain satisfying mixture of solace intertwined with the feeling of open freedom. This was the life!

Dad had never been far out in the water, much less deep-sea fishing. The look in his eyes after hooking his first swordfish remains etched in my memory. No one could have helped him at that instant while his catch, several hundred feet away, struggled for freedom. A personal tug-of-war took place between a fish and a stubborn seventy-year-old man. It couldn't fit any better than his: a sabbatical, if only brief, from the confinement of life in the fast lane and the pressures of leaving one culture while entering another.

Still with these successes, there was a telling hollowness in the few of us experiencing life's traditions, feelings that came from enjoying certain pleasures in life that others couldn't. They served as a reminder of what other family members lacked, what close personal friends could only imagine, but maybe never possess.

These interacting forces took their toll on Latino managers. Having better-paying jobs also carried a large emotional and psychological price. Some individuals found themselves spending more time at work than with their children and spouses. Others worked tirelessly to open doors for Latinos who wanted similar government jobs or increased government funding for Latino nonprofit organizations in the community. Whatever the motivation, the consequences followed well-defined patterns.

Burnout ran high. After two to three years on the job, several started returning to their hometowns from Austin to Dallas, my hands suddenly started trembling. The more I attempted to control myself, the worse my hands shook. I finally reached the front porch steps of my home, but all I could do was get in the car and head for the nearest hospital emergency room.

A week later I sat in the psychiatrist's office attempting to make sense out of my confusion. Having made the move from Austin to Dallas represented the final change from what had previously been a life filled with Latinos every day of my life to one that was culturally cold and unfamiliar. In what seems one instant to another, my life became an existence of living in an Anglo community, attending Anglo church, and sending my kindergarten-aged son to a mostly Anglo elementary school. With the exception of a couple of professional Latino friends who lived across town, my social network was mostly Anglo, including co-workers and neighbors. Everything was different and uncomfortably permanent.

"Is this what it means to be a Latino professional?" I used to think to myself. "Is this what people mean who make it professionally?" No doubt, I enjoyed more money, better material comforts, and more economic security. "For what?" I'd ask myself. "What's the sense of living alone in a community of strangers, not being around those I loved, seeing them only on holidays, no longer being part of their lives?"

Several years of confusion and sudden midnight panic attacks passed before I caught a glimpse of what was going on inside my head. Answers didn't come from my Dallas doctor. Although he was thoroughly professional in his work, his advice and counsel was confined to his understanding of an Anglo world. Dr. Lymon Phillips, an Austin Latino psychiatrist who grew up in Corpus Christi, was better prepared to understand my stress and needs.

My weekly encounters with Lymon led me to eventually make a critical decision regarding how I wished to spend the rest of my life. The alternative to a healthier mental and emotional state of mind meant leaving government forever and returning to the familiarity of a prior world. There were no compromises. It was time to go back home. Change meant reintegrating into a culture that had been my life as a child.

While I served in an executive role in the state government, I discussed the conflicts and tensions of culture clash with Rudy Flores, special assistant of Governor Dolph Briscoe. One of Rudy's goals was to increase the number of Latinos in middle- and upper- management jobs in state agencies. His influence as a member of the governor's staff made change possible.

During lunch breaks and after work, whenever we had a moment to talk, I'd remind him that watching Latinos make the transition from home to the life of government could be tracked with a stopwatch. After five or six months on the job, a known on my office door indicated a need to talk. "Hey man. Can I talk to you?" someone would ask.

Like me years before, the strained looks on their faces and the first words uttered served as reminders. There were discernible indications of mounting cultural and emotional conflicts. Arming these young men and women with the training to cope and better understanding the forces at play became initial impetus for NHI's work in 1979. It was easy for me to identify with these pressure and feelings of cultural desperation. I was living proof.

Sponsoring stress management intervention programs became the first initiative of the National Hispanic Institute. It took place at Stephen F. Austin Hotel on 7th Street and Congress Avenue in downtown Austin. NHI offices were located on the second floor. The response to our outreach campaign was nothing short of amazing. Over 200, mostly Mexican Americans, attended the inaugural session at a cost of $250 per person. Seeing the initial interest, we immediately planned to sponsor similar sessions in Dallas, El Paso, Midland-Odessa, and Houston.

The problems, stresses, and dilemmas of young Latino professionals were carbon copies of what we had witnessed in Austin. To the participants, it was the workplace: Anglo superiors who didn't understand them culturally and didn't appreciate the impact of high-pressure jobs on their emotional makeup. No one understood the difficulties young Latinos were facing in making the transitions from culturally familiar environments to lives on the fast track of mainstream America. As an organization bent on having a clear purpose and identity, we considered our work important and especially relevant to an upwardly mobile Latino community facing difficulty transition challenges. We were well acquainted with their needs.

We wanted participants who had paid the high registration fees to leave as satisfied customers who would take special insight from our training to their jobs. To achieve those ends, we invested considerable time and money finding trainers with experience in culture conflict and cross-cultural relations. These individuals also had to be powerful, dynamic speakers and presenters. Paying them was not as much a consideration as it was locating quality trainers who understood the changing needs of the emerging Latino professional.

Dr. Roberto Jiménez, a psychiatrist from San Antonio, became our feature trainer. His training and credentials were not typical of Latinos who had gone from the dusty roads of barrio life to the professional world. A distinctive Boston accent that came from years of studies at Harvard, Roberto carefully delivered his message mixed with a Spanish word or two thrown in on occasion. He kept audiences glued to his every utterance. He commanded center stage when it came to understanding the dynamics of the changes that occur whenever people work outside the comforts of their cultural realities.

Jimenez described the phenomenon of cultural transition for Latinos as occurring in four phases. He called them the Initial Phase, the Awareness Phase, the Devitalization Phase, and the Revitalization Phase. Jimenez developed this presentation with Latinos specifically in mind. The personal confusion and stresses of Latino professionals struggling to bridge the gap between competing - as well as clashing - cultures could finally be explained, and the depressions and misgivings of the Latino professional could finally be understood. From the training, they were able to accept the phenomenon and dynamics of culture conflict not as an aberration or something unusual to the individuals, but normal to the human experience. For us, as an organization presenting its inaugural program, Jimenez gave NHI a special place and meaning. The Initial Phase was described as "the high" Latinos get from making the crossover, landing the big job, or having "made it". He highlighted the feelings of this phase as losing touch with the distant past and future and focusing instead on the rush one feels from having accomplished an important feat and experiencing the payoffs.

The Initial Phase was described as "the high" Latinos get from making the crossover, landing the big job, or having "made it." He highlighted the feelings of this phase as losing touch with the distant past and future and focusing instead on the rush one feels from having accomplished an important feat and experiencing the payoffs.

"We don't measure our personal achievements,They get this feeling the first time they read a letter acknowledging their admission to a dream college. At that moment, nothing is more important or exciting."

Jimenez explained the similarity of feelings Latinos were experiencing in the professional world. "The euphoria lasted days, even weeks. Everything around is exaggerated and wonderful. Enjoying the world, walking around on a cloud, paying attention to everything seen or touched is part of the experience, of having accomplished the big dream. The person feels special and contented, sometimes for weeks, even months."

Jimenez would then take the audience to the second phase- the realization part of the journey when one gets the first inkling that things might not be as well as first thought. He associated the Awareness Phase, as he called it, with the feelings one gets inside the pit of the stomach after getting the first bad grade in school or having a confrontation with a supervisor at work.

"Do you remember that first D or even F in chemistry or philosophy in college?" he would ask. "Do you remember the time you were called in and maybe even chastised for something you did wrong at work, when you were made to feel different, no longer included in the whole? The Awareness Phase begins as you recognize that maybe what you thought was wonderful at first is not exactly what it was cut out to be. It's that time when a question mark pops up in your mind and starts altering your previous environment, not with the people, but with you."

Jimenez spent considerable time on the third phase called Devitalization. As a Vietnam veteran, he littered his explanations with accounts of soldiers on the battlefield who, after losing arms or legs thought about devitalization as being the time in the person's life when letdowns in life, personal demise, and feelings of abject failure are present.

"This is when you start questioning why your life has become such a cruel experience," he'd say. "Why me? In some cases, you even begin to sense that there are people around you who don't have your best interests in mind, maybe even wish to hurt you. In college, students change majors because they determine that a particular professor doesn't like them or they don't have a sufficient grasp of the coursework requirements to pass. Some stop hanging around close friends. They start sticking mostly to themselves. Some go back home, maybe transfer to other colleges. In more severe cases, they start drinking, becoming sexually promiscuous, maybe even start doing drugs. On the surface, they seem to enjoy being different, standing apart from the rest. Depending on how severe the depression, some even consider suicide. They create their own realities, their own truths and beliefs about the world in which they find themselves."

Jimenez reviewed examples in the workplace, making sure that the participants fully understood the Devitalization Phase as having the potential to become dangerous when it came to consequences.

The fourth phase, Revitalization, was described as being more introspective and lasting for those able to shift over.

"The Revitalization Phase," Jimenez said, "is the human instinct to survive, to shake off the past, to hang those things that burden us in life in exchange for a fresh start. In revitalization, people no longer think everything is possible as they did during the initial phase. Instead they start thinking of what's possible for them for them as individuals."

Jimenez defined revitalization as a soul-searching experience for different truths, the discarding of the old, and the beginning of the new. Jimenez also described revitalization as a journey in which the individual controls the environment, their interactions with others, and the outcomes they expect to achieve.

"In revitalization," he would instruct the participants, "feeling capable of laying out a personal life agenda is an exciting, even exhilarating experience. You're no longer enamored by a life out there, beckoning you to join by adhering to the expectations and standards of others. You become your own architect, the designer of what makes you happy and content with yourself. You take charge and start surrounding yourself with people who love and want to be with you. Your family and former neighborhood buddies take on a new meaning in your personal life journey."

The success of these first-time stress management sessions was immediate. Participants returned to their jobs realizing that at last there was an organization like the National Hispanic Institute that understood their feelings and conflicts, and could help them better cope with the pressures of "being minorities constantly struggling in a majority world." Jimenez became a popular presenter, often asked to give the same lecture to different organizations and groups around the state. Word on NHI quickly spread.

At the institute, we weren't satisfied. Despite the temporary relief many experienced from participating in our stress management programs, the "affliction," as we described the problem afterwards, remained. Gaining awareness for the emotions triggered by culture conflicts at their jobs was important to the participants in our view. Most would return to their jobs better equipped to cope with the conflicts that invariably surface in diverse cultural settings. Gaining insight, however, wasn't the final answer. It was only a partial response to a larger challenge.

In our estimation, tensions would remain high primarily because "cultural clash" is nothing more than a euphemism that describes a struggle for cultural dominance in the workplace. The fight for dominance doesn't go away until the influences least able to sustain the pressure finally give way to the more powerful ones.

In our view, understanding the dynamics of these interactive influences might temporarily help young professional Latinos in the workplace. The training, however, wouldn't help solve their concerns, not to their satisfaction.

Months of discussion brought us to another observation. By twenty-five years of age, Latinos in mainstream jobs might no longer be trainable as leaders of the Latino community. The psychological damage of long-term, unresolved culture conflicts at work and in the community was forcing them into permanent modes of reactive behavior that made therapeutic counseling a more needed service.

The extent of influence that mainstream work environments seemed to be having on Latino young professionals turned our efforts towards high school youth. Our work needed to start with young men and women who were not yet prisoners of mainstream jobs. Our new challenges were evaluating the best ways of approaching this age group, determining which type of youth would be good prospects as future Latino leaders, and analyzing the kind of training need to attract and sustain their interest.

Over the next year, Jimenez and I spent countless hours evaluating NHI's direction. The stress management programs had given us a live laboratory to observe and analyze workplace problems facing Latino professionals. It didn't matter whether these young adults lived in Houston, Dallas, Corpus Christi, or Odessa out in West Texas. The conflicts and issues they described followed the same patterns.

Other outcomes came from NHI's early training experiences. The success of our start-up programs steered us away from traditional sources of funding, like grants. We didn't need to portray Latinos in a negative manner to obtain financial assistance. As a friend often reminded me, "You don't have to tap dance or do Bojangles to create attention. You don't have to make someone feel bigger than they really are in order for them to help." Well-designed professional training services aimed at the needs of certain sectors of the Latino community could potentially generate the financial resources required by NHI to sustain its work.

By becoming enterprising and self-sustaining in our development, we started to uncover a treasure of Latinos in the academic community. Several were conducting important research on the mental health and educational needs of the Latino community. Most were interested in having a connection to the professional sectors of the community. The institute provided them with a means to connect directly with Latinos in the workplace, something that was not an everyday experience in the classrooms of American colleges and universities where they taught. For us at NHI, however, these early experiences in training were crucial. They allowed us to further illuminate the role the institute could potentially play in Latino community life.

One of our first conclusions was that NHI would not become a politically involved community activist group advocating for the underprivileged. That much was clear. Instead, the organization would concentrate on the specialized needs of young men and women who had the intellectual capacities and potential to operate at higher levels of community life. An oversight in our thinking was in not stopping to first evaluate the amount of friction and arguments this direction would cause among staff, the NHI board, and people in the community whose help we would need the most to get started.

"What are you doing to work with drop-outs, young people who don't have skills to get jobs? What about drug addicts, runaways, and pregnant teenagers? What are you doing about them? Why are you concentrating on youth who have it made, who don't have problems?"

These were questions asked by friends. They were also teachers, long-time friends, community leaders, and heads of organizations that knew us. Their historical understanding of community service was to work with the need; not those who didn't need help. They insisted on an explanation. Why weren't we doing the same, like other organizations in the Latino community? Why did we want to be different? What was there to be gained? Why were we turning away from Latinos with more urgent needs to work with youth who didn't really need help?

The answers to their questions weren't easy. Despite our attempts to explain, we often stayed up late at night thinking about our decisions. It took a few more years to believe in our instincts.

We determined that NHI wasn't established to work with Latinos facing the always-difficult circumstances of not having the education, training, or skills to attain gainful employment. Our job also wasn't to work with the needs of low-performing youth being kicked out of school, dropping out, or getting pregnant. We weren't here to guide high-performing Latino youth in making the jump to mainstream either. It wasn't our responsibility to prepare them for life outside of the Latino world. There were more institutions than we could ever imagine which were much better prepared and more able than NHI to do that job.

Instead, we saw our mission as guiding our more gifted youth back towards the Latino community. They were our top candidates with the potential to give our community a much-needed boost in intellectual leadership. Eventually they would also have the abilities and know-how to use their skills and expertise to grow new businesses in the Latino marketplace, possibly participate in crafting a new identity of Latinos as a global culture. They also were able to think critically and hopefully would cause a shift in Latino thinking from dependency on the larger system for solutions towards self-direction and self-enterprise.

Making this mission part of our institutional challenge was exciting. But it was only part of the equation. Our overall concepts and approaches still needed to be hammered out. For a Latino community historically conditioned to advocate for the underdog, making a case for the needs of intellectually gifted Latino children would not be immediately embraced. The conventional wisdom was that Latino youth with good grades in school didn't need help. Those children could easily make it on their own. The suspicion was that NHI's hidden motive was to "cream the top" and take public credit for students already poised for success. Others would go so far as to contend that NHI had abandoned the needy, instead adopting an elitist attitude towards the rest of the Latino community as a way of buying into the pocketbooks of corporate America.

While discussions during these early years at NHI were sensitive to these sentiments, we also weren't overly concerned. Instead, we concentrated on the special challenges that high-ability Latino youth would face when approached to consider becoming leaders in the Latino community. As Gloria de Leon would argue during late-night discussion sessions at the office, "Leadership in the Latino community is not something you do as a hobby or passing interest when you have time. It's not something you put on your resume. It's a way of life that's based on a deep, motivating appeal for people you enjoy, love, and want to be with."

For the caliber of youth and families being considered a NHI's primary market audience, life in the Latino community would probably not be seen as an appealing alternative, especially when compared to the lifestyles and attractions of the corporate world and the glamour of the fast lane. Training for future leadership roles in the Latino community could easily be interpreted as being socially and economically confining. Some would see it as being forced to work with the underprivileged and undereducated. Our task as an organization was to devise an attractive appeal for the more mobile and intellectually gifted child, painting a Latino culture that was much more positive and appealing than the negative images portrayed by the media.

The constant tug between putting old beliefs to rest and adopting new ones left us with little energy. The motivation for giving and becoming involved in Latino community life in the 1960s had previously come from the perception of Latinos being seen as economically and socially disabled people with enormous needs. To counteract these views, we had to devise something different and create a set of beliefs and truths that could give Latino youth a healthier and more productive understanding of themselves and the many roles they could play as future leaders. And with prior rates of failure being high for those who had been willing to risk the crossover, we concluded that years, perhaps generations, would be needed to see the first seeds of change start to appear on the horizon.

Setting the stage for new thinking to evolve was only one small step. The task would be enormous and ambitious, beyond the capacities of any one individual to shoulder. NHI could no longer see itself as an advocate for community change, not in the civil rights sense, like other Latino organizations could. The National Hispanic Institute needed a different role, a calling of its own. Injecting a different social direction into the thinking of the Latino community would act to challenge Latino youth intellectually, emotionally, and spiritually. A new Latino reality would also have to be crafted, not one confined to barrio depiction of gang wars, drugs, violence, and suffering. Instead a new panorama of opportunity tied together by a global culture of people who daily share a common heritage, language, and history had to be forged.

NHI's role would be to introduce high ability youth to these possibilities, stimulate dialogue regarding the promise of the future Latino world, and create the means to bring Latino youth together. The institute would also introduce these young men and women to a different Latino reality in order for them to better appreciate the promise of an emerging twenty-first century Latino world. In these roles, NHI would become a central force in shaping and influencing future Latino leaders in their quest to lead healthy and productive lives as individuals, and to provide the guidance and advice needed by those willing to journey back as leaders.

After all these years, I finally had a small, but important glimpse of individuals with so little education accomplishing so much in such a short span of time. I now understood the reason they spent so much time together visiting at home at the kitchen table, why they were up at all hours of the day and night.

"*Crear otra vida para ellos,* (Create another form of life for them,)" Dad would often observe at home while sipping coffee, enjoying his pan mexicano.

"*Solo eso los inspira. No es jugar pelota en el parque. Es tener un nuevo motivo para vivir afuera de lo que han entendido.* (Only that will inspire them. It's not playing ball at the park that matters.

It's in having a new motive to live outside of what they've understood.)"

Gloria and I had a lot more talking to do, a lot more to share with each other, many more hours to spend together, just like Mom and Dad.

Chapter Four: Conflicts in Identity

1. Write a brief story that explains which of Dr. Jimenez's four stages you are in right now. Describe what you think about this and how this feels for you.

2. If you decide that you want to move on to the next phase, what do you intend to do for yourself now?

3. Describe a situation in which you have (or you anticipate you will) experience a cross-cultural clash. What challenges did you (do you imagine you will) confront?

4. Write a brief description of the life purposes that you currently wish to fulfill. Remember, this is provisional, so you will probably change this statement in the future- possibly many times.

5. What do you imagine you would think and feel if and when you realized these life purposes?

6. What do you imagine you would think and feel if your efforts fell short of realizing these life purposes? What would you do?

Chapter Five
Tejano Millionaires

Young Latinos struggling to start and manage their own business often go at it alone, without anyone to advise them. Older Latinos with a wealth of experience in the business world aren't readily available to mentor younger ones through their first crucial steps of development. The relationships needed to avoid costly mistakes are few and far between.

For the majority, the knowledge of business is mostly learned through trial and error, through the pain that invariably comes from having made the wrong decisions. There are no maps to success, or beacons to light the way. Mostly, the entrepreneurs live in a reality of having to go it alone, carefully measuring every step along the way. Most instinctively know that one slip could potentially spell the difference between survival and failure. In 1979, I found myself in the same predicament, alone and with no experience in nonprofit management.

"Mira Nieto, (Look at it this way, Nieto,)" the rough and tough Liberio Hinojosa from H&H Meat Products in Mercedes, Texas, told me a few years after NHI got started, *"Si tus servicios no son suficientemente buenos para que te vaya bien y puedas sobrevivir los primeros años, debe de morir tu organización.* (If your services aren't good enough to help you weather the first few years, the organization should die.)"

"¿La discriminación? ¡Olvídate! Tienes que estar ciego a eso, pero también te tiene que gustar trabajar duro (Discrimination? Forget it! You have to be blind to it while being driven to a work you love to do,)" added Willie Salinas in 1982, an owner of the family-run Ideal Derrick in Odessa.

Once I took up starting the National Hispanic Institute, my time was mostly spent ensuring the organization's survival, putting out little brushfires, and staying connected to people who could potentially throw business our way. The wait-and-see game demanded alertness for opportunities, stamina, and patience.

My background and training didn't include business management. All four of NHI's founders were former government employees. Before that, I had been a community organizer and, prior to that, a classroom teacher. Organizing the infrastructure to run a nonprofit organization was not part of my professional repertoire. NHI was my first introduction to business, my exposure to the world of offering our services and products with hopes of making enough money to grow and eventually prosper.

Losing my state job and the accompanying loss of income and deciding to head NHI made life difficult. The change was sudden and glaring. A newly established organization needs daily tending. NHI was a new organization with no track record, no money, and no immediate prospects of obtaining funding. We didn't have an office or even a typewriter. We lacked the cash to meet payroll, make business trips, and pay rent.

At first, the illusion of an NHI for Latinos outmatched the challenge. It was going to be difficult, but not impossible. All it would take, it seemed, was to use the correct marketing techniques, connect with the right movers and shakers in the Latino community, target the right consumers, and deliver quality services.

I was also young and arrogant enough to believe that because I had a degree, I would avoid the same mistakes that older, less-educated Latino businessmen made. The fact that I lacked an understanding of what it really takes to start a business never entered my thinking. Appearances were far more important as I was hell-bent on projecting the public image of a trained executive talented enough to master his world.

Adopting that attitude nearly drove NHI to an early grave. We didn't consider capitalizing our efforts for the short or long haul. We didn't know how to construct a basic business and marking plan to support our efforts. We operated mostly on ego. Before, I had been an executive in government who helped create the policy that funded local projects throughout Texas. Now the tables were turned, as I was the person making the requests for a struggling NHI. Someone else was going to determine the legitimacy and worthiness of our ideas and proposals. The uncertainty of not being able to guarantee some modicum of stability for those who left secure jobs to join me added even more stress.

A couple of other problems also got in the way. In 1979, I was a year removed from divorcing my first wife. I was still trying to adjust to no longer being able to see my children every day. Back at NHI, it was "vato management" (seat of the pants management), full speed ahead, and don't look back, carnal (brother). We kiddingly called this approach "Chicano business theory." By the end of the first year, only a few dollars had come in. Bills piled up. My personal credit was ruined. The phone stopped ringing, and the walls started closing in.

By the end of 1982, everyone who started with me left. Richard Hamner went back to then-State Representative Gonzalo Barrientos. Gonzalo resigned as chairman of the board in reaction to my decision to dismiss a young Lena Guerrero—who later became a Texas Railroad Commissioner. And both Arturo Gil and Arturo Moreno found new employment with the state.

Seeing my condition, Dad advised me one day: *"¿Por qué no vas con amigos tuyos, señores de confianza, que conocen negocio y pueden darte consejos?* (Why not work with friends you can trust who know business and can provide you with counsel?)"

I saw his wisdom. I shouldn't be trying to get a business off the ground without guidance. This was a time to let go of my overgrown ego and stop being *"chingon"* (big time) by seeking good counsel. Besides, the advice would come from my own kind, individuals with similar life experiences who understood how to run a business in the Latino community.

By late 1982, NHI had the most "Who's Who of Texas Latino business owners" on its board of directors. They were people known in the Latino community for their success. They weren't doctors, lawyers, or politicians. They were individuals who had come up the hard way by working sixteen-to-eighteen-hour days. They were men who understood what it meant to work years to reach their goals.

Liborio Hinojosa and Pete Díaz, Jr. came from the Rio Grande Valley of South Texas. "Libo," as his friends know him, ran H&H Meat Products in Mercedes, Texas, a well-known family-run company. Pete Díaz, Jr. owned several grocery stores from Rio Grande City to Brownsville. Sam Moreno's company was Petroleum Energy Equipment Corporation with oilfield equipment supply stores in Texas and Louisiana. Abraham Kennedy had El Gallo, a popular South Austin restaurant. Phil Garza and his brother, Rey, ran a transport services business in Houston, USA Delivery. Pete Dominguez, originally from Austin, had developed a chain of Mexican restaurants in Dallas. By far, the most colorful were the Salinas brothers, Mario and Willie. They manufactured oil derricks in Odessa in West Texas.

Each time this cast got together for board meeting, their rugged Tejano business character always went on display. Outside NHI offices on North Lamar, the parking lot was lined with Cadillacs and Lincolns. Several flew to the meetings in private planes. Once together, they spent more time trading stories regarding their business exploits than attending to the needs of the institute. It wasn't my place to complain. To the contrary, it was a rare opportunity to be in the same room and company with such well-known, experienced Mexican American businessman.

Listening to them give each other advice on special business matters beat any M.B.A. program. There was no business theory here. No one talked politics or suggested that we affiliate with either political party. It was an opportunity to hear real problems and witness real people collaborating with each other on different ways to solve them. They never seemed to be jealous of each other either.

Though wealthy and influential men, they were genuinely interested in each other's successes, often recommending their personal accountants and lawyers to each other. The only differences were their personalities and their life experiences. The bond they shared was in the difficulties they had encountered in getting their businesses off the ground. All of them understood what it meant to start with nothing.

Only Liborio had been in the meatpacking business before as a young man with his father. It was the combined efforts of his family that took H&H Meat Products from a small local operation to a national scale. Sam Moreno had a college degree. Each of the board members spent years inching his business to the top, against enormous odds. All of them understood what it meant to do without, to deal with hostile banks, and to be discouraged. Each had a personal journey to describe.

Whenever an NHI board meeting was called, I never knew exactly how they planned to travel. It was always a guessing game on how they would get to the meeting. *"Tú no más dinos el día y a qué hora tenemos que llegar, y allí nos vemos,* (You just tell us what day and what time you want us be there, and we'll see each other,)' Liborio would often say. He was a man of few words. The ingredients that got him to the top were being unafraid of work, not being scared to get his hands dirty, and demanding quality and commitment from anyone who wanted a role in making H&H Meat Products a national success story.

Board member Willie Salinas also became intensely involved with us. He was particularly interested in our leadership program for young professionals, often showing up with his wife and chauffeur. Once at the training, he would sit motionless through the entire presentation, always in the back row, dressed in his customary black West Texas cowboy hat, blue jeans, boots, and leather vest, always available to help.

"¿Van a la comida, Nieto? (Going to supper, Nieto?)" he would ask. "Alguien necesita algo? (Does anyone need anything?)"

As with most early NHI board members, Willie understood what it meant to start with almost nothing. He and his brother, Mario, were born in the United States; however, they were reared in Agualeguas, Mexico. The need to provide for their family forced them to quit school early. As teenagers, they found work in Houston as welders for an oil derrick manufacturing company. They soon concluded that they could make oil derricks themselves. One day, they bought eleven acres on the outskirts of Odessa and moved there to start their own business.

"Al principio, nadie nos quería dar negocio, Nieto, (At first, no one gave us any business,)" Willie would recall. *"Pero yo mis carnales le metíamos todo el santo día, jalándole, buscando quebrada. Poco a poco, allí íbamos. Primero, no más nos querían como mecánicos, cuando algo se les quebraba. Pero cuando veían lo que estábamos haciendo, y también el precio, pues ¿que iban a hacer los güeros? ¡Allí esta!* (But my brothers and I would work days on end, for hours, working every angle possible, looking for a break. Slowly but surely we kept going. At first, they wanted our services, but only as mechanics when their machinery broke down. But when they saw the quality of our work and what we charged, what were Anglos going to do? That was it!)"

Whenever business took me to Odessa, Texas, Willie refused to let me rent a car. He owned several, ranging from pickup trucks to Cadillacs. For me to spend a night in a hotel while in town was, to him, clearly out of the question. "Tu te quedas aqui, carnal" (You stay here, brother, at my home!) he would demand. "Aquí en mi rancho. (Here, at my ranch.)"

Willie lived close to Mario and their business, Ideal Derrick. A huge sign that read "Willie's Ranch" marked the entrance to his place. He designed everything, including his home. The house included a large den, open kitchen, and plenty of bedrooms. A two-story structure next to it was specially built to entertain friends, called "Willie's Cantina," the décor in the lounge was a loud red. Drinks and food were always free. It was also not unusual for him to order a calf slaughtered and barbecued for friends after a golf tournament or other special occasions.

Having family and friends around was important to Willie and Mario. They had come a long way from Agualeguas, surviving years without money. Now it was time to celebrate and share a little wealth with buddies.

Willie and Mario Salinas were throwbacks to the old days when people never lost their sense of loyalty and appreciation of others. They understood that it was their workers who were behind their climb to the top. These were the people who didn't argue when asked to stay behind to work or spend entire weekends to fill back orders. It was clear why the Ideal Derrick annually sponsored an all-expenses-paid, weeklong resort outing at the Chandler Ranch in deep West Texas for all employees and their families to enjoy. It was also easy to understand why bonuses were shared. Ideal Derrick was not only a business: everyone was treated like family members.

Most of their employees were newly arrived Mexican immigrants willing to sacrifice, clawing at every opportunity to do better. Willie and Mario understood this experience. They understood what it meant to uproot one's self, move to strange surroundings, and feel totally and completely alienated from the environment. They knew the loneliness involved the depths of despair that a person undergoes after making enormous personal sacrifices.

This was the human side to the Salinas brothers that only those close to them witnessed. Too much was made of their individual accomplishments by local newspapers, Latino magazines and organizations in the community. Their everyday human side and their feelings about success and failure were often ignored.

During special moments of reflection and celebration they would sometimes express their thoughts about life. Well hidden in their strong, unyielding characters were their abilities to find humor in their struggles. It was their way of surviving countless disappointments.

The Salinas brothers reminded me of something Dad once shared with me. "When you hear the coyote howl at night," his grandfather used to tell him, "he's not really crying, but laughing at the moon. Laughing is his way of keeping from crying, from accepting failure on this earth. That's his way of surviving. That's what keeps him going. El Mexicano does the same. Because in this life we fail more than we succeed, we learn to rely on humor to keep moving forward, to continue our individual journeys until we die."

When I was a guest at his home, Willie reminded me one day that none of the food at his place was bought at the store.

"Aqui en Willie's Ranch, se rinde todo," he would say proudly, *"res, puerco, verduras, lo que necesita.* (Here at Willie's Ranch, we harvest everything, beef, pork, vegetables, anything that's needed.)"

One particular morning, while visiting Odessa, he woke me up before dawn. *"¡Levantate, Nieto! Ya esta almuerzo,* (Get up, Nieto! Breakfast is ready,)" he said, his voice booming over the home intercom system.

The aroma of eggs, coffee and freshly made tortillas permeated the house. There was a special feeling that comes from the wide open spaces of West Texas, a kind of down-home feeling one gets when relaxing, half-asleep in the early morning stillness, sitting around a kitchen table, muttering about meaningless incidentals.

"Dormiste bien anoche? (Did you sleep well last night?)" Willie asked.

"Como que no, Willie, (Of course, Willie,)" I responded. *"Pero tuve que levantarme anoche para usar el bano y nunca halle el lavatorio grande, nomas el chiquito de ninos.* (I got up to use the bathroom but couldn't find the large lavatory, only the little one you built for your children.)"

Willie stared for an instant as though ready to say something, but unsure of my reaction. His slow chuckle broke the silence. The house had two major structural flaws, he confessed. The fish and vegetation bond immediately inside the door entrance was originally built to be a swimming pool for his children. The same problem happened when putting in a hall bathroom. It wasn't built for his kids. It simply came out too small for adults, but big enough for children. In particular, it wasn't meant for a long-legged, six-foot-four guy like me.

"No, hombre," he confessed that morning, completely red-faced. *"Yo fui el ingeniero y el arquitecto. El swimming pool me salio muy chico, asi como el baño. Pero cuando me di cuenta, ya estuvo muy tarde.* (I was the engineer and architect. The swimming pool came out too small, just like the bathroom. When I finally realized what had happened, it was already a done deal, too late.)"

Listening to the story was too much for me to take. Willie had a humorous style of recanting incidents in his life. He didn't mind poking a little fun at himself or admitting errors in his way of doing things.

"Oyes," he suddenly asked, *"¿Como estan los tacos?* (How are the tacos?)"

"Estan ricos Willie, gracias, (They're really good, Willie, thank you,)" "Bien ricos. (Really tasty.)"

"Pues orale (Cool)," he responded. *"A mi me encantan huevos con conejo.* (I love eggs with rabbit.)"

My frozen face said more than words would ever describe. This was Willie. There was nothing pretentious about him. He was a homespun man who considered himself lucky to live in a huge house, having a thriving business that provided him with lots of money, and have the opportunity to fool around with friends laughing at life. He could have easily become arrogant and self-absorbed. Willie dared the odds and enjoyed life in ways few people ever enjoy.

Sadly, he died at forty-eight years old of age from alcoholism. I never understood whether his drinking problem came from not knowing how to handle success or from other unresolved issues. At times, he talked about feeling overwhelmed by the responsibilities of always taking care of others and always having to be in charge. Sometimes, Willie got caught up in the loneliness of wanting to be cared for, protected, and comforted.

Gloria and I flew to Odessa for his funeral. Mario was there along with several other brothers and sisters, accompanying Willie's wife and their children. A mariachi played traditional Mexican songs at the cemetery while hundreds of friends and business acquaintances paid their final respects. As his coffin was quietly lowered to its final resting place, Willie's favorite, song, "El Rey" (The King), was played by the mariachis.

> Yo se bien que estoy afuera,
> pero el dia en que yo me muera,
> se que tendras que llorar.
> Llorar, llorar, llorar, llorar.

> I may not matter much,
> but the day that I die,
> you will cry.
> Cry and cry and cry and cry.

Two years later, Mario died of lung cancer.

Willie and Mario were typical of early NHI board members. Rough, rugged, and driven by an unyielding desire to succeed, they were accustomed to the hard work of long hours. This was their simple, uncomplicated formula for success. It took sweat, occasional tears, and the ability to get up from defeat time and time again.

"Mira, Nieto, (It's this way Nieto,)" I remember Willie saying, *"Cuando nos venimos para Odessa,*

no era raro levantarnos a las cinco de la manana a trabajar todo el santo dia. No te miento. Asi en el solaso, tirado de rodillas, weldiando todo el dia en el pinche calor. ¿La discriminacion? ¡Olvidate! Tienes que estar ciego a eso y te tiene que gustar trabajar. No hay lugar para huevones aqui, gente que nomas quiere estar sentada mientras los otros se chingan. (When we came to Odessa, it wasn't rare for us to get up at five in the morning and work all day long. I'm not telling a lie. We were here in the hot burning sun, working on our knees, welding in the damn heat. Discrimination? Forget it! You have to be blind those things and you have to enjoy working. There is no room here for laziness, people who want to sit around while the others are busting their asses.)"

Other NHI board members shared Willies' sentiments. Working fifteen and eighteen-hour days, seven days a week, was not unusual to them. Instead of complaining, they paid their dues through long grueling hours. They pushed hard and demanded that everyone around them be as focused. They never expected to get something for nothing. To these Tejano entrepreneurs, their businesses were their way of life. They either worked or it was over for them.

When discussing issues in the Latino community such as being poor or not having an education, all of them shared similar opinions when it came to work.

"El problema, Nieto," Liborio Hinojosa from H&H Meat Products used to suggest, *"es que el gobierno ha creado toda una generacion que no quiere trabajar. ¡Prefiere que les de el gobierno todo asi, gratis! Te trabajan, pero si les conviene. La pregunta basica es, ¿cuanto paga? Si no les conviene, pues ¿que mas? Tienen la seguridad del welfare, el chequecito. El gobierno ha creado una generacion entera de gente que esta acustumbrada a pedir para no trabajar.* (The problem, Nieto, is that government has created a generation of people who no longer want to work. They prefer that the government give them everything for free. They work if it's to their advantage. If not, why should they bother? They have the security of welfare, the government assistance check. They government has created an entire generation accustomed to asking for help so they don't have to work.)"

Except for an occasional contribution from the Salinas brothers, the Institute didn't receive donations from any of these board members. On occasion, one of them paid for a meal. Despite having the resources to contribute thousands of dollars, they were more interested in whether or not the Institute's products had the potential to work. Their message was clear: "Expect nothing from us, expect the knowledge that if you work hard and pay strict attention to your business, there is a chance that the National Hispanic Institute might survive. Otherwise, you'll soon join the thousands who try and fail."

According to them, survival was for those who didn't make excuses about life and braved the odds. They had a collective disdain for banks, for laziness, and for people who expected a free handout. They weren't in the business of giving their hard-earned money away. They ran in small circles of close friends. They enjoyed serving on boards and commissions, but only if it didn't interfere with business or personal time. They viewed life simply and pragmatically.

"If you want special privileges from life, go out and work for them," Phil Garza from Houston often said. "Don't make excuses. Do something! Don't just wish or plan. If you fail, try again, again, and again. Who you are is not as important as what you do. Don't mind the long hours if it's you who expects to enjoy what your business gives you. Never worry about what others say. It doesn't matter how many times you fail or get knocked down, only how driven you are to get up off the canvas and go back to it again."

These lessons from men who did something special within their journeys continue to ring loud in my ears. Liborio summed it up one evening while we shared dinner in McAllen.

"Mira, Nieto, (Look at it this way,)" he said. *"Espera nada de nadie. Si NHI da buenos servicios, la gente viene y va querer mas. Ellos pagan porque les importa. Si das malos servicios, no te vienen aunque les ruegues. Si la hace NHI, va a ser porque pensaste en tus productos y servicions e hiciste algo*

para asegurar los beneficios a tu clientela. (Expect nothing from anyone. If NHI gives good services, they will come and want more. They will pay because it's important to them. If you give bad services, they won't come back even if you beg them. If NHI makes it, it will be because you thought about your services and products and did something to ensure benefits for your customers.)"

Liborio was talking social Darwinism. If NHI were to thrive, it wouldn't be because of our cause or appeal. There was a bottom line, and it was to work with people's self interests. The moment we stopped doing that, NHI would die, and, as he reminded me, it should. These discussions did much to change my views, the way I approached the world. Earlier, my beliefs were to appeal to government, point out the needs of Latinos, and make a case for funding. That wasn't Liborio's view of the world, nor Sam Moreno's, nor Pete Diaz, Jr.'s. They preferred NHI to be market-driven and self-enterprising. We had to take our chance in the marketplace, understand its rules, abide by its requirements, and either thrive or fail in the process.

From the original group of NHI board members, only Sam Moreno remains. Even today while in his seventies, his mind is as needle-sharp as the first time we met almost thirty years ago in Dallas.

"¿Hay Nieto," he continues to ask in his always inquisitive humorous manner, *"en que te metiste ahora?* (What have you gotten yourself into now?)"

At times, while making the daily twenty-eight mile drive from Austin to NHI in Maxwell, the faces and lessons of these people run through my mind. There is a certain security in having been their student, in having learned from the best. Here were a group of successful Tejano millionaires who went from having virtually little to nothing as young boys to developing sizable, well-respected businesses. Their success did not come from asking for handouts. It came from being highly focused, having amazing stamina, adjusting to the changing conditions of the marketplace, and having the will to "get up off the canvas when knocked down," according to Phil Garza.

"True champions always know that somewhere along the way, they're going to get knocked down. It's getting up that makes the difference between those who win and those who lose."

For Gloria and me, it wouldn't be until 1985 that we finally felt the confidence to become a little more public with our efforts. Until then, we shared very little about our personal business with others. In between, there were times when NHI couldn't pay us a nickel for our work. My salary in 1980 was $8,000 for the year. The only two things that kept me going were pride and hope. There is a certain unwillingness to fold tent and run when looking straight into the eyes of defeat. If you take that step, you know that you will never recover from it. You lose your self-respect and the capacity to face yourself.

In our most desperate times, my thoughts would wander off to Willie, Mario, Phil, Sam, Pete, and, especially Liborio. Phil and Sam were always available to talk. But it was Libo's philosophy that bothered me the most about our survival. "If your services aren't good enough, your organization deserves to die."

These weren't words of comfort or encouragement. Liborio was describing a result, a predictable outcome for those who didn't pay attention to their businesses. There was always something or someone else ready and willing to take your place. You might be remembered or missed for a moment. Life, however, has a way of moving on to the next person.

While Latino entrepreneurs of the future will continue facing similar circumstances, perhaps the environments in which they develop their individual business ventures will not be as openly hostile as the conditions and attitudes faced by their predecessors. Conversely, Latino business leaders could consider fostering the development of a different economic playing field. With the growth of the Latino population in this country, it's very possible to establish exclusive ethnic business districts that have carry-over attraction to other consumers as well.

Chinatown in San Francisco and La Villita in Chicago are good examples. These places allow both sophisticated initiatives and mom-and-pop startups to have better chances of surviving the rigors of business. It's not always the best strategy for new Latino startups to compete in open markets, against well-established companies with years of experience and large war chests.

For young Latino entrepreneurs of the future, the challenge of business will be different and new. The Internet will undoubtedly play a key role. Under-financed companies will have greater chances of impacting the consumer without the overhead requirements of sophisticated storefronts, marketing sales forces, and large inventories.

The greater challenge for these future business leaders, however, will be obtaining a better working knowledge of the emerging Latino consumer market. Latinos have spent an entire century first working to understand the American mainstream and then learning to survive and thrive within it. A new, changing era dictates the need for another strategy. The America of the twenty-first century will consist of a diversity of cultures and competing worldviews. American companies will no longer depend almost exclusively on the traditional American consumer for profits or labor supply. Globalization will paint a scenario distinct from anything we've known in the past. The growth of Latinos in the United States and Latin America will increasingly become a major consumer factor in determining profits and dividends for all sectors of business and industry.

The success of future Latino leaders will depend on how well they understand and prepare for these eventualities. This means letting go of old perceptions and adopting new ones. It means retooling our thinking as a community. It means turning our attention to better understand the "new American."

Certain business principles, however, will remain the same, especially the Libo Principle: "If your services or products aren't good enough, your organization deserves to die."

The Willie Salinas Principle will also continue: "Discrimination? Forget about it! You have to be blind to it. If you want to succeed, you first have to enjoy working. Forget about anything else."

Phil Garza's view of the world will also be key: "True champions always know that somewhere along the way, they're going to get knocked down. It's getting up the makes the difference between those who win and those who lose."

Chapter Five: Tejano Millionaires

1. Write a brief description of your relationships with any persons who have served as your mentors, coaches, or members of your support groups.

2. How did you find, engage, and negotiate working relationships with your mentors, coaches, or support groups?

3. Describe your typical interactions with your mentors, coaches, or support groups – for example, what do you get from them? What do you give to them?

4. How do you think you have benefited from your interactions with your mentors, coaches, or support groups? What did you learn:
    a. About yourself?
    b. About helping relationships?
    c. About setting priorities?
    d. About making sacrifices?
    e. About achieving your life goals?
    f. About learning from your experiences?

5. How have you avoided potential mentors, coaches, or support groups who try to work out their own problems through you? How have you made sure that these people do not have a hidden agenda that serves their purposes but not yours?

Chapter Six
Potomac Fever

Generally, U.S. Latinos have a historical view that we live in a society with a considerate and responsive government. It was government that stepped in and saved the nation during the ravages of the Great Depression. It was government that intervened in the 1960s to level a playing field that purposely kept Latinos, Blacks, and other American ethnic groups from enjoying the same rights and privileges as Anglos in our nation. Therefore, our 1979 trip to Washington to plead a case on behalf of the National Hispanic Institute was not unusual. To the contrary, Washington was the place to go when all else before failed.

We found the nation's capital every bit as magnificent as anyone could imagine. Its people reflected the culture of countless political interest caught up in an ongoing struggle to gain an edge, a foothold. Some were involved in large and complex political machinations. Others participated in more subtle transactions away from public eye, in the privacy of nondescript government buildings. Somewhere in the interplay of trade-offs and favors, Latinos were involved. It didn't take long, however, to figure out that they were at a disadvantage in a game where --- at best --- they could only gain minimum payoffs.

Nothing was more descriptive of this dynamic to me than NHI's Washington experience. Being turned down for funding was not as bitter a pill to swallow as realizing how little power Latinos over the years had acquired. The Black community was far more powerful. Anglos continued to enjoy most of the spoils of the systems.

In contrast, Latinos seemed to still be pinching themselves for having a presence. Any influence was better than having none. Being in D.C. for a week ended any notion that substantial headway been made. The experience forced me to realize the wisdom of Dad's observation that NHI's success would never come from political deal making. The institute needed to rely on its deeds in the community and make believers out of the youth and families being served.

Despite the advice, going to our nation's capital meant new possibilities for NHI. Washington, D.C., was our final plea for help. Three of us made the trip: Arturo Gil, Richard Hammer, and me. Rather than flying, we left by car one misty Monday morning, from Austin to make the 1,800-mile trip to Potomac. We gathered the few dollars our families could afford and set out on the decisive eastward journey.

I had been to Washington only twice before, once while an employee with the Federal Regional Office of Economic Opportunity in 1970 and then as part of the Texas Department of Community Affairs in 1977.

On my first trip, I served on a policy panel on migrant education programs. Latino federal government employees were asked to suggest policy on migrant education. Being there brought me into contact with several able and articulate young professionals who had a lot to say about education policy and the special needs of migrant and seasonal farm-workers. On the second trip, I represented the Governor's Office of Texas at an education conference. Both trips were brief, allowing only enough time for a quick tour of the sites. Making the long drive the third time around allowed us to dream out loud about returning home with funding. It didn't matter much which agency or person was willing to work with us. All we wanted was to bring home the "Washington Gold."

Once on the way, we made the most of our trip. We wanted to see the Smokey Mountains and taste the flavor of another part of Americana. We stopped in an occasional small rural town to observe people and to experience people from different backgrounds.

Exhausted after almost twenty-six hours of nonstop driving, we found ourselves lost in a rural

Virginia village. It was time for lunch. Getting out of the car to get directions from the manager of a local convenience store, I noticed two men eating at a shaded picnic table about fifty yards away. Conjunto music (traditional, rural Mexican music) – the kind familiar to the South Texas border towns --- sailed out of their open car door. I made my way over to get directions and make small talk.

"*Buenas tardes,* (Good afternoon,)" I said, "*Andamos peridods. ¿Nos podrían decir el rumbo para Washington?* (We're lost. Could you direct us towards Washington?)"

"*Cómo no,* (Of course,)" one responded. "*Se van aquí por este camino otras veinte y cinco millas, hasta el camino número cincuenta, y voltean hacia su derecha. Washington queda unos cuarenta minutos de allí.* (You follow this road another twenty-five miles, until you reach Highway 50. You turn right. Washington is about forty minutes from there.)"

"*Gracias,*" I responded. "*¿Oigan, que andan haciendo por aquí tan lejos?* (Say, what are you doing out here so far?)

I really didn't understand the directions. I was curious about why these two individuals, apparently undocumented immigrants, had come this far.

"*Pues trabajando.* (We're out here working.)" one of the men responded.

"*¿Y de por aquí son?* (And you're from around here?)" I asked.

"*No, somos de México,* (No, we're from Mexico,)" was the answer. "*Usted save, la vida* (You know sir, trying to make a life for ourselves)."

No further explanations were needed. Their eyes told the story. They worked for their money two thousand miles from their homes, separated from family, with only each other. Survival for them was real and hard.

Their need, like ours, had pushed them this far and as our paths crossed we looked to them for directions. After peeling away the titles and credentials, there was little that separated us as people. They had traveled long distances in their struggles to make a living. We were doing the same. They had expectations and aspirations for their efforts. So did we. They were taking an enormous chance of ending up with nothing. We shared the same possibilities. They were from Mexico and we were from the United States and suddenly that made little difference.

"*Cada cabeza su mundo,* (Every person's head forms its own reality,)" Dad used to say. "*Todos aprovechamos la vida en la manera que mejor entendemos.* (We all approach life in the best way we know how.)"

Washington was an amazing place to visit. People and cars rushed in all directions at the same time. The numerous buildings stood out in their magnificence. Giant statues of American heroes rose out of manicured lawns and colorful gardens. This was Washington, D.C., our nation's center of power and influence.

The apparent energy of the city and the natural excitement that comes from being there to flavor it, however, soon gave way to other more basic needs. Finding parking was the first problem. To us, the winding streets all blended together. A wrinkled city map, indecipherable federal building names and addresses, and parking lot attendants who seemed to point in every direction but the right way confused the situation. Herds of people constantly flooded across streets with an authority that threatened our tired bones. No one paid attention to each other as though detached and too intent on getting to their individual destinations to look around or signal any form of human acknowledgement. As Tejanos, whose customs drive them to show recognition even to strangers on the highway, we found D.C. impersonal. This was a place to conduct business and leave, and not where one met people and cultivated relationships.

Eventually, we fumbled our way to a meeting that had been arranged with Lionel Castillo. Lionel was from Magnolia, one of my old neighborhoods back in Houston. He had grown up in the barrio and had risen to political prominence as comptroller for the City of Houston. He was always in the newspaper taking public issue with the spending habits of the City Council. He didn't run from a public fight either. He was known for his cool-headed approach and his ability to capture the sentiments of the voters. Everything he did and said was carefully thought-out and weighed in advance.

Over time, Lionel became a respected Latino leader throughout Texas. When Jimmy Carter ran for president in 1976, Lionel became one of his top political advisors and supporters. His reward was being appointed director of the Immigration and Naturalization Service. Despite his political influence, Lionel was never one to be above others. We felt confident that he would receive us well and do everything in his power to help. He was down-to-earth, hard-working, a special kind of person you could look to help.

Lionel was in a large office building not too far from the Capitol. Security guards inspected our briefcases before leading us to his big spacious office. Big, leather chairs welcomed our aching bodies. After exchanging greetings and enjoying cold refreshments, the conversation drifted over toward illegal immigrants. Lionel touched lightly on his agency's plans, even suggesting that there has been talk in the administration about building a fence-like structure along the Rio Grande from El Paso to Brownsville.

"Part of my job is to help keep the illegals outside our borders," he said. "But the problem isn't going to go away like that. It's almost out of control."

Arturo, Richard, and I fleetingly glanced at each other, all three of us apparently thinking the same thing: the two men at the convenience store in Virginia.

"Hey, carnal," Arturo said. "We're not trying to rain on anybody's parade, but a couple of *carnales de Mejicles* (brothers from down Mexico way) just finished giving us directions to Washington."

"Really," Lionel answered. "Where?"

"A couple of illegals working fifty miles from here in Virginia, vato," Arturo responded.

The next several days were spent visiting federal agencies, looking for grants. We went to every office imaginable, including Early Childhood Development, the Small Business Administration, the Migrant Education Office, and the Office of Economic Opportunity. Ed Gutierrez offered to take us in for the week.

Ed's apartment wasn't far from the district. We even took time out to host a small cookout for several D.C. friends. Word got around fast. Everyone eagerly showed up at the celebration. We played golf and traded stories. Most of them wanted to know the latest on friends back home, whether or not a particular individual was still involved in "La Causa" (The Cause). Most yearned to return home. They were recent transplants from Texas, attracted to D.C. by the lure of enjoying a little more power and influence. Their plans were to eventually move back.

Before the Washington trip, several state agencies and private foundations in Texas had turned down our funding proposals. The narrowness of our work and lack of a track record and reputation were often cited as the reasons for the rejections. Not having an identity as an organization meant no funding and, conversely, no income. On top of these problems, were also young and naïve in understanding the politics of "grantsmanship." Our only alternative was Washington.

Soon after being there a few days, we realized that Latinos in career government jobs had little influence in the new Carter Administration. Several of the new appointees were still unpacking boxes. It never occurred to us that we were insignificant in a city that customarily dealt with national and international issues. NHI was nothing. It was merely a tiny organization in a world of enormous political power and influence. Washington was a place with a unique culture and identity. Few people ever fully understood it. We weren't Washington insiders. At best, our chances of gaining a tiny foothold were negligible. All we offered was a few nebulous and hard to understand concepts.

The weeklong experience taught us several lessons. One was not to expect special favors from officials on the basis of sharing a common heritage. As interested as our Washington friends seemed in our work, they were there to serve the interests of their superiors. They weren't advocates for Latinos as we thought. If dealing with organizations like the National Hispanic Institute advanced these interests, then there might be ways of working together. If it didn't, we were shown the door with a handshake and small talk. Washington brought us face-to-face with this reality.

Before Jimmy Carter, Republicans occupied the capital for eight long years. Nixon, and to some extent Gerald Ford, appeared to make politics a personal and private experience. Ideology only mattered on the surfaces. What really counted was deal-making and leveraging power. Getting an audience with top executives depended on the size of the constituency and voter turnout potential. Everything relied on knowing how to play the game.

To us, the Carter Administration meant the possibility of returning to the old days when you could count on people's help. Thus, our priority became making early contact with the new administration. We thought that we had a couple of advantages up our sleeves through Rick Hernandez, special assistant to the president, and Lionel Castillo. Both of them were Houstonians. They knew my parents and me personally. Rick played basketball on Dad's teams in Houston's Denver Harbor. Now both of them were in high and influential places. We potentially had someone on the inside to protect our interests, or so we thought. We absorbed ourselves with the notion that doors would automatically open.

In the end, nothing took place. We accepted the inevitable. No help in the amounts we imagined would be forthcoming. A small community grant might be thrown our way to keep us surviving. Nothing more.

The return trip to Austin gave us time to reexamine our thinking. Our core beliefs needed to be questioned, maybe changed. Government as a traditional fountain of help could no longer be the focus. The philosophy of government was beginning to shift away from the old ways of doing business to something new.

There was a clear distinction in what was going on in Washington for Latinos by 1980 when compared to previous eras. There were two types of Washington Latinos: carry-overs from the golden years of the Johnson Administration who survived the derailing of federal programs by the Republicans and the new breed of young men and women experiencing the Washington scene for the first time. While it appeared that important changes were in the making, it became clear that many of these new appointees were mere window-dressing. Someone else controlled the strings. Someone else held the power.

Latinos were present. They occupied a few public positions. A few favors were dispensed to community agencies back home through grants, but not in significant amounts. This wasn't like the Johnson Administration before. In the Carter years, Latino presence was subtle. Under Lyndon Baines Johnson, there was a call to duty, to mobilize Latinos across the country, to awaken the so-called "Sleeping Giant." Latinos appointed to key positions were there to make things happen. In the Carter Administration, appointments to jobs seemed more reflective of "political payoffs" rather than a national agenda for Latinos. Jobs were dispensed to individuals who represented special interests at local levels. There was little or no interest in jelling together a cohesive national working group. If they responded at all, it was to the people who got them there.

For the National Hispanic Institute, an unknown and politically unproven entity, lacking a constituency, it was clear that nothing important would ever happen. No funds would be directed to a small, insignificant organization like ours. While the people we visited were kind and appeared genuinely interested in our efforts, they also had little influence in providing us the resources needed for our work.

In retrospect, we never understood how the "Washington game" was played. Maybe we didn't say the right things or see the right people. Maybe we shouldn't have made the trip in the first place. The anticipation and excitement of running around with the rich and powerful was quickly over. The short-lived journey made us feel small. We were at the bottom of a political food chain where feeding the larger powers was all that mattered.

We concluded that our survival as a small, start-up nonprofit organization could no longer depend on public or even private funding. We needed other strategies to capitalize our efforts. The focus had to shift from the grantsmanship game to the community we wished to serve. We needed to develop and identify the services and products that the Latino community needed and could afford. Our style and manner of working with Latinos also needed an overhaul. For now, however, finding solutions through politics was out of the question. Instead, we needed to concentrate on studying the Latino marketplace.

The more challenging question would be in determining what to sell to the community, learning how, and where to get started. Deciding to move away from seeking solutions through politics meant changing the playing field for our infant organization. It also meant completely revamping our business and marketing approaches. For the National Hispanic Institute to make it, Latinos could no longer be treated as clients in need of government services. From now on, they had to be seen as valued customers who possessed the economic power to make or break us. Making the shift from the way we were accustomed to doing business posed our biggest hurdle.

NHI could no longer be tied to the political world. Washington would remain the same, a place where Latinos are essentially pawns in a game of constant political power brokering where they play small roles in a larger process.

The approaching new millennium signaled an opportunity to consider a new approach. Taking sides as partisans would no longer be the way. Despite the work by the Latinos to gain a modest foothold inside our nation's political structures, the results only made minimal impact on Latino quality of life. A better choice was to work on redefining the relationships that were bringing Latinos together. To achieve this end, Latinos would have to be willing to divorce themselves from the larger system, no matter how difficult or painful the process.

The master-servant method of politics for Latinos had to end. The next step would be to look at the future through a different political telescope that was not based on partisan relationships. Intellectual, cultural, and economic wealth building in the Latino community had to become the most important priority. Bridging differences rather than maintaining partisan relationships that kept different sectors of Latinos apart would be another strategic decision. Finally, a new model of Latino community collaboration had to be defined, especially one that provided youth with a compelling social, civic, cultural, and economic rationale to invest their talents and energies both as valued citizens and future Latino leaders.

NHI's Washington visit, the historical view of Latinos towards government, the era of the Latino civil rights movement combined to prove that the problem had not been Latinos not being able to work together. The problem had been the ways in which Latinos had gone about attempting to reach those goals in a changing political climate.

Washington, D.C., was the answer in the 1960s. However, it was too big, too impersonal, too detached in the 1980s to have any direct impact on Latino community life. And in the year 2000 and beyond, it would play less of a role.

The choice was to search for other channels where Latinos could be in greater control of the processes and outcomes they most desired.

Chapter Six: Potomac Fever
   1. Consider a situation when you were planning how to realize your life goals. Write down the assumptions you made about the sources and kinds of support you thought you would need. That is:
      a. Who did you assume would do what to help and support you?
      b. Who did you predict would compete with you or create obstacles to prevent you from reaching your goals?
      c. Who did you assume would pretend to agree with you in public but privately withhold support or sabotage your efforts?
   2. How did you test the validity of your assumptions and expectations?
   3. Which of your assumptions and expectations turned out to be accurate, valid, and realistic? Which turned out to be reasonable but false and unrealistic?
   4. If and when you discovered that some of your assumptions were false:
      a. What did you think?
      b. How did you feel?
      c. What did you do?
   5. What were the consequences of your responses to discovering that some of your assumptions and expectations were accurate, valid, and realistic?
   6. Where you were confronted by the discovery that some of your assumptions were false and some of your expectations were unrealistic, you probably were also confronted by the unpleasant reality that some of your beliefs about the way the world is supposed to work were also flawed. Write a brief description of this challenge, including: what you thought (in what ways your thinking changed) and how you felt (in what ways your feelings change.)
   7. In what ways, if any, did these confrontations and changes in your beliefs and feelings affect and change your aspirations, life goals, strategies, and action plans?

Chapter Seven
Lonely Road Back

The movie Born Free springs to mind whenever I remember my first experiences running the National Hispanic Institute. In the movie, a scientist couple working in Africa runs across a female lion cub abandoned by its mother. The couple fears she won't survive, so they adopt her. Eventually the cub, Elsa, reaches full adulthood, but lacks the experience and cunning to cope in the wild. The couple has to wrestle with the decision to either keeping the lioness in captivity at an enormous economic price that they cannot afford or releasing her into the bush, where there is almost no chance of making it. Eventually, they train the lion to hunt, under the realization that she never developed the natural instincts to either feed or defend herself against predators.

These were similar to the circumstances that I faced in 1979. At no time before did I feel more intimidated and outside of my element than during my first attempts to run a new organization. Years of work as a community organizer in federal government environments had not prepared me. It became a "learn-as-you-go" experience where one false move meant a long way down to the bottom with little to no chance of recovery.

Between graduation from college in 1964 and starting NHI in 1979, my income had come essentially from public school and government jobs. Whether my work was satisfactory, or not, there was always the certainty of a paycheck. This mental understanding of what it meant to work didn't make the changeover any easier. As executive director, I was on my own, like Elsa, learning to hunt for funding, for survival.

The problem was that no one had ever taught me to be on my own. Dad had tried, but I was too self-centered and self-absorbed to listen, what with me having a college degree and all. Besides, I was thirty-nine years old by now and had been in the professional world for sixteen years. Certainly this counted for something?

In those years, NHI was little more than a collection of ideas looking for believers. Three or four of us daily got together to hash out and attempt to describe cloudy thoughts that were difficult to articulate. We had lunchtime discussions, evening talks, and weekend marathons that seemed to have no end nor came to any realizable conclusions. Afterwards, everyone went back to the security of their jobs and their families.

For me, it was back to the reality of no income and no path to follow. Six months went by without any progress. Three more months passed. NHI's office was nothing more than the living room of my apartment, a telephone, an answering machine, and a second-hand electric typewriter that was always on the blink.

To keep moving forward, I became my own solitary cheerleader. "Remain focused, keep going," I used to think to myself each night. "Just don't give up."

Had it not been for Conrado Cruz, Jr. in Laredo or Robert Aguilar in Corpus Christi, NHI would have abruptly ended the first year. These two old, trusted friends faithfully stood by me the entire way. They understood my personal financial situation and supported my idea of an institute for Latinos. They saw NHI as being something good for the Latino community, and they were willing to lend a hand. For years, both had served as executive directors of employees, and being a state executive had not given me the necessary background and skills.

Responsibilities to employees, making certain that the organization had sufficient funds to operate, being on top of state and federal regulations, implementing field programs, ensuring that the organization stayed within its mission, and working with a board of directors weren't part of my previous training. Making payroll and opening and closing the office also were new, as were giving an organization a solid sixteen-hour day and guiding employees to work in teams to achieve crucial organizational objectives.

Like the lioness in the movie, I too had developed a captive view of the world where everything was provided from eight to five during the regular work week. As a government employee, I may have looked like a lion and even roared like one when challenged to support Latinos, but for the most part my environment gave me safety, security, and predictability. My hours were regulated, my work supervised, and the paycheck to feed my family and pay bills predictably disbursed at the end of the month. When thrown out and faced with being on my own in the real world of other more experienced hunters, I felt frightened and abandoned. I was clueless and without direction.

My goal in the early 1960s right out of high school was to get the degree behind me. "All you need," I used to think, "is to get a college degree to get started. After that, it's smooth sailing ahead." After four and half years of studies, I walked across the stage to receive the sheepskin. I believed that it would somehow give me a special advantage over others. I never thought that a degree would only help open doors.

Initially, the college degree started me higher on the salary scale than my friends back in the barrio. It also threw me into a pool of similarly credentialed competitors, who were as highly driven and ambitious as I was. At these levels of professional employment, I was constantly involved in power frenzies where devouring others was not only a normal part of the process; I was getting devoured as well. In other words, I was both the hunter and the hunted.

No one ever told me it would be this way. No one ever guided me or helped me understand how to be effective in those work large anti-poverty community organizations and had access to federal and state grants that could be used to hire me as a consultant to assist them with different needs.

Despite the difficulties of making NHI work, progress was made. Sometimes the steps forward were tiny. For me, each little victory was cause for celebration, including the first-time purchase of an electric calculator, a second-hand government-issue metal bookcase, and a used desk.

An office rental agreement was hammered out with Gabriel Gutierrez, an Austin lawyer who had offices on Interstate 35. For $100 a month, the National Hispanic Institute finally moved out of my apartment living room to a place of its own. The space was less than a hundred square feet, with barely enough area to walk around. NHI, however, had an office to conduct business.

Later in the summer of 1980, Arturo Gil, Richard Hamner, and Art Moreno made the transition over to NHI. Like me, Moreno also became victim to a shake-up by the incoming Republican administration of Governor Bill Clements. Arturo Gil resigned his post with the Early Childhood Division of the agency where we all worked. Richard wanted to find something more challenging besides being an administrative assistant to State Representative Gonzalo Barrientos.

Our immediate decision was not to pursue federal or state funding to underwrite our work. Instead, we preferred an organization that was different, more enterprise-driven in developing its financial resources. The initial goal was to become a firm focused on the special needs of Latinos being brought into first-time management and supervisory positions with government and private corporations.

Our business plan centered on making needs assessments of Latinos working in management roles in the Austin area and then conducting nation-wide searches for Latino professionals in the various specialty fields to serve them. Much to our surprise, the concept immediately took off. Over 200 Latino professionals from both public and private sectors showed up tour first "Stress Management Series" at the Stephen F. Austin Hotel in downtown Austin.

Seizing the moment of having so many people attend the first session, we convinced the owner of the hotel to give us office space for $400 a month in exchange for guaranteeing him at least six full training conferences a year. To our surprise, he agreed. NHI immediately moved to downtown Austin. Being on 7th Street and Congress Avenue, only four blocks from the state capital became a personal triumph and a step forward for an organization desperately looking for a little public recognition. We had a "place to hang our hats," a conference area for meetings, a 24-hour answering service through the hotel switchboard, a café on the premises to relax and chat, and a suite of former hotel rooms serving as offices.

For the moment, life couldn't have been any better. It didn't matter that the offices were slightly worn and the hotel not too popular with out-of-towners. Being in the business district was far better than answering phones from my living room or being stuck in a tiny office.

After settling in, we visited the Southwest Education Laboratory, a half-block from the hotel. The lab was a large outfit that primarily served Texas and surrounding states. Established back in the early days of the Johnson Administration of the 1960s, most of its work concentrated on developing new teaching materials for school-age children. It also had the latest in video production capabilities, something we were interested in for our programs.

The price tag for these services immediately killed our chance to pursue the idea further. We did manage somehow, however, to meet for a few brief minutes with the executive director. He turned out to be a friendly person who seemed to be genuinely taken with the explanations of our work.

After listening for a few minutes, he suggested going over to his warehouse to pick out any stored furniture that would help us out. This was an improvement over the old, broken furniture the hotel loaned us. Nothing matched when we first moved in. The furniture was either old or faded or had been weakened by years of use. Besides, these weren't furnishings designed for office use. The lab's offer made it possible for us to take another step forward.

Over the weekend, David "Hamburger" Terrazas, a friend from East Austin, helped load several shiny desks, book cabinets, credenzas, a conference table, chairs and other equipment that we needed. David and I went back several years to his high school days in 1968 when LUCHA, a new Latino organization in Austin's East Side was first starting to replace the Old Guard. LUCHA was the organization that helped elect Richard Moya as the first Mexican-American county commissioner in Travis County, Gonzalo Barrientos as the first Mexican-American state representative from Austin, and John Treviño as the first Mexican-American Austin city council member. All of us belonged to LUCHA and dutifully attended meetings at the Salvation Army on Holly Street.

David was the youngest LUCHA member and also had carved out quite a football career for himself, having made All-District for Johnston Rams. Well-known as an all-star catcher for community fast-pitch softball team that played around Texas at various Mexican-American state meets, he weighed in between 260 and 280 pounds on a five-foot-eleven-inch frame. Although his physique gave an impression that he was not agile, once on the field, David was every bit a star athlete.

Over the years, David developed another side to his personality--- politics. He occasionally stopped over at a political watering hold called Rabbits on East 6th Street for a few beers and to "talk smack" about different politicians in the community. On Sunday mornings, we'd meet for breakfast or he'd come over to my apartments to watch NFL games on television.

There was little I could ask of David that he wouldn't do. He printed NHI's first official letterhead, never asking for payment. Other times, he would show up at the office after work with reams of white bond paper. His only request was that we not ask him where he got it. Whenever playing golf against each other, our voices could be overheard accusing each other of cheating. "If you ain't lying," he'd say, "you ain't trying."

Today, a pencil holder on my desk has David's photograph pasted on one entire side with that "burlesco, vato loco" (fun-loving, crazy guy) look on his smiling face. Nicole, my daughter, laughs every time she sees it. Pasted across the bottom of the picture is David's statement "Hamburger, A Legend in His Own Time." Each time I see his photograph, I imagine David laughing out loud with his captivating roar, stopping only long enough to remind me, "What can I say brother? When you got it all, what can I say?"

Support back then didn't come from friends in high places in government or business. It came from friends like David. It came from "down home" individuals with whom I enjoyed a special connect that went beyond politics or business dealings. All of them had grown up in the barrios like I did back in Houston. Recalling our sports exploits as youngsters was far more important than understanding the philosophy of NHI. I played weekend basketball on the Joker's basketball team. We shared bee talk together recalling our "locuras" (craziness) in barrios as youngsters. Only on occasion did our discussions turn to concerns in the community.

For me, these special opportunities provided a sense of connection to the community, a special protection that one needs when feeling vulnerable and alone. I could never convey enough thanks to friends like Hamburger, T.C., Sub, Pinaco, Fancy, Crow, Coon, Mañas, Dapper, Manuel "Roomie" Ledesma, Pelon, and countless other East Austinites for being there when life for me turned rough and dark. They never excluded me, always acknowledging my presence through a special friendliness when I felt most isolated and lost.

But there were others as well, like Ray Benitez, who loaned me his pickup truck to move borrowed furniture to our newly acquired downtown offices.

A couple of weeks before, I fractured my arm horse-playing with my children at the apartment swimming pool. One Saturday afternoon Roy tried pushing me, causing me to slip on the wet pavement and jamming my arm. After picking up my daughter Nicole at the airport on her return trip back home from visiting an aunt in Mexico City, the swelling became noticeable and painful. A quick trip to the emergency revealed that my arm was broken in two places and required a cast for several weeks.

Realizing the dangers of removing the cast before giving my arm a chance to heal, I decided to take it off anyway. David needed help carrying the furniture up two floors our new offices. We spent almost an hour with a hacksaw carefully cutting through the cast.

The next week, Arturo Gil showed up with a neatly wrapped article hidden in brown wrapping paper. It was a small five-by-twelve shingle with "National Hispanic Institute" inscribed on it. We proudly placed it at the front entrance of our office.

Despite having permanent offices, NHI continued wrestling with different challenges. There wasn't enough money at the end of the month to cover salaries. As primary wage earners, the four of us had family responsibilities. Pressures to produce earning mounted daily. After several weeks of long distance phone calls and writing back and forth, Arturo Gil finally landed a small grant from the Office of Education. The money, however, only helped pay rent, telephones services, and made a few hires possible.

As the grant writer, Arturo Gil was the project director. Our business manager, Arturo Moreno, was paid part-time to oversee the financial aspects of the program. There wasn't enough funding for either Richard Hamner or me to be included.

Friends again were there to help. Rudy Flores, an NHI board member and former special assistant to Texas Governor Dolph Briscoe, returned to Uvalde to work as senior loan officer at the governor's bank. More than once, he let me sign unsecured personal loans to pay bills. Phil Garza from Houston also pitched in. As owner of a trucking company that moved materials and equipment for different freight forwarding companies, he needed an outside salesman to broaden his customer base. Growing increasingly desperate for income, I took Phil's offer and became a consultant salesman for USA Trucking. The caption written across his flag-draped trucks read, "USA Delivery: We Deliver Everything But Babies."

In months that followed, selling trucking services for USA Delivery meant leaving Austin each Tuesday by four in the morning and driving three hours into downtown Houston by seven to avoid traffic jams. The day's routine involved making cold calls in a market completely unfamiliar to me. Never had I personally experienced so many turndowns, disappointments, or slammed doors. Plainly speaking, I had no concept of the trucking business, selling transportation services, or bidding to move thousand containers from ships that were being unloaded daily on the docks of the Houston Ship Channel. Everyone else seemed to know how to sell except me. Everyone seemed familiar with how to make things happen but me.

Neither the trucking services nor the shipping industry were the issues. Phil accompanied me on almost every sales call, always offering to pay for lunch or parking and even giving me spending money for the day. He was giving me the opportunity to crawl out of a hole. Even with these advantages, I still couldn't sell or close a deal. Younger salesmen from other companies did much better and ended up with the larger contracts. They knew the business, the ins and outs. My life was on the other end of the spectrum, despite the college degree and having previously served in government executive roles.

After six months of constant lets downs, the sum total of my sales revenues hovered a little under $6000, gar less than Phil and I had previously predicted. A secretary working the telephones could have done far better for fewer dollars.

The problem was clear. The skills necessary to sell, stalk the prey, and make the kill were absent from my sales repertoire. I wasn't prepared for the business jungle, to look out for myself, and hung on natural cunning and instinct. The entire time, the previous fifteen years of being a so-called professional, my ability to subsist depended entirely on being handed a check at the end of the month.

Before, reporting to work on time or coming in a few minutes late didn't matter that much. I was high enough in the ladder to set my own schedule. Performing well on the job, or simply passing the time away on meaningless chores never endangered my position.

My former work with state government required little accountability, outside of filing reports, attending occasional community meetings to make speeches, and responding to the needs of my superiors. When circumstances placed me into a different environment, in a jungle of fiercely competitive interest furiously fighting to gain the advantage over the other, I found myself lacking the savvy to make my own way.

Earlier Dad had expressed concern over this problem from the moment I started NHI. "¿Creíste que iba a ser fácil, verdad? (You believed it was going to be easy?)" he asked during one late-night talk.

Despite the difficulties, he preferred that I not depend on others. In his view, making my way in life had to come from within, from my instincts and abilities to be observant, to recognize opportunity, make split-second decisions and be in full command of the outcomes. Being asked to leave my state job, not knowing how to sell trucking services in Houston, or not knowing how to create business for myself finally clarified my situation.

It was apparent that I needed to first look inside myself, to critically evaluate the beliefs and values driving me. If life was to take a different turn, it had to start with changing my perceptions, my relationships with others, and my understanding of business world. It was up to me to find and seize opportunity. It meant creating my own pathways and patiently setting up opportunities to make the final kill.

Not everyone out there was my friend for me to pour out my heart or to share my complaints. Life also didn't have to be played naively. Caring for and feeding myself were my responsibilities. These duties didn't belong to others.

Being on my own for the first time in my life forced me to start seeing myself as my own best provider. Besides, life wasn't meant to be fair. Survival had to be within my own control. There were no search parties out there to save me from the cold.

"Cada cabeza su mundo, (Every person's head is his own reality,)" Dad used to say. This meant having the courage to meet the world head on, to survive your own mistakes, to be resilient and confident.

"No es pecado fallar, mijo," he'd say. "Pecado es doblar las manos y no aprender de tus errores. (It's not a sin to fail, son. Sin is folding your hands to give up and failing to learn from your mistakes.)"

In retrospect, the Houston experience was a remarkable opportunity to evaluate my approach to life. I had seen people with much less create a lot more out of life. Bobby Garcia, a skinny little guy from my neighborhood in the Northside, had become the owner of a well-known and respected freight forwarding company. Alfred Hernandez, Jr., M.D., had grown up with me in the barrio. Johnny Mendoza and one of his brothers, who grew up only a block away from our home on McKee Street, became attorneys.

Gilbert Moreno, who lived across the street from us, turned his mother's small tortilla business into a popular restaurant and Mexican food products company.

Dad had his own unique way of describing opportunity in Houston. "En este pueblo," he would humorously underscore his lessons to me, "hasta los perros pueden hacer dinero. No mas es el querer. (In this town, even dogs are able to make money. Want is the only requirement.)"

After Houston, I returned to Austin and NHI more determined, more willing to take risks. Everyone immediately saw me become distant and not wanting to share all my plans as before. I was no longer the last in line to get my share of the rewards. When the Washington grant ended, Arturo Gil left. Shortly after, Arturo Moreno, our business manager took another job. Richard Hamner returned to his old post. The only persons left were Olga, a part-time secretary who was attending the University of Texas, and me.

By the end of 1981, I quietly packed NHI's belongings and moved the office from Guadalupe Street to North Lamar Street, a few blocks away. Less office space meant cheaper rent. Moving to a new location also meant starting all over again. NHI was down to either survival or extinction.

In less than twelve months, I went from the romantic perception of everything being possible and everyone being involved to a reality of being left out in the cold alone to fend for myself. None of my early partners were to blame for my despair or failures. We all tried our best. The problem was inside me, my approach to building an organization.

Soon after, however, changes started to take place. Before, the fear of failure was the prime motivation for working long, hard hours. After all, I had been tossed out on my ear from my government job only a couple of years earlier while at the same time going through a painful divorce. Time also has a way of healing as well as failure being a painful, but excellent, teacher. I was ready for whatever life tossed across my path. Besides, waiting for opportunities to be given to me or falling in my lap was no longer a part of my thinking. My childhood friends in Houston kept creeping up in my mind. If they could create meaning out of their lives after having started with so little, so could I.

NHI remained at the North Lamar office for a year through 1982. Ricardo Sanchez, a Chicano poet and former Brown Beret from El Paso, and his friend, Dale McCollough, briefly joined me. Ricardo was a breath of fresh air in my life, another vato loco (crazy guy). He laughed at life, enjoyed telling stories of his days as an activist, and wrote poetry effortlessly. Many times, we spent hours theorizing, being self-critical, looking at our community, and peering into the future.

As quickly as he came, he left one day. He just packed up. He left me a personally inscribed message on one of his favorite books. Ricardo was a reaffirmation of my childhood in Houston. I always found affection for the lifestyle of those guys. There was something mysteriously attractive about "la pachucada" (street guys). Not all of them were as bad as we were led to believe as youngsters. They weren't people to avoid. Most were neat individuals who didn't walk to the same drumbeat of the larger society. They created their own reality, their own culture, and their own perceptions of life.

Ricardo described this life through his writings, the celebration of being free souls. In a strange way, there was a correlation between vatos locos of the past and working with Latino youth. My work was not to be the bridge for our young to become like the rest of mainstream. It was to help them shape a reality that preserved culture, gave an identity as people, and made us competitive and valued citizens on our terms.

Ricardo and I remained in touch for several years afterwards. He ended up at a university in the state of Washington where his work was eventually archived.

One day, I received a message that he had gone back home to El Paso to die. He was diagnosed with an incurable cancer. I didn't go to work the day my friend passed away. I stayed at home, in an upstairs bedroom, seeing him in my mind, imagining his laughter, privately weeping, and at the time clutching the book he left me.

Friends like Ricardo Sanchez gave me the energy to continue my journey, to craft my vision, to remain strong in my will to create an institute for Latinos despite the disappointments and setbacks. Like my parents, he taught me to laugh at failure, to endure, and to not turn my back on my dreams. I can still hear his words when alone in the privacy of my thoughts.

"Ese vato, tienes que ser como el coyote. De día, buscas de lo que la vida te da. De noche le cantas a la luna con tus alaridos. (Hey dude, you have to be like the coyote. During the day, you take from life what it gives you. At night you sing to the moon with your howls.)"

In surviving the first couple of years, something else happened along the way. At various intervals in the beginning, there were times when the end seemed all too obvious, plain for me to see, inviting me to quit, to give in. On other occasions, the inability to make my ideas work became overwhelming frustrating. But it was not being able to provide my children with the lifestyle I had given them before that proved to be the most disheartening.

Everything I owned was either broken or second-hand. The little house on Farm-to-Market Road 1626 in Manchaca, just south of Austin, was not only old, it also was rundown with broken windowpanes and a leaky roof. Even having enough food to eat for the week became a problem. With these challenges, my children and I made it somehow. Ten-year-old Nicole would come over on weekends to sweep, make beds, and cook hamburgers for her three brothers. Roy and the twins helped with yard work, washed the car, and made do with what we had. None complained, except for Marc, who one day wanted me to know that the little television that sat on the chair in the living room was broken. It didn't have color.

"That's okay, son," I remember saying. "We'll get it fixed next week."

Little did he know as a six-year-old that the TV set was a second-hand black and white.

"Nothing else could possibly go wrong," I used to think. Something always did. In 1980, I began to notice that my bed was covered with sweat whenever I'd get up in the morning. My weight started going down steadily from a previous 230 pounds to slightly over 180 pounds. Dark rings started to appear under my eyes. At night, my heart would beat up to 120 times a minute while asleep.

One weekend, during a visit to Gloria's parents in McAllen, I awoke not being able to lift myself out of bed. After I managed to get dressed, Gloria rushed me to the hospital emergency room. A few tests later, the attending doctor advised me to immediately return home to consult with my personal physician. He suggested the possibility of a developing brain tumor. Back in Austin the next day, another episode of sudden and unexplained exhaustion left me with no strength to stand up. An endocrinologist finally diagnosed the problem. I had developed a severe thyroid condition that had come close to killing me.

In addition to taking radioactive iodine to attack my overactive thyroid, the doctor's orders included plenty of bed rest, no exercise except slow walks around the block, and extreme caution in walking up and down stairs.

My recovery was going to take time. In the end, everything worked out. I slowly regained my strength and finally went back to my work.

In June of 1982, we staged the first Lorenzo de Zavala Youth Legislative (LDZ) Session among the high school youth enrolled in NHI's first leadership project, the Austin Young Leaders Conference (YLC). Weeks before, YLC students spent long weekends listening to guest lecturers and taking tours to observe city and county governments. Though they were courteous and attentive, boredom was written on their faces. LDZ, a mock youth legislative session, was designed as the fun part of their participation, their reward for being dutiful and conscientious in their attendance. Besides, this was our first attempt at doing something different in the Austin Latino community, working with a different audience of youth.

At this time, Gloria de León also came into the picture. We had met several years before in 1976 when we both worked for the Texas Department of Community Affairs. Both of us had gone through divorces and had seeing each other regularly. We even contemplated marriage earlier, but there were other problems involved.

By 1982, she was thirty years old. I was twelve years her senior with four children. Two years before, she left the Governor's Office of Energy Resources and Conservation to join State Senator Peyton McKnight's staff in his bid for governor. We both felt that the election of Senator McKnight to the governorship would not only enhance her career, but also possibly strengthen NHI's prospects for state funding. Without warning, the senator suddenly withdrew from the race, leaving her out in the cold with no job. Soon after, Buddy Temple, the state railroad commissioner, took up the challenge of becoming the new Democratic nominee. Buddy called on several occasions encouraging Gloria to consider becoming a member of his campaign staff. After several discussions, she consented, only to face his withdrawal from the race weeks later.

Disheartened from these setbacks, Gloria and I spent long hours going over our future. Whenever she wasn't looking for jobs in San Antonio or Austin, she was at NHI, involved in planning the youth session.

As the Young Leaders Conference project grew, Gloria became more involved. Ken Sheppardson, Senator McKnight's former legislative assistant, helped us with the legislative format and procedures. Days were spent writing drafts for Ken's review. We wanted a format that was close to the real legislative process, but obviously not demanding or complicated. These young kids had never before participated in policy.

It was Gloria's idea to name the legislative project the Lorenzo de Zavala Youth Legislative Session, after the first vice president of the Republic of Texas. Assisted by her cousin, Edward De León, we decided on a process that began with a two-day student convention at the LBJ School of Public Affairs at The University of Texas followed by a two-day mock session at the state capitol. Students were given the entire week prior to negotiate the rules of the convention and form their political parties.

All of the participants were honors students from Austin high schools. They weren't there because they needed help. We recruited them because we needed their energies and talents to also include the Latino community. Most neither spoke Spanish nor had any real life experiences in the barrio. They came mostly from middle class families that measured success by grades in school, membership in school organizations, and college and career plans. Student volunteers did most of the support work. We invited parents, kids, and friends, to get involved. The first problem was not having enough students to make the experience meaningful. We needed more participants than the sixty in the YLC. Everyone was asked to recruit friends and cousins to bring the numbers to at least one hundred. Roy and Nicole, who at the time were fourteen and twelve, were thrown into the pile. To make the youth government process more interesting, we asked college graduates who had participated with NHI the previous years to participate as the program's youth mentors and advisors.\

Each night before the convention, the lights at NHI offices burned late, many times past midnight, to accommodate students arguing over rules. The counselors and advisors became intensely involved. This was the early foundation of what was to eventually become a legacy for thousands of other Latino youth to follow. Instead of rules being created by adults, the students became the designers of procedures, the persons responsible for the program.

By the time the first LDZ session took place, we counted 165 participants, including forty migrant high school students attending a summer program at nearby St. Edward's University. By the end of the 1982 session, both students and parents alike stood in awe of their accomplishments. This was not a program imposed on the students and counselors by someone else. It was their creation, their own unique experience.

Toward the end, the Austin students discovered that the migrant participants hadn't yet received their government stipends. They were away from home without money to wash their clothes. Quietly, without attracting attention, they collected $70 to help out. This wasn't an act of pity. These were young people with a genuine care for their newfound friends.

No matter how much they tried after the program, letting go was difficult. From the state capitol, the entire delegation of youth went to a barbecue place across the street from St Edward's. Several hours were required to say good-bye. Repeatedly they went over the session, day-by-day, event-by-event. They relived the experience over and over, stopping only on occasion to request that NHI sponsor the LDZ as a statewide program. Never did they imagine that one day the National Hispanic Institute would become nationally known and would even conduct programs internationally. The LDZ class of 198 laid down the first cornerstone of an experience that today continues to capture the imagination of thousands of youths.

The LDZ also gave Gloria and me firsthand insight into a particular sector of Latinos. These youth were more mobile, more focused, and more ambitious. The majority of them had difficulties with Spanish. Most had parents who expected them to do well in school. There was never a question regarding getting a college degree. Their biggest hurdle was in selecting which college to attend. They belonged to numerous student clubs and were respected by their peers. But there was a problem involved. They didn't see themselves as future leaders of the Latino community. As a matter of fact, they didn't necessarily relate to Latinos at all, outside of sometimes acknowledging a cloudy and distant relationship.

The social model they used to measure their success was joining the National Honor Society, holding high posts in student government, being head cheerleaders, and being ranked among the top of their high school classes. Latino culture and issues, speaking Spanish, or seeing themselves as playing a role in the life of other Latinos wasn't in their plans.

This didn't make them bad or uncaring kids. To the contrary, they were decent young men and women who were modern-day, All-American types. Seeing the world differently set them apart from other Latino youth. Their destination in life was going to a big-name college or university and eventually getting a solid job that gave them economic security. Achieving these dreams outside of the Latino community was what set them apart from the rest. It made them different, more attractive to the larger society.

Our work as an organization was to expand their view to include Latinos, to make the Latino community part of their vision for the future, and make Latinos integral to their realities. We never imagined the resistance our ideas would encounter along the way. It caused us to question whether or not we were out of sync with our more successful role models.

High-risk Latinos--- high school dropouts, pregnant teenagers and underachieving youth, those not making it in life --- understood their personal dilemmas. Their parents, school officials, the community in general, and the media made certain to remind them each day of their situations. They operated near the bottom of society and desperately needed help to have half a chance of making it. In contrast, the young people we decided to train as future Latino leaders were different. How do you criticize making straight A's or being ranked in the top ten percent of a high school graduating class? How do you question a young person whose vision of the future is to eventually become a physician, attorney, or engineer?

Gloria and I knew what lay in store for a young, struggling NHI, which lacked the support of a community more accustomed to dealing with problems than opportunities. The National Hispanic Institute was an organization that had not yet learned how to make a compelling argument for its more developed youth to come back to the Latino community rather than constantly working to leave it.

It all boiled down to one common concern --- the economic survival of NHI. We could have easily worked with troubled youth and received all the funding we needed, especially with the help of our politicians and friends in the government. Discussions on this topic didn't last long. The decision was to continue with our direction, hoping that along the way someone would realize that maybe our instincts were correct.

Much to our surprise, the support came from youth we first considered only remotely interested in Latinos. It didn't come from our established leaders. They were too caught up with the demands of being public officials, responding to community issues, and attending meetings.

In contrast, we saw young people who were genuinely interested in what we had to say.

Inside their psyches was a cultural imprint left by parents, and perhaps, grandparents. Once this part of them was touched, it awakened a spirit deep inside, a special energy that made them want to become involved and linked back into the community.

A thought flashed across our minds: maybe in setting themselves apart from the rest of their Latino peers though studies or though their activities at school, they no longer felt wanted. Maybe they needed to have someone carve out a role for them.

These early NHI experiences will be remembered for years. Like the lioness in the movie, there were time when all I wanted was to turn back the clock, to return to a secure job. Even the pay mattered very little. Job offers came from Washington, D.C., and Houston, but leaving my children behind was out of the question. They were too much a part of my life, too important to my sanity to be apart.

At times, in frustration, Gloria would demand that I find employment elsewhere, even if it meant working at a convenience store part-time. Several times there wasn't enough money to pay bills or provide for my children's needs on weekends.

Seeing no other alternative, I finally took a part-time assistant coach's job at St. Edward's University earning $5.25 an hour. Although being on the basketball court brought back many found memories of my youth, I left soon after completing the first season, going back to NHI to continue my search.

It was too late now to turn back, even if it meant losing the little pride that remained, even losing Gloria. My mind was set. There had to be an answer and the only way for me was to continue my journey not knowing the outcome.

Chapter Seven: Lonely Road Back

1. Briefly describe a desired state you want to create or achieve. What is it about this desired state that is, for you, attractive, compelling, and desirable?
2. Write a brief story about a time when you felt afraid that you could not achieve your vision or goals.
   a. What did you think about the situation and about yourself?
   b. What did you feel?
   c. What did you do?
3. Write a brief story about a time when you were surprised to discover that you did not know something that you did not know.
   a. What did you think?
   b. How did you feel?
   c. What did you do?
   d. What did you learn from your efforts to cope with this surprise?
4. Write a brief story about a time when you were surprised to learn that you had to figure out how to run a social or organizational maze (that was created by others) in order to become effective and successful.
   a. What did you think?
   b. How did you feel?
   c. What did you do?
   d. What did you learn from your efforts to cope with this surprise?
5. What are you willing to sacrifice or delay now in order to create the future world in which you want to live?

        a.   What did you think?
        b.   How did you feel?
        c.   What did you do?

6. How do you know what knowledge, skills, and attitudes (KSAs) you will need to do what you want to do – now and in the future?

Write a brief story about a time when you first realized that it was you – and you alone – who was responsible for producing tangible, measureable results in order to be successful.

Chapter Eight
Proceed Only on Faith

When experiencing success, there's often the tendency to be cautious, sometimes conservative, because of the fear that something will go wrong along the way. Between 1988 and 1991, NHI grew quickly. We understood the growth potential of the Lorenzo de Zavala Youth Legislative Session as a project that could be replicated elsewhere in the nation. An increasing applicant pool each year demanded that we consider expansion to other states. Our problem was that we did not know where, how, or with what money.

New Mexico was first selected for expansion of our programs. There were several reasons to start an LDZ project there. The state bordered Texas. Latinos played visible leadership roles in the community. Being next-door neighbors meant students being turned away from the burgeoning Texas LDZ could easily be routed into another NHI program.

There were, however, a few reservations. We didn't know if Latino leaders and organizations from New Mexico would consider getting involved in helping an unfamiliar program get off the ground. We also questioned whether the state had the critical mass needed for the long term.

The population of New Mexico, by Texas standards, was small. Less than a half million Latinos lived there with almost fifty percent being in the Albuquerque metropolitan area. These numbers were tiny in comparison to the more than four million Latinos in Texas. We didn't know anyone sufficiently familiar with New Mexico Latinos who could offer us guidance and support.

The more hidden reasons for being so cautious had more to do with our inner fears of failure. Gloria and I had worked eight long years to take an organization through a painstaking process of becoming statewide. The commitment caused us to live without money for weeks at a time. Hard times leave an indelible impression on a person. It made us conservative, sometimes unwilling to gamble away the small gains we had come to cherish.

There were other questions needing answers. What if the students didn't want to attend a New Mexico LDZ? Were New Mexican families willing to pay for their children to attend? Did Latinos in New Mexico share the same sentiments as Tejanos about wanting their children to be involved in the Latino community? Were there any differences between our two cultures that could conceivably stand in the way?

On a trip to Santa Fe to talk with officials at St. John's College, we arranged a meeting with a high-level Latino official from the University of New Mexico (UNM), Dr. Alex Sanchez, the academic dean. He was also in the city, testifying before a New Mexico legislative committee.

A conservative-looking, medium-built man who fit every popular description of people from academia, Dr. Sanchez expressed immediate interest in involving his university. We had lunch together at the Bull Ring, a popular restaurant frequented by politicians in the heart of downtown. I had been in Santa Fe in the late 1960s when George Gonzales was mayor.

The city hadn't changed that much. It was still filled with people in their business attire, privately chatting, huddling over deals, oblivious to another world outside. Out on the sidewalks, tourists perused the shops, cameras strapped over their shoulders, casually looking though the countless boutiques and outside restaurants that give Santa Fe its internationally know Southwestern flavor.

After lunch, he made a few calls to the university and came back to our table with instructions for us to visit with Dr. Matthew Padilla, associate director for student services at the university.

"He's waiting for your call," he said, as we got ready to leave. He was in a hurry to get back to the capitol. "Stay in touch with Matthew," he reminded us on his way out. "And good luck."

The next morning, we drove south to Albuquerque and UNM. From Tome, a small community south of Albuquerque, Matthew's look and demeanor was more descriptive of New Mexicans who came from the northern regions of the state. His questions were pointed and direct. Underneath the tough-minded veneer, however, there was genuineness in his makeup, a sincere concern for people. Though open to the idea of a leadership program at UNM, he wasn't quite ready to accept us at face value, not without first putting us through a rigorous question and answer period. In the end, however, he consented. We had an agreement.

Gloria and I were thrilled, but nervous. The discussions in Albuquerque meant taking NHI beyond Texas. The move would allow us to serve more students, test new ideas, and make NHI even bigger. We knew that students, once given the chance to experience the LDZ, would like it. How to get them to the University of New Mexico was the question. And the best thing to do was not to waste time.

Three weeks later, we were on our way back. Plans included hitting every town possible. Gloria and I started in Santa Fe one morning and moved north to Farmington, Raton, Las Vegas, and Espanola. Afterwards, we headed south to Las Cruces and Deming. Then we turned to the southeast part of the state to visit schools in Roswell, Hobbs, Carlsbad, and Artesia before returning to Albuquerque. Going to so many schools in such a short period of time would have been impossible without two key people, Ernesto "Netti" Ramos and Jerome Block, both from Santa Fe.

Netti and I went back years to the early days of the Office of Economic Opportunity (OEO) in the 1960s. He and his family lived across from Whit Rock Lake in East Dallas, about a mile from our home where we first moved after leaving Austin. On weekends, we'd get our children together to barbecue, play backyard basketball, or spend the evening playing guitar and singing old "ranchera" songs. Our kids enjoyed being around each other, as did our wives. All of us became close friends, like family. Years later, in 1986, Netti's youngest daughter Gina became the first New Mexican student at the Texas LDZ. The experience started talks about the LDZ eventually being taken to New Mexico.

Jerome Block was a corporation court commissioner when Netti introduced him to me. His father, Johnny Block, was a well-known Latino businessman from Santa Fe, whom I had met several years earlier. Jerome and I became instant friends. He and Netti worked tirelessly to get NHI's first New Mexico program going. They accompanied us at meetings to endorse our programs, made presentations on our behalf, and made their contacts throughout the state available to help open the doors for us. Their most important contribution was validating NHI's presence.

A few months later, 178 high school students from New Mexico, Texas, Arizona, and Colorado helped celebrate the inaugural LDZ at the University of New Mexico. Gloria and I were more relieved than excited. Our senior counselor staff was tiny and our junior counselor staff consisted of only three high school students: my daughter Nicole, Michael Soto from Brownsville, and Judy Salinas. Everyone worked around the clock, only getting a few hours of sleep. Every available volunteer was asked to pinch-hit as needed, often assuming multiple responsibilities.

In the end, the experience paid off. Eric Barbosa from Weslaco, Texas, became the first New Mexico governor; Michael Padilla from Los Lunas was the first lieutenant governor; Jennifer Olguin from Round Rock, Texas, the first speaker of the house; and Amy Lopez from Santa Fe, the chief justice of the supreme court.

Similar to the Texas program, students found it difficult to leave. Lasting friendships were formed. It didn't matter whether a student was from Texas, New Mexico, Arizona, or Colorado. They shared in a common experience that bonded them together. They competed against each other in an intense learning environment and enjoyed it. They spoke out about different issues regarding Latinos in the United States. They voiced opinions about subjects that would have been difficult and intimidating to the average sixteen or seventeen year old.

As the week drew to a close, the magic of the LDZ was obvious. It had worked one more time, creating a special chemistry, unique to every group that would eventually follow in the years to come. Worn out from eighteen-hour work sessions that lasted eight consecutive days the staff limped back to Texas exhausted but pleased with the results. Everyone grew and matured a little bit in the process. We were proud that our ideas had worked.

The next year, the LDZ was taken to Colorado, then to Iowa City, Iowa, in 1991. A year earlier, the first Collegiate World Series project for high school seniors was conducted at Southwestern University in Georgetown, Texas. The high school freshman Young Leaders Conference was also expanded to New Mexico and then the Midwestern United States after 1995.

We also expanded beyond high school programs. Two years before, the Collegiate Leadership Network was founded in El Paso. The National Conference of Community Leadership Councils for parents came in 1964. NHI also sponsored its first international program in 1996 in Monterrey, Mexico. Two years later, a second program for Mexican college students was started in Guanajuato. Between 1987 and 1998, NHI went from an organization that served 200 students a year to over 3,500 in eighteen states and Mexico.

The most important lesson learned along the way was the role that confidence plays in taking risks. Making the jump from Texas to New Mexico was the turning point, a special moment in NHI's development when eyes were closed and leaps were made into the unknown. Success in New Mexico provided the impetus for success in other states. Until the step was taken no one knew if the idea of a leadership institute for Latino youth had a chance of making it.

Gauging the impact of NHI training programs on the thinking of students was difficult. New Mexico gave NHI the opportunity to look beyond Texas. The realization was that the National Hispanic Institute could create a national following in the Latino community. This understanding forced an inward look at our work to understand the dynamics of the programs, to more fully understand organizational issues needing correction if growth was to continue in the years that followed.

New Mexico forced a close, critical look at our operation, from approaches, to the methods being used in relating with youth, to the outcomes everyone expected and wanted, and the philosophy and beliefs driving the organization. It was already known that the LDZ was able to touch the hearts of students. The experience and participation gave them a means to connect to the community, in a setting where everyone was Latino, where those in attendance shared a common culture, past, and history.

New Mexico also provided an ideological rationale for NHI's expansion that went beyond just serving more students. New Mexico, as a state and setting, symbolized the institute's work. If the mission was to help train future leaders for the Latino community, New Mexico represented a homeland where crafting a new public message and direction for future Latino leaders was at least remotely possible.

For Gloria and me, New Mexico was an exciting step in the evolution of NHI. We never realized that the mountains and people would also start a personal healing process in our lives.

For Gloria, New Mexico came on the heels of two devastating family tragedies. The summer of 1988 was only two years removed from the deaths of her sister and father. She wasn't quite ready to pick up and start over again. Her sister Lisa had lived across the street from us in Austin for several years. Both sisters frequently visited their family. Everything changed from one moment to the next.

Lisa was tragically killed in an accident while on the way to work. She had taken a day off to drive from Austin to McAllen with Gloria to surprise their dad on Father's Day. When a call came to our home early in the morning from the hospital emergency room, Gloria was only slightly concerned. Once at the hospital, we were hurriedly taken to a sided office and told the shocking news. Lisa had suffered permanent brain damage and wasn't expected to live more than a few hours. Only a few hours were left to gather the immediate family and pray for her. Then, Lisa was gone.

Twelve hours afterwards, her father suffered a massive, fatal heart attack at our home. Witnessing his daughter's resuscitator being turned off by the attending physician was too much for Gloria's dad to bear.

For the next several months following her sister's and father's burials, Gloria did everything possible to maintain control of her emotions. In an instant, however, she would start crying uncontrollably. For more than a year, Gloria was in a cloud of confusion and stress, attempting each day to gain enough strength to keep going.

Family setbacks were not our only challenges. Friends familiar with New Mexico repeatedly told us that as Tejanos we would never be fully embraced, and NHI programs would never work there. Instead, we found an altogether accepting environment. Unlike when in Texas, who we were as an organization was never questioned. We found an immediate appreciation for our services and the benefits our programs meant to Latino youth and the community. We weren't prepared for an open welcome, not after being continuously warned.

When compared to New Mexico, ethnic tensions in Texas between Latinos and the majority community were more apparent. Sometimes school districts flatly refused to open doors to NHI programs, especially in communities like West Texas, Dallas, and Central Texas. At times, the institute's nicely printed student brochures were sent back to Maxwell with personal handwritten notes scribbled all over them. "What about programs for Whites?" they would say in bold, red ink. "What about programs for Blacks? Why are you a racist organization?"

In one particular instance, the person who wrote a similar message wasn't smart enough to remain anonymous. Although the envelope didn't have a return address, the post office had clearly showed its origin. It came from Hereford, Texas.

In New Mexico the climate was different. We were never scrutinized regarding our motives. No one ever asked us what we did with the funds, and whether we had the organizational capacities to deliver on our promises. Instead, we were embraced at face value and given the support we needed. Serving youth was the overriding concern for everyone. The more familiar we became with New Mexico, the stronger our efforts about taking the LDZ to other states.

An undeniable realization was the impact that New Mexico could potentially have on Latino youth nationally. Everything about New Mexican culture was Latino. Whether in the larger towns and cities or in small mountain villages of northern New Mexico, the influence was obvious, easy to see, taste, and appreciate. Latino culture was in the music, the architecture, the art, the food, and the look. Even the smallest, inconspicuous villages publicized their founders and when they were first established.

An important distinction about New Mexican Latinos and their counterparts in other U.S. states was that they were landowners with long community and family histories dating as far back as 500 years. The tradition of land ownership rooted the people deeply into their living histories. Large and small plots of land had been passed through the generations. With only the smallest of examples possibly in California, no Latino community in the United States could lay claim to the same. New Mexico stood as an exception, the one place in the nation where a community of Latinos had been able to carve out their own cultural niche, formed their own history, and developed their own unique identity.

For the National Hispanic Institute, New Mexico was a gold mine of U.S. Latino history for other Latinos throughout the nation. Before other states could lay claim to having the first Latino mayor of a major city, the first speaker of the house, the first governor, or president of a university, New Mexico had a already long ago celebrated those victories. They had poets, artists, composers, large Latino-owned companies, people with land holdings, attorneys, and dentists. The social and cultural environment of New Mexico, in other words, was a model to appreciate and study in constructing a new reality for Latino youth. New Mexico freed us to imagine the possibilities.

Years before, Dr. Roberto Rodriguez, a friend of ours who served as a superintendent of a Texas Rio Grande Valley school district described Gloria and me as having started the POOF Theory.

"I've known Gloria and Ernesto for year," he would tell friends. "Every time we talk, they tell me about just having finished adding another program to their repertoire of services. NHI is constantly growing and expanding. The amazing part of this work is that NHI doesn't have any money to speak of, only the students and a few parents who become involved. My wife Judy and I used to talk about this all of the time. One day we realized what Gloria and Ernesto meant by snapping their fingers and hollering "poof" when confronted with tough challenges. Poof to them means "Proceed Only on Faith."

Roberto was correct. Many times, NHI proceeded only on faith to reach a goal. Being keenly aware of the organization's abilities when compared to the requirements of the tasks, large or small, was also important. Ultimately, however, it was faith that produced the courage necessary to dive into the unknown.

Through the years of guiding NHI, Gloria and I were forced to uncover the inner strength in us to be risk-takers. Our backgrounds as young children and growing up in tough neighborhoods prepared us for this role by constantly having to overlook repeated failures for the one opportunity to emerge. When left with little to offer from the standpoint of economics or connections, trust in our instincts became our trump car in high-risk situations.

We trusted other Latinos, and the importance of our work. Gaining faith in working with others didn't change the playing field or guarantee success. Trust meant approaching relationships with a different mindset, letting our defenses down, and being open and frank in dealings with others. It also meant concentrating more on relationship building.

Throughout the years, NHI had become accustomed to looking outside the Latino community for answers rather than inward. The decision was made to remain inside and expect answers from Latinos as the experts with special skills and knowledge. They had the abilities to understand tough questions and to provide meaningful answers. Latinos could no longer remain the people with the problems. They needed to control and manage their own solutions.

While encouraging this thinking at our programs, Gloria and I made similar changes in our beliefs. It no longer mattered whether the young people being invited to join NHI were from New Mexico, Colorado, California, Illinois, New York, or Florida. If they preferred to call themselves Latinos or Hispanics or if they insisted on being Mexican American, Chicano, Spanish American, Puerto Rican, Cuban, Colombian, Nicaraguan, or any other Latino nationality, also didn't matter. Our role was building trust, learning to step across barriers that separated us. It meant looking for common ground rather than being overly sensitive to individual differences. It involved working together to craft a broader, more inclusive vision of Latinos instead of limiting NHI's work to regional considerations.

Not everyone was in accord with this direction or willing to let their defenses down in their interactions with us. Rather than criticize, Gloria and I became accepting, preferring silence when confronted by individuals who weren't ready to work with Tejanos. We learned to move on and become more selective about whom to involve. After all, Latinos were as diverse as anyone else was. They didn't all look at the world the same way or agree on the same issues. Not all of them shared the same philosophies and outlooks.

This was normal, not unusual or weird. Some Latinos could only deal with their immediate communities. Others suspected anyone from outside their community. Some had personal and historical reason for their feelings.

The challenges weren't discouraging to us. We already knew there were people in the Latino community who would listen, who were willing to participate in a common vision, and who would gladly contribute their time, energies, and skills to become part of the work. Trust building was the main objective along with the finding the right people to involve.

Running into individuals who shared similar concerns and who had been searching to connect with an organization like the National Hispanic Institute was always cause to celebrate. Some of the supporters lived in small rural towns like Antonito, the San Luis Valley of Southern Colorado, or Penasco in the mountains of northern New Mexico. Others worked in the anonymity of the large urban centers of Los Angeles, Chicago, and Houston. A few were doctors, lawyers, and business owners, successful individuals who wanted their children involved with NHI. The majority was made up of everyday, hard working parents who understood the responsibilities and demands of family and parenthood. They wanted nothing more than to participate in crafting a different future for their children.

This chemistry of people who shared our vision and were willing to work together to make dreams come true for their children helped establish the foundation of what was to become one of the largest organized constituencies of Latino youth and families in the nation. It first started by learning to trust our work, trust others, and also trust ourselves.

This sense of community gave NHI the faith and encouragement to cross barriers and to pursue dreams. It served as the impetus to take risks and feel sufficiently cofortable with the unknown to move forward even when all of the details had not been fully worked out.

It was also at this juncture of our development in 1988, while in New Mexico, that Gloria and I were forced to address another critical question regarding our views as the principal leaders of NHI. We had to turn away from government and the philanthropy of the private sector to help us with our needs. Instead, we had to rely on our own resourcefulness to move ahead and reach our organizational goals. And, if anything, those resources had to come in the form of human capital from the Latino community.

It all came down to having faith in our ideas and our capacities to motivate others to join us. If we couldn't find the way to trust our own instincts, our intellectual capacities to think big, and our problem solving, motivational, and organizational skills, there was little we would be able to do in teaching Latino youth to also think differently. Our most important responsibility was to guide them to first have confidence in themselves and then the Latino community.

In making this decision, we no longer would be able to depend on others to guide or assume responsibility for NHI. Failure would come not from lacking a vision or failing as strong-willed, energetic leaders. It would be from not trusting ourselves enough as two individuals to take a leap of faith into the future knowing that faith in the Latino community was the only assurance to move forward.

Chapter Eight: Proceed Only on Faith (POOF)

1. What do you think – and feel – about the POOF theory?
2. What would you be risking to POOF? Are you courageous enough to take those risks? What would it take for you to POOF?
3. What does it take for you to learn to trust yourself? Other people? Your work?
4. Briefly describe a situation where you wanted to achieve some goal but everybody told you it would be too difficult. You doubted that you could be successful. Yet you tried and you succeeded.
    a. What did you think?
    b. How did you feel about yourself?
    c. How did you feel about those who thought that your success was unlikely?
5. When you achieved results that were beyond what you and others expected:
    a. What did you think?

        b.   How did you feel about yourself? About others who thought that your success was unlikely? About those people who helped you to succeed?
6. How did your success influence your aspirations and plans for your future?
7. What, if anything, did you do to follow up on and leverage your success?
8. Describe a time when you were identified and recruited by one or more people who wanted you to share their vision and aspirations.
        a.   What did you think?
        b.   How did you feel?
        c.   What did you do?

Chapter Nine
The Turmoil of Change

The amount of mental, emotional, and psychological effort required for me to change from my previously held perceptions about my work in the Latino community was immense. Years were consumed taking baby steps forward in crafting a new and different role for NHI. The journey was filled with doubt, fear of the unknown and unpredictable outcomes. Gloria and I knew only to proceed on faith, guided by the knowledge that they ways in which we had done things for most of our lives were ineffective.

At times we felt as though we were shooting at a moving target, until we suddenly stumbled across another insight. It wasn't only our thinking that had to change. The mental framework through which information was being received, processed, and interpreted also had to be unraveled.

By 1990, Gloria and I concluded that in order for the National Hispanic Institute to succeed, it would have to create an authentic and positive purpose in the Latino community. Our work also had to be distinguishable from other Latino groups. It had to serve a definitive mission. And crafting an identity, purpose, and role for the institute could only come from us.

We never stopped to analyze the difficulties we would encounter. We never gave a second thought to the changes we would have to undergo. We rarely stopped to contemplate how long it would take for us to craft a community purpose that was compelling enough for others to follow, and how painful it would become at times to alter core beliefs that had guided us since childhood.

In the 1960s, I had seen my community role as being similar to a warrior who defends his people, a person demanding answers and action. Once home from college, I got wrapped up in the civil rights movement in Houston, appearing before city councils and school boards and pointing to the unfairness of the system.

There were plenty of unresolved issues to get mad about. The Latino community needed answers not next year, not next month, not next week. Solutions were needed now! Fresh with a degree in hand, my drive was to give something back, represent those with less, change the system to become more tolerant and inclusive of people.

Working in government became the means for me to gain access to the system in order to change rules of how people dealt with the Latino community. The higher my position, the more influence I could assert over policy matters and affect change. This reasoning drove me to work hard at quickly moving up the professional ladder into management. One day, however, fourteen years of work came to an abrupt end. I was out on the street. This abrupt firing was an important reality check in my life.

There is no real need to analyze the factors leading to my dismissal in 1979. The reasons were easy to understand. A new administration had come into power after an election. A Republican governor won over a Democrat. The transition team needed to vacate positions for the supporters, and I was high enough on the ladder to be affected. It left a gnawing feeling that someone had sufficient power over me to affect my career and the quality of life of my children. That realization burned pretty deep inside.

The second reality check came soon afterwards. There was nothing particularly marketable about my capacities to negotiate. I had no tangible skills. A college degree from a respected institution was important; however, it didn't make competing at certain levels of employment easier or provide me with career longevity.

There were other concerns smoldering in my mind. Through the years, I had become part of a working world where conformity and being a good team player were the only expectations. More importantly, I wasn't the person in waiting, the next one in the lineup. An invisible ceiling was in place that would ultimately keep me frozen to certain levels. My father tried to warn me one day in 1971 that eventually a choice would face me regarding the world in which I preferred to live out my life.

"*Si quieres ser Mexicano, mijo,*" he said one day while visiting me in Dallas, "*todavia seras mi hijo. Si quieres ser parte de otro modo de vivir, en otra cultura, todavia seras mi hijo. Esa es tu decision. Solamente tu puedes decider tu cultura, la vida en que tu prefieres vivir. Pero no puedes vivir en dos mundos. Cada decision tiene sus ventajas y sus desventajas. Una cultura tiene que dominar y si no, es posible perder la mente constantemente cruzando de una realidad a otra.* (If you want to be a Mexican, son, you'll still by my son. It is your decision. If you choose to become part of another culture and way of life, you'll still be my son. Your challenge is to decide in which world you prefer to live. Either choice has its advantages and disadvantages. But you can't live in both realties. One culture has to play the dominant role or else you'll go crazy jumping from one side to the other.)"

Dad understood my crisis, the stress of one day living and adjusting to one set of cultural roles and expectations and then having to do a turnabout to live in another reality. In one world, I was the minority person, different from the others. In those settings, I always felt uncomfortable, and out of place.

"How do you spell your name again?" I was asked in that world. "Do you mind repeating it? Are your parents from Mexico?"

"This is what Dad meant," I used to think to myself.

One day I was in an office wearing a white shirt and tie, working next to strangers. Hours later, it was nothing for me to be back in the old neighborhood hanging with friends, absorbed in a completely different reality. For me this wasn't simply having friends from different backgrounds. This meant having to constantly juggle contrasting worldviews of how relationships were build. Having to move back and forth was mentally and emotionally exhausting. It caused tensions in my personal and married life. It created difficulties in how I interpreted and approached my work. It influenced my selection of friends, where I went to relax, where we lived, and how I planned my future. Dad saw the impact these pressures were having on me. He didn't like what he saw and was suggesting that I choose one or the other.

"*Seguiras siendo mijo,* (You'll still be my son,)" the words kept echoing in my mind. "*Pero decide una o la otra. No puedes brincar de un lado al otro. No puedes estar en medio como una cerca, o la presion te destruira.* (But choose one or the other. Don't keep jumping back and forth and don't straddle the fence or the pressures will eventually destroy you.)"

Years later, a similar dilemma was in play. This time, however, Latino youth of the 1980s and 1990s were involved. The confusing circumstances facing them were similar to those encountered by my generation. They too had to contend with the tensions of simultaneously living in two competing cultures. They were doing everything possible to attend the best universities to ease their transitioning into mainstream society. They felt pressured to criticize the very stream they were attempting to join for not being more inclusive. While making the crossover, however, they faced accusations from peers in the barrios for having abandoned their cultural community and roots. These conflicting struggles had been tough on Latino youth. Their modern counterparts were feeling the same pressures.

Making matters even more stressful were political demagoguery against affirmative action, the contention that the few gains being made by Latinos were due to a lowering of standards. These problems brought back memories of my own struggles as a young man attempting to decide which direction to take.

In 1960, friends encouraged me to leave home and go on to college. "Mira vato," my friend Robert Reyna used to say. "You've been offered a scholarship to play basketball in college. ¡*Avientate ese!* (Go for it!)" A month after I returned from college, he and other friends criticized me for having changed, forgetting my roots, and for looking down on them. On a similar trip back to the neighborhood the next semester, I made efforts to fit in. The attacks were different.

"Mira este buey. Se va y no cambia. Todavia esta como nosotros. (Look at this dumb fool. He leaves and refuses to change. He's still like us.)" These challenges embroiled NHI in internal ideological battles. One of our tasks was to create clarity for young people experiencing the age-old phenomenon of upward mobility and the accompanying emotional roller coaster ride. The conflicts were between one style of life that was culturally familiar and comforting and the stresses that come from moving out and away.

Even at a young age, NHI participants were already starting to feel the enormous burdens of dual cultural expectations and being challenged to become future community leaders while they still lived in mainstream environments that neither embraced them nor saw them as equals.

NHI was doing little to settle these inner conflicts. In fact, it was contributing to the problem by compelling them to pursue leadership through the same processes as past generations. The conflicts that emerged were virtually identical. It was the second verse of the same song. The outcomes were predictable. In the end, our future leaders would have no alternative but to become accustomed to trickle-down opportunity, cultural separation from the Latino community, and the emotional and mental anguish that comes from constantly having to straddle and balance two realities.

NHI had to determine a course of action. One alternative was to stand on the side of mainstream Latino youth. Bringing successful Latino role models to the attention of the NHI youth or inviting them to special conferences to develop an appreciation for life in the larger U.S. society would be easy. Gaining admission to the well-known institutions, obtaining degrees in highly specialized fields, and mastering the requirements of mainstream culture meant increasing their probabilities of having higher incomes, more secure jobs, and acquiring better material conveniences.

A second choice was to become cause-driven, focusing on the poor and those who needed special advocates championing their needs. From our vantage point, this alternative was too narrow and too emotionally and psychologically draining to sustain efforts that consumed years with only minimal victories.

Strangely, both choices led to the same dead-end. Both meant encouraging our best and brightest to focus on the crossover. Nothing new would come of these approaches except a constant drain on the brainpower of the Latino community. It would perpetuate the belief that to remain behind meant living an existence of limited opportunity and higher prospects for failure.

In order for the institute to create a role for itself, another alternative had to be found, something more profound than the first two choices. NHI needed a compelling rationale for the future, an attractive choice for young people to become involved and to experiment with different possibilities.

We also knew that these ideas had to stand the test of time, extend well into the new millennium, attract participation from the various sectors comprising Latino community life, and create the common grounds within the different nationalities that comprised an emerging U.S. Latino culture. Reaching these goals would demand that NHI make important changes in its philosophy and educational goals. It also meant gaining a much deeper understanding of the beliefs and views held by youth being recruited to participate.

The beliefs and values young men and women held towards their own community were mostly in place. We had to find ways of arming them with a new set of social lenses to see Latinos from a different perspective, as a modern and attractive world culture, not as a minority artifact of little value. The prevailing view of a Latino community being a damaged society didn't fit NHI's goals for the future.

A third reality was needed, one that would lead our young to shape a different Latino community. They no longer needed to spend time reacting to issues outside their control. Efforts had to concentrate on reshaping and recreating a different self-identity and belief, one that enthused youth about their future in the Latino community. Accomplishing this work carried an important, but unstated understanding. Fostering the creation of a different belief system would require patience, constant reflection, and analysis and experimentation. The old could no longer serve as the means of chartering the new.

In the enthusiasm to start, neither Gloria nor I saw what later became apparent. Changing the views of young people was not the most important obstacle. The fact that young people were not fully shaped by the influences of a modern day society made change possible for them. They weren't prisoners of almost unalterable view of life, not yet.

Gloria and I were the problem. Did we have the capacities to make the crossover to a different mindset? Did we have the mental discipline and stamina to alter our historical mind-set towards our community? And, did we fully understand the emotional, psychological, and mental rigors that come from looking inward for solutions instead?

Months of work turned into years as Gloria and I took first steps towards a destination that had not yet been determined. Between 1992 and 1995, a period we came to know as the "dark days of NHI" set in. Many times Gloria and I found ourselves on completely opposite sides, bickering and arguing endlessly over the meaning of our work. Gender became a political issue as some argued that at NHI programs, Latino culture was being overwhelmingly influenced by men. Mexican machismo was held up as evidence of the current status between men and women. A senior counselor once argued at a Colorado LDZ program, "All Mexican men want is to have their food on the neck of their women."

There were also attempts during programs like the LDZ to promote female participants to top elected positions either through favoritism or lessening the roles of men in the administration of the programs. The battle lasted almost two years at a severe loss of confidence among staff. It strained relationships that threatened to destroy NHI and the marriage that Gloria and I had worked so hard to build.

Other concerns also consumed valuable time. Endless debates took place over the involvement of middle class Latino youth in NHI programs. Were they capable of eventually becoming leaders in the Latino community, given the fact that they didn't come from barrios? And what about children from mixed marriages, especially those with Anglo parents? Wasn't it easier for them to make the switch over without ever having to contend with their identity as Latinos?

Neither of us took steps to compromise or look at the issues causing the rift. Our feelings were more important. This attitude caused suspicion among staff and volunteers towards one another that sometimes ruined close friendships.

Earlier issues were different in comparison to the 1990s. Back then, Latino youth who were participating in institute leadership training needed help in coping with the psychological and mental stresses of upward mobility, adjusting to the requirements of moving from Latino environments to mainstream settings. At times questions surfaced regarding the readiness of middle class Latino youth to assume leadership roles in the Latino community. One view held that highly skilled young Latinos, already trained to deal with difficult challenges and disciplined enough to be creative represented the best possible candidates.

Others took an opposite position, instead supporting the idea that NHI should concentrate on developing the leadership capacities of youths who lived in the barrios and were more familiar with the needs of Latinos.

Ten years later, NHI was becoming embroiled in a different battle. This impaired our ability to see the larger picture. We were instead blinded by the same jealousies and internal conflicts that had caused the demise of other Latino organizations in the past. There was no one to blame but us. The options were to either stop the fighting or kill our dream.

NHI drifted for several months. Only time could heal the wounds that remained after hostilities subsided. In early 1993, the Collegiate Leadership Network (CLN) conference for undergraduate NHI alumni was unveiled in El Paso as a national project. A year later, the first parent National Community Leadership Council Conference was conducted in San Antonio.

My daughter, Nicole, left for Mexico to pursue her M.B.A. at El Instituto Tecnologico y de Estudios Superiores de Monterrey. While studying at the university, she started testing the possibility of a Mexico Language Program for high school students. Later, she added the Graduate Consortium to our undergraduate college initiatives. Carlos Hernandez, who was in charge of the Young Leaders Conferenceexpanded into New Mexico and the Midwest.

Roy, my oldest son, came back from a brief stint in professional baseball to take over a failing Collegiate World Series and made it an important revenue stream for the organization. Ileana Perez was hired to direct the College Register, turning a previously small collection of colleges and universities that participated in summer fairs into an organization with significant influence on NHI and its educational affairs.

By then the "Triangle Theory" had been introduced to LDZ students in Colorado. This concept was used to evaluate student feelings regarding U.S. Latino social mobility, social class, and culture conflict. Its intent was to stir discussion on whether participants perceived admission into the American mainstream as primarily driven by skill and individual effort or determined more by race and ethnicity.

The discussion on these subjects became long and exhaustive. Students nervously acknowledged that as Latinos they were members of a community that historically had been relegated to the bottom rungs of society. They easily related to the changes that occurred for those moving away from the community for the sake of finding better jobs and lifestyles. Most understood the price involved to gain admission and the psychological and emotional impact they would have to endure in making the changeover. They were living proof of these conflicting emotions and were desperately searching for answers.

Mostly they talked about the guild that came from being seen as "illegitimate" in both the Latino and Anglo worlds and being caught in the pressure cooker of living in two distinct –sometimes- conflicting – cultures. Most of them wanted to see themselves as future Latino leaders, but didn't have any ideas of where and how to begin. Most couldn't speak Spanish and felt anguished about not knowing anything about their own culture and history. They wanted in, to feel validated and be included.

NHI's slow healing process began in late 1995. Our intent was to take the institute to another level and in a more defined direction.

By then, we had become less defensive about our work, more conscious of our personal motives, and individual beliefs. We were better able to accept differences in our view and opinions.

In retrospect, we jokingly called this phase of introspection "self-imposed lobotomies." Old beliefs were questioned and new ones took their place. Simple as this process may have sounded to some, in truth, the reality was excruciatingly painful, emotional, and physically draining. Surrendering old beliefs and truths was hard. Crafting something new to replace the old was similar to the dynamics of converting from one religion to another. There have to be compelling reasons to cause the changeover.

The emotions that accompanied our conflicting views and beliefs must have been similar to those of hundreds of other Latino organizations that sprang up during the 1960s. A few brave individuals introduced thinking that did much more than demand changes in the system. It drove entire sectors of the American community to forever alter the ways they thought of themselves, the roles they wanted to play in society, and the rewards they sought for those born in the future.

Civil rights shook the very underpinnings of how we believed as a people. It caused tremors in the lives of every American who had a point of view regarding race and race relations. The impact of the civil right movement as a social force affected every institution of our nation.

A crucial ingredient of this movement was its impact on the people who were driven to change the system. Before seeking changes or going beyond the conventional problem-solving wisdom, they first had to look at themselves in the mirror and critically analyze the beliefs that drove them. More importantly, they had to risk the ultimate price that paralyzes most people from pursuing their destiny in life. They had to face up to the possibility of ruin and failure.

In the late 1960s and the early 1970s, young Latinos in Crystal City, Texas, took issue not only with the beliefs of the local school district, but also the practices of the school board and school administration. The people in power back then thought that Latino youth weren't cut out for certain leadership roles. They questioned whether the youth had the right stuff to become cheerleaders and class officers. The fact that Latino youth were left out or placed at the bottom made these views even more apparent to their parents. School requirements were applied to reward the Anglo elite and to place Latinos at the bottom. Learning to win and experiencing victory were not the lessons shaping the beliefs of Latino youth.

Today, we know Crystal City as the "birthplace of the Chicano Movement." Beyond the dramatics of the famous student walkouts and the media attention that city eventually received, a more profound change took place in the self-perceptions of the Latino community. One sector of people was unable to perceive Latinos as having any role in the affairs of the larger community. Latino youth not only called these beliefs and practices into question; they defied the very rules that governed them.

Twenty-five years later, NHI was undergoing its own conflicts in views and philosophies, though not openly in the community and certainly not at the level of the civil rights movement. This time the fight was internal. Still, it was an important turning point in the life of an organization that was at a critical crossroad in its historical evolution. We knew then, as we know today, that fresh new approaches were needed to address old, complex human problems and challenges. The first step, however, was to create a new mission statement. What worked in the twentieth century may have been good for those times.

History taught us an important lesson. We needed a different understanding, a new rationale to train our future leaders, especially if we were going to make quantum leaps forward as a community and if we expected to thrive as an organization. Other Latino organizations in the twenty-first century would have to tackle these questions and issues in the same manner. Approaching problems through past strategies and practices made the decline of the traditional civic and political structures of the Latino community life apparent and self-evident.

There was an important lesson to learn: It was not so much that Latinos in the twenty-first century were losing interest in their communities as much as Latino leaders of the past either being unable or unwilling to train new leaders with new ideas and different possibilities.

Chapter Nine: The Turmoil of Change

1. Write a brief story about a situation with which you were dissatisfied and you very much wanted to change. However, you were not clear what your desired state should be or how to change your current state.

2. What was it about this situation that was dissatisfying for you? What was dissatisfying for others?

3. To what extent were you able to create a specific, compelling vision of a desirable future?
   a. How did you try to clarify your desired state?
   b. What other people were involved in crafting this vision?
   c. Were the other persons cooperative or competitive in working together to create the common vision? What was the basis of the conflicts?
   d. How did you deal with those who disagreed with you?
   e. How often and why did you modify your desired state?
   f. What was the result of your efforts?
   g. What did you learn about the value of creating a common vision?
4. In addition to yourself, who else was dissatisfied and willing to commit themselves to cooperate in attempting to create an acceptable and viable plan of action to achieve the common vision?
   a. How did you develop a strategy and a plan of action to achieve your desired vision?
   b. Who, beside yourself, was involved in setting strategy and developing an action plan?
   c. How cooperative or competitive were these people in working together to create a common action plan? What was the basis of the conflicts?
   d. How did you deal with those who disagreed with you?
   e. How often and why did you modify your desired state?
   f. What was the result of your efforts?
   g. What did you learn about the value of creating a common action plan?
5. What did you learn from your efforts to bring dissatisfied people together to co-create a compelling vision of the future, a set of meaningful goals, a realistic strategy, and a workable action plan?

Chapter Ten
The Will to Endure

For years, Mom wondered how immigrants from Mexico, with virtually no money and little education, could move to the United State and open a successful restaurant within months. At least it seemed that way to her years ago while living in East Houston's Magnolia in the late 1940s and early 1950s.

"Esto tarudos aqui, (These Mexican American dummies, here in our own country,)" she would say, *"hay están saliendose de la escuela, trabajando por nada. Llegan los Mexicanos del otro lado y en un tris-trás, tienen sus negocios. ¿Y los Mexicanos de aqui? Son flojos. No quieren batallar ni sufrir para avanzar. Ese es el problema.* (They're leaving school, working for nothing. Mexicans from across the border get here and in no time, they have their own businesses. And the Mexicans from here? They're lazy. They don't want to be bothered or suffer a little in order to advance. That's the problem.)"

Mom's observations haunted me years later as NHI struggled. What she observed about Mexican Americans in the United States seemed to apply to me as well.

By the end of 1982, the National Hispanic Institute could talk about only a few accomplishments. Programs were developed mostly on instinct and management of those programs was done through trial and error. We were following an unpredictable road.

Towards the latter part of the year, economics forced us to move again, this time from our North Lamar location. We found office space at Concordia Lutheran College in an old annex building. All it needed was a good paint job and new carpeting. The staff consisted of a part-time bookkeeper and me.

Gloria continued volunteering. By now, we were more than just close friends. She was a breath of fresh air in my life, a connection to a past that had been absent for years. There was no denying it. Gloria had gotten under my skin. I was hooked.

In her usual positive demeanor, each morning she'd show up bright and early to help with whatever needed to be done. Sometimes she'd reconcile our financial records or answer letters. Most of the time she spent it being a patient and supportive listener. No longer working for state government, she was looking for work in a tight Austin job market.

Several things went wrong that year. She left state government to work in a couple of failed gubernatorial campaigns. The few job openings that interested her paid considerably less than she had been making. She also wanted to remain in Austin a little longer. All of these problems added to several other challenges we'd face later. I had little income and four children to support.

Gloria was living off of her unemployment benefits. Each week, she'd go over to the state employment agency to file papers showing that she was genuinely looking for a job. This was part of the process for her to receive her check. It meant sitting for hours going through an interview to explain her status, and looking through countless pages of available openings that mostly paid hourly wages.

On one particular morning, on the way to pick her up for lunch at the agency, I saw her among several other people listening for their names to be called. Gloria always dressed professionally, her hair in place and her face made up. There she was asking the government for help, trying to convince some entry-level, state bureaucrat that she was doing everything in her power to find work. It was more than I could stand. This wasn't what we had gone to college for. This wasn't why our parents had worked and sacrificed. Stories of my parents from the 1929 Depression came rushing back. One of Dad's most important victories during those times was that he never stood at a soup line and that he never sought government assistance.

Once inside the building, I went directly over to Gloria and gently took her hand. "Let's go to lunch, honey," I said. Outside, I explained my feelings. This could never happen to us. We weren't people who needed that kind of help. And while we might have little in resources at the time, there were always answers, other possibilities.

We spent the rest of the afternoon talking. Sometimes we were overwhelmed to tears by the moment and by the fact that we'd lost our way. We drove for hours around the Hill County west of Austin, holding hands, captured in the silence of our thoughts. We had truly grown to love each other and wanted to spend the rest of our lives together. This was much more than running a struggling organization or being unemployed. Our bond was personal. It was time to make permanent changes our life as a couple. The dreaming and excitement of running NHI together was no longer the point.

It was time to set a course and make a commitment that had real consequences. Of course my new work was important, but I couldn't imagine it without Gloria next to me. She didn't want me to go it alone either. We decided that day to roll the dice, first by becoming life partners and second by making NHI our life's work. No other choices were needed. As long as we remained together, NHI also would work.

Our first challenge meant Gloria and I learning each other's management styles and how to work through conflicts. For the most part, we managed. However, our relationship was tested to the breaking point. These feelings, however never lasted long. A special chemistry, a deep affection for one another, drove us back together. Many times at night, after sixteen-hour days at the office, we'd walk over to the Star Restaurant on the I-35 service road across form Concordia Lutheran College, to drink coffee, grab a bite to eat, and continue talking about our work together. This was standard practice. We were determined to make our relationship and ideas work. We were past the point of no return. The challenges we were facing were eventually to make us inseparable.

Outside of my parents, no one ever influenced me more than Gloria. Her approach was different. Dad and Mom were Socratic. They taught me to ask myself the tough questions. They never had answers. I had to listen attentively and think through different possibilities.

In contrast, Gloria was much more confrontational. She had opinions and views on everything. Sometimes I had to raise my voice over her statements to stay in the discussion, much less prevail. Her style would eventually force me to act beyond the confinements of words. Her presence in my life and work gave me a confidence I never had before. It was worth the sacrifice. Before, others sometimes found my ideas difficult to understand. Through the years, something always seemed to go wrong between thought and action. Gloria gave me the confidence to do, not just talk. Her "you can do it, honey" attitude eventually began to work.

Today, after all those years of giving life to a struggling concept, Gloria and I still argue over differences. Beyond the trivialities of life, however, she remains my barrio girl, the one I always wished for as a teenager.

At twenty-seven years of age in 1979, she was already strong in her beliefs. The Rio Grande Valley to Gloria was "the place where the sun rose and set." This region of the state was perfect, the place where you could see people in transition, from those barely slipping across the border from Mexico into the United States to well-off attorneys and doctors.

There was a particular innocence and naiveté in her that was carefully balanced with a strong belief in her roots. Gloria was never one to turn back on poor people. Mom used to say that Gloria was not scared by what she saw in life. This back human trait attracted me to her. Despite the twelve- year difference in our ages, she was a throwback to something I always admired and never had as a young man growing up in Houston barrios.

It was strange how our paths crossed one day. The occasion was a brief and quick drink with friends after office hours at a local bar where staff from our state agency gathered. Neither one of us knew about each other's troubled marriages at the time. We both married outside our culture and were in the last steps of divorce. When we came face to face for the first time, we acted as though we had shared a past life together. Something immediately stirred inside. A connection was instantly made. Words weren't needed.

At first, we became inseparable friends, many times taking long walks and sharing common experiences we had as children growing up in the barrios of McAllen or Houston. An attraction was present from the beginning that has kept us constantly together. A couple of years later, I couldn't imagine life without her. She expressed the same sentiments about me. Later in our relationship, when bitterly engaged in differences over the direction of the institute, the need to share life together as a couple always overcame our individual egos.

We've never fully understood how events brought us together. Everything about our backgrounds pointed us in opposite directions. She was from the Valley. I was from Houston. She came from a family of five girls who annually migrated to Pecos, Texas, to harvest melons. I was brought up in a family of all boys and spent summers helping my parents at the parks in Houston barrios.

Gloria's vocation was as a social worker involved in alcoholism prevention. I studied education in college. She was born in 1952, while I was twelve years older. Gloria never had children. I brought four into our relationship. Even friends and family discouraged us from marriage. It wouldn't work they said.

Both of us, however, were driven to be involved in the lives of those with whom we shared a history and culture. We also wanted to share life and grow old together. Gloria was my inspiration, my reason to work hard. She gave me the courage and a spiritual comfort. She was the person in whom I could entrust my most delicate and private feelings, the one in whose arms I could openly dream and sometimes despair and at times cry.

In planning the 1983 LDZ, our more immediate task became figuring out how to get enough Latino students from throughout the state interested in an eight-day program in Austin. We needed at least 150 youth to attend. Would they pay tuition? Could they afford it? How were we going to convince high school teachers and counselors that the Lorenzo de Zavala Youth Legislative Session was an important educational experience for their students? More importantly, how were we going to finance the program?

We had to figure out a way to pay for the costs of food, housing, local transportation, facility rental, and handbooks. We put in a funding proposal to Curtis Meadows of the Meadows Foundation in Dallas who two years earlier gave NHI $10,000 to expand its management series for young Latino professionals to other parts of Texas. Ralph Quintanilla, executive director of the Texas Department of Community Affairs (TDCA), also offered to help. Additionally, we submitted a proposal to Austin United Way, hoping that a few dollars could be thrown our way.

To our surprise, however, Ralph called NHI one day to announce that TDCA was taking the offer back. A local Latino legislator didn't want us funded. A similar call came from the United Way. The same legislator had gotten wind of our submission and blocked us. If there was no money, there was no support. As it was later told to us, "Ernesto Nieto doesn't vote on the legislative floor. This one does." No reasons were given other than it was better to forget the entire matter. Although Senator Hector Uríbe of Brownsville tried to help, nothing changed.

To compound our problems, NHI was hit with an IRS audit. We never found out what caused the audit except that we received a letter announcing that our books needed to be examined. With the first statewide Texas LDZ only months away, NHI's checking account showed a balanced of $3,000. Late one evening at the office, I broke the news to Gloria. No help was in sight. Also there were no signs to indicate the Meadows Foundation had considered our request.

Gloria and I sat on the baseball bleachers at Concordia Lutheran College trying to figure out our next step. Our toughest estimates showed that we were going to be $15,000 in the red after expenses. It must have been almost three in the morning before we called quits and went home. Nothing else could be done.

Late the next morning, I went by to pick up the morning mail at the old downtown post office. "More bills," I thought to myself as I took a small bundle of letters from NHI's post office box.

Hidden among the other envelopes was a surprise. There was a letter from the Meadows Foundation that contained a grant announcement. The cover page had no more than three or four sentences. It congratulated us on receiving the award and expressed best wished on our first statewide LDZ. Neatly folded inside was a $30,000 check!

The changeover from despair to exhilaration was instant. My car couldn't move fast enough down the freeway to share the good news with Gloria. The entire world was suddenly lifted from my shoulders. Once home, both of us repeatedly read the letter. In between, we'd stop to hug, high-five each other, and dance around the dining room floor like two crazy people.

For the next several weeks, our energies remained in high gear. Instead of driving home at night, we'd take pillows and blankets to sleep on the office carpet after late-night sessions of writing student handbooks and organizing training curriculum.

During the workday, we called every conceivable high school in Austin, Dallas, Houston, West Texas, El Paso, Corpus Christi, South Texas and the Valley. We also called LULAC and the American G.I. Forum Chapters, Hispanic Chambers of Commerce, community action agencies, anyone else who could possibly aid us in getting students to sign up.

We spent hours on the telephone trying to gain the confidence of the parents. How long was the program? Where would the children stay? Who was responsible for supervising them? And how well prepared were we to respond to an unforeseen medical emergency? These questions repeatedly had to be answered.

In between calls, we also mobilized volunteers to help. Gloria's sisters, Nila and Lisa, became our registrars. We talked to the president and a couple of student members from The University of Texas Mexican American Business Student Association to see if they would chip in as senior counselors. A few days later, they called NHI with a list of members who wanted to help. Dr. Ricardo Santos from San Antonio, a well-known historian, was contracted to give a special talk on the history of Mexican Americans in Texas. Alumni from NHI's Austin Young Leaders Conference also dropped by to help stuff envelopes, run errands, and answer phone calls. Everyone got involved as the days drew near for our very first LDZ. If anyone else happened to drop by, it wouldn't take but a couple of minutes before they were put to work.

On the day before the program, Gloria and I didn't sleep much. We couldn't. Instead, both of us tossed around all night, suddenly waking up because of something we forgot or overlooked. At times, we'd lay staring at the ceiling while the clock kept ticking away. Every so often, in a completely dark room, one of us would ask a question out loud, knowing that the other was also awake.

"Was there a last minute detail we might have overlooked?"

"How are you feeling right now?"

"You think everything's going to be okay?"

The anxiety of not being able to predict the turnout increased our tensions.

"What if no one shows?"

"What if the entire program in a failure?"

Anything over 100 students would have been considered a huge success.

By five in the morning of the first day, we no longer could stay in bed. It was better to shower and leave for the office. It didn't matter that it was still dark outside.

Student volunteers started drifting in by seven. Some sat on the front steps of the office quietly talking, waiting for assignments. By nine in the morning, a couple of parents and students rolled into an empty parking lot. Concluding that maybe we were about to experience a bust, I hustled over to the airport to get away. It was nearing 10:00 A.M. by now. To my excitement, fifteen to twenty students were waiting to be taken to campus. I drove back in time to see a couple of school buses filled with excited students wheel in the parking area. By three in the afternoon, NHI had 184 students registered as the first official class of the 1983 Texas Lorenzo de Zavala Youth Legislative Session.

The week became a blur. On Tuesday evening, the third day of the program, Michael Dennis Marín from Canutillo, Texas, near El Paso, became governor, edging Abel Salas from Austin. The air was filled with excitement when the winner was announced over the loudspeakers. Students on the winning side cheered. Those on the losing side looked stunned. In the middle of the commotion, a delegate jumped on stage and started playing "Happy Days Are Here Again" on the piano as the winners wildly danced and hugged each other.

The next day, everyone went to the Texas State capitol to be sworn in to office and listen to the keynote address of a former Houston civil rights leader and national president of LULAC, Alfred J. Hernandez. Alfred was a well know Houston lawyer. He was also a close, personal friend to my parents. He had been the voice of the Houston civil rights movement. He was there when the first Raza Unida Conference was held at John F. Kennedy High School in 1967. He had also risen to national prominence and on several occasions visited the White House to consult with Presidents Kennedy, Johnson, and Nixon.

To me, Alfred J. Hernandez was the perfect pick to speak at our inaugural program as LDZ delegates made their first commitments to leadership in the Latino community. What better examples than to have these young persons interact with a man of such national stature?

Seeing the delegates gathered attentively in the House Chamber, Alfred found it difficult to maintain his composure. His voice quivered for an instant, causing him to remain silent for several seconds before delivering his remarks. The LDZ was a dream come true for him. He always wanted someone in the community to train youth to become leaders in the Latino community. He never thought that the work would come from the son of Santos and Esther Nieto. It was important for me to have this aging warrior at the podium, to have him see the work, to have him understand that the vision and dream were not over. It was just beginning.

On Saturday, the students attended a private college fair. Later that evening, they received handmade awards at a banquet. When dinner was over, students climbed on buses for the Governor's Ball at a private, downtown club overlooking the state capitol. Gloria and I stayed back to remove linens and put away dirty dishes and trash. There we were, Gloria in her stunning evening gown and me in a dark business suit assisting her. Earlier in the evening we were the masters of ceremonies and now we were the janitors.

The impact of the program had been worth every bit the effort, the contributors of the many volunteers who helped, and the hours spent in planning an event that would eventually become a special moment in the lives of thousands yet to come. Exhausted but happy at the success of the first LDZ, Gloria and I sat down momentarily to savor the moment. The gymnasium suddenly looked huge and empty without the youth, and their laughter and applause, and the sounds of excitement. The look in our eyes told the story, described our inner thoughts. We had run the race and crossed the finish line. Along the way, we had experienced a few bumps and setbacks. In the end, however, the dream that drove us had prevailed.

On Sunday, the final morning of the training, on the campus grounds of Concordia Lutheran College and the site of the first LDZ, former Austin Young Leaders Conference student Ray Alba stepped forward and played "Taps." We made a circle around the flagpole to witness the official lowering of the LDZ governor's flag and its presentation as a special memento to the first governor. When J.R. Gonzales, also from Austin and chief of protocol for the program, stepped forward to officially announce the end, no one moved. They stood silently together, tears streaming from their eyes, exhausted from the week, realizing that something special had just happened in their lives. All of us were affected. All of us shed tears.

It was 1983, almost 150 years after the Alamo in San Antonio; 135 years after Texas had become a state. Although no one knew it at the time, this was the first youth leadership session for Latino students that had ever been conducted in the House and Senate chambers of the state capitol. Our best and brightest had come from over 100 Texas high schools.

Another custom had changed also. The LDZ wasn't to reform or rehabilitate youth; its intent was to bring in successful role models. These kids were winners, youth with positive outlooks on life. They were helping to mark an important milestone and sending a revitalizing message to the rest of the Latino community and their youth peers: if you wish to be part of a new tradition and custom for Latino youth, you also have to commit to excellence in your personal development.

When everyone finally went home, Gloria and I quietly walked around the Concordia campus, each of us privately engaged in the memories of young people laughing, scurrying around the campus making speeches, hanging around in groups and enjoying a newfound freedom. It was over now. Only the silence remained.

Hundreds of scenes repeatedly played in our minds. Laughing faces and personalities were permanently etched in our minds. Gloria and I had won an important personal battle. LDZ had taken place without being dependent on the uncaring attitudes of a few politicians or government officials. Instead, a Latino community had responded.

Dad was right: *"Si tienes fé en la comunidad, si tienes buenas intenciones, y si tienes un actitud correcta, la comunidad responde.* (If you have faith in your community, if your intentions are good, and if you have the right attitude, people always respond.)"

The Lorenzo de Zavala Youth Legislative Session gave many young Latinos first-time insight into a different reality of decision-making in which they determined outcomes and made rules. The experience helped develop a fundamental grasp of power, negotiation, and influence. They learned to respond to challenges that come from being at the top. It was also an opportunity for personal growth, self-discovery and self-validation.

Alongside the lessons gained by the students, Gloria and I also went through our own personal growth. We experienced what it meant to give ourselves permission to act, to control outcomes, and to take risks. Given our backgrounds in government employment, this was new to us.

The challenge that was sure to follow was in determining where to take the National Hispanic Institute next. We could either remain local or be satisfied with operating only in Texas. There was also the prospect of becoming national or even international in scope. Although thoughts of becoming a large organization seem a little far-fetched at the time, we also understood that the decision was mainly ours.

I could still hear my father say, *"Tienes que soñar, mijo, para inspirarte a ti mismo. Sin inspiración, no es possible alcanzar suenos grandes,* (You have to dream, son, so that you can inspire yourself. Without inspiration, there's little chance of achieving big dreams.)"

Where we took NHI was not a matter of chance. If it succeeded, it would be because of our efforts. For the moment, I understood what immigrants from Mexico must feel when confronted with an alien environment and not knowing which way to turn. At first, the thoughts are frightening and oftentimes run away and hide. Then your own instincts to survive take over. Eighteen-hour days are nothing. You take whatever work comes your way. You don't shirk the responsibilities of opening the front doors to your business at seven in the morning and keeping the lights on until nine at night.

Your priority is to create satisfied customers who go back and pass the word around to their friends. Mom was also right. You become blind to *"la batalla"* (the battle) when you start seeing the fruits of your labor take shape.

Several days after the students left, Gloria and I spent hours and days reading the letters students sent to NHI. We wanted a deeper insight into their thoughts and understanding of the LDZ experience. More importantly, there had to be special reasons for their tears when the program came to an end. Their reasons were strangely similar to those of Alfred Hernandez the first time he stood in the House Chamber and saw the seats filled with brown faces. These tears were not only from students leaving or having to say good-bye to newfound friends. There was something else involved.

A letter from a young woman from West Texas answered our questions. Before the LDZ experience, she was part of a predominantly Anglo girls' dance team. She lived in a mostly Anglo neighborhood. Her friends were all Anglo and her social life revolved mainly around doing what her Anglo friends did. This was the first time in her life she had been around all Latino peers. At first what surprised her was how smart and articulate they were.

She also wrote that she had discovered the hostility she had previously harbored towards her own community and culture. The guilt of seeing herself as being prejudiced, especially towards her own community, overwhelmed her. She also had misunderstood Latino culture and, as a result, had allowed a distance to develop with her grandparents, cousins, even her own parents. She was deeply bothered by this attitude and wanted us to know that LDZ had provided her with the encouragement she needed to finally return to her culture, her community and her family. Other letters revealed similar discoveries. We finally understood the tears.

The session had not only been a student legislative program on public policy. It might have appeared that way to the outside world. Instead, it was a cultural and emotional exploration that led Latino youth to peer inside themselves. At the LDZ, they were able to talk freely about their private world in terms that would never be shared with friends, parents, or at school. Somehow the LDZ offered a protective veil that compelled the students to speak without concern for criticism. They discovered that they weren't alone in harboring particular views about other Latino youth or the problems faced by the Latino community. Other peers sitting next to them in the session thought the same. Most were at the top of their class in school. All of them also enjoyed a special status of importance in school life as athletes, cheerleaders, and heads of student organizations. The question they had to answer for themselves was the price they were willing to pay in the end. Was the quest to accomplish life dreams worth the price of losing their culture, language, and identity?

It didn't take them long to understand when they heard or saw the U.S. media portray their limited views of Latinos. The low-income Latino community faced special problems and challenges. Some of the issues were being perpetuated from within the Latino community. External forces imposed others. But the low-income Latino community was only part of a much larger Latino world and reality. There was much more to being Latino than simply poor people living in poor neighborhoods. There were opportunities to create, share, and advance. The possibilities were endless and exciting.

A new Latino world was emerging. Seeing Latinos from a completely different and healthier perspective was uplifting to these youth. But seeing the Latino community from the positive side also causes them to reflect and focus on what had driven them to turn away. It was not about becoming Anglo that was causing them to grieve. It was in not wanting to be Latino!

Chapter Ten: The Will to Endure

1. Describe a time when you were well along a pathway that seemed to be leading to

a future that you valued. But, in this process, you became aware of unexpected, conflicting views of the world, events, and conditions that challenged your sense of the validity of your assumptions, expectations, beliefs, and values.
        a. What did you think?
        b. How did you feel?
        c. What did you do?

2. Describe how you made sense out of your unfolding, unexpected, challenging life experiences.
        a. Which of your beliefs, values, or assumptions were threatened by these unexpected challenges?
        b. How did you respond to these challenges? Did you react instinctively (attack or withdraw) or did you mindfully reflect on your challenges and your reactions?
        c. What aspects of your worldview did you modify in order to take these unexpected challenges into consideration?
        d. What aspects of your worldview did you keep intact and unchanging despite these unexpected challenges?

3. Briefly describe a relationship you developed with a person you admire and trust, a person with whom you feel comfortable saying whatever you have on your mind without censoring or editing your hopes, fears, assumptions, aspirations, and values.
        a. Is this person reliable enough for you to trust him or her to say what she or he believes even if you get angry when you disagree?
        b. How did you and the other person develop this trusting relationship?

4. Write a brief description of the times and places where you felt safe and made sufficient time to look inward, inquire, explore, discover, reflect, analyze, and reevaluate your view of the world, life goals, strategies, and plans.

5. Briefly describe whatever ideological conflicts emerged – within yourself or between you and others – as a result of engaging your emerging challenges?
        a. What were these ideological conflicts?
        b. What did you think about when confronted by these conflicts?
        c. What did you feel?
        d. What previously unrecognized issues became evident as a result of the conflicts?
        e. How did you make use of the issues that emerged during the conflict?

Chapter 11
The House on the Hill

When we were children, Mom and Dad would take my two brothers and me riding around Houston's upscale Lindale and River Oaks communities at night to see brightly decorated homes during Christmas. Even back then, in the late 1940s, the expense and time families invested in decorating their homes resulted in homes elegantly adorned in colored lights and fixtures that conveyed stateliness and elegance. Others had Santa waving from a sled pulled by reindeer. There were also the traditional Christian nativity scenes of the Holy Family sitting alongside the sheep, cows, and donkeys.

My brothers and I amused ourselves by playing an imaginary game of owning the larger and more elegantly decorated homes. The family pilgrimage always started in Lindale, which was not too far from where we lived. The more expensive and spacious homes were farther west in River Oaks. Albert, Roy, and I took turns being first to select the homes we felt were the best and most creatively decorated.

Even as young boys, we knew deep inside that the neighborhoods where we lived offered little to brag about. Life was strikingly different for those of us who lived in barrios like Magnolia, the Fifth Ward, or Northside. Our first home on McKee Street was small, with only two bedrooms for five people. The house on Cochran was only a shell without sheet rock to cover the inside walls. The common space was a large open area that also served as the bedroom, living room, and kitchen all at once. Mom handwashed our clothes outside in large *"cubetas"* (tin buckets). We had outdoor toilets and cold well water. It wasn't until Dad bought a small frame house in Magnolia in 1949 that we finally enjoyed indoor plumbing and warm running water. Riding around the more affluent neighborhoods in Houston, especially during the holiday season, was our private reprieve, a temporary escape from the realities of our everyday lives. Lindale and River Oaks were the reminders of what others had and we didn't.

Seeing the house in Maxwell many years later in 1985 rekindled those memories, The Schawe Mansion was built at the turn of the century in 1903, the same year Dad was born in Laredo. It was out in the countryside, away from the city, on a hilltop, beyond the noisy sounds of people with its white columns and two porches. There was a connection to a former era of slower and comfortable lifestyles when relationships were personal and permanent.

Maxwell eventually became my private hideaway from everyone, a retreat where I could kick back, think, and stare off into space for hours. The town was not easy to find. Getting there required going through a maze of winding farm roads that eventually end up at an unnoticeable gathering of homes with few commercial establishments.

Art Millicam, a friend who worked with me in state government years earlier, was the real estate agent who found the place. He called one day about a house for sale with twenty-seven acres.

"Hey Ernie," he said in his broken Dutch- accented English. "I have this house that's really interesting. It's a pretty good deal but I have to warn you; it needs work, and it's way out in the boonies."

By now, we were in the third year at the Concordia Lutheran College campus in Austin and were already concerned about finding offices elsewhere. The administration had called, requesting the building back to accommodate a growing student enrollment. Art's find couldn't have come at a better time.

Gloria and I left one Saturday afternoon excited to see a place that also came with land. It took us an hour to locate Maxwell and another ten minutes or so driving trying to find the place. There was no "For Sale" sign to guide us. The house was several hundred feet from the road and could barely be seen because of the trees that surrounded it. An industrial hurricane fence that ran across the property line for a hundred yards separated the property form the Nagle Company, a manufacturer of wooden coat hangers. Mostly Mexican American families who lived in the area worked there.

The Schawe Mansion was an authentic Texas Victorian home that possessed the look of the early twentieth century. The structure consisted of two-and-a-half stories, a steeple roof, two porches, eleven rooms, and a gorgeously constructed staircase leading to the second floor. The rooms were large with fourteen-foot ceilings and wood doorframes that were made out of Heart of Texas pine. Nothing was structurally wrong with the eighty-two-year-old house.

At one time it must have been a spectacular home, certainly the talk for miles around. Legend had it that a German immigrant who had become wealthy cotton grower built the home at the turn of the century. He not only farmed his 5,000-acre property with an abundant supply of cheap Mexican labor, but also owned the local granary and a Maxwell bank. During the 1929 Great Depression, he lost his fortune, except for the fifty-acre homestead. The house stood empty for twenty years as title jumped from bank to bank. A party house. C.W. "Shorty" Grumbles became the owner afterwards. By then, twenty-three additional acres had been sold off to other area investors interested in cheap land.

The moment Gloria saw the place she instinctively said, "Buy it if the price is right."

There really wasn't much else to see in Maxwell. The old downtown area, a few hundred yards down the road, was little more than a few deteriorating building, a beer joint, and a rental place for farm equipment. Maxwell was so tiny that it appeared empty. The only attractions were an old Lutheran Church that was probably built in the 1920s and a fenced cemetery with a towering tribute where Old Man Schawe was finally laid to rest. Outside of that, Maxwell was little more than a barely noticeable agricultural community where cotton was still king.

When Shorty Grumbles said he wanted $363,000 for the place, I thought to myself, "Not worth it." The amount of repair work needed was going to drive up the costs even more. Still, we walked around and peered underneath to see if there were any rotting beams. We banged walls with our hands to detect vibrations. We even crawled around the attic to make sure the house was solid. On the way back home, Gloria insisted that we not wait long to do something, at least offer a price for the place.

"Who knows honey," she said. "You never know what people will take." A week later, Shorty and I met again. He and his wife Norvel had lived there until each of their children graduated from high school. Although Shorty had the look of a rancher, he didn't run any livestock on the place except for the few cows he needed to get his agricultural exemption. In the rear of the property, by a clump of trees, he had coops for his chickens an old rusty building used to hang homemade sausage. In the front fields, Shorty had built a loading pen made of cast iron pipes to load cows for market. He and Norvel loved country living. The old house and land, however, were too much for them to take care of now that their kids were grown. Besides, looking after her aging mother made moving to San Marcos a necessity for Norvel.

"I'll give you $200,000 for the whole place," I told him to test out his interest and maybe find out what he was thinking. This was nothing more than a starting point for negotiation.

"Can't do it," he responded." Got too much invested in the place. But I'll come down to $300,000. That's about as far down as I can possibly go."

Shorty was a nice man who understood hard work. Friendly looking, burned by the sun, easy to get along with, he had homespun character written all over his face. He wasn't a Philadelphia lawyer. But he also didn't act like a hard-core investor on the take for fast money. He was an honest looking gentleman, a family man doing nothing more than attempting to arrive at the best possible deal.

"Let's half your offer," I said, smiling back. "How about $220,000?"

Shorty stared down a few seconds, kicked a couple of small rocks with his right foot, and then looked up with an inquisitive, but humored, look on his face.

"Say, where did you learn your math?" he asked. "Halfway between $300,000 and $200,000 is $250,000."

"It's half to me," I remarked, half laughingly." At least that's the math I learned back where I grew up in Houston."

We weren't arguing math. We both knew that. We were talking price. "Gimme $240,000 and the place is yours," he shot back. "That's my final offer."

Without uttering another sound, I stuck my hand out and we shook on it. Art Millicam, the real estate agent, stood there for an instant, looking at both of us. He had arranged the meeting between Shorty and me, but never figured that an agreement would be so quick. The next step was working on the papers to finalize the deal. Shorty was willing to owner-finance the purchase, amortize the note over thirty years with a ten-year wrap, and even went a point and a half less than the prevailing interest rate. There was only one final catch. He wanted a $40,000 down payment.

"No problem," I responded and we again shook hands.

On the drive back to Austin late that afternoon, I started questioning myself, "Where am I going to get $40,000 for the down payment? And besides, how are we going to make the $2,000 a month note?"

As soon as Monday morning rolled around, I was up early, ready to see the president of United Bank in East Austin, originally chartered as a minority-owned bank. Gilbert Martinez, one of a few Mexican Americans in Austin in the banking industry, had been particularly helpful in supporting my efforts to keep NHI afloat in 1979 and 1980. He made several small, unsecured loans to help us pay bills at times and extended our credit lines even when NHI wasn't doing well. Still, he had faith in what we were trying to do and could count on our word to pay back whatever we borrowed. However, Gilbert was no longer with the bank, but earlier had introduced me to the president. My hope was that he would at least remember my face.

When I got there the secretary told me that the gentleman was no longer with the bank and had recently taken a new job with a different company.

"Mr. Graeber, out in the lobby, is our new president," she said, pointing to him.

Instantly I realized that this particular "Mr. Graeber" wasn't a stranger. He was a childhood friend from Houston. We had attended the same elementary, junior high, and high school together, and played basketball and football on the same teams. We recognized each other immediately. After hugging for a few moments and laughing out loud on how amazingly small the world is, we walked to his office to catch up on old times. A couple of weeks later, I met Shorty and Norvel at the mortgage company ready to close the deal with a $40,000 check in hand.

For us, buying the Maxwell house was the biggest transaction of our lives. Our home in Austin cost only a fraction of what we had just completed. NHI was now the proud owner of an eleven-room, turn-of-the-century, Texas Victorian home that sat on nearly thirty acres out in the country.

The Grumbles had done as much as they could to make the place livable, but the amount of work required made keeping the place up pretty difficult for two people. Despite these challenges, the Schawe Mansion remained the center of attraction for Maxwell, including visitors who happened to find the little town by accident. The moss-adorned Texas wild oaks that surrounded the place had worked their magic for years. Old timers in the area would say that former governors and legislators used to ride out from Austin on horseback and buggies to spend an afternoon drinking cool lemonade on the front porch and discussing business with Old Man Schawe.

Years later, the National Hispanic Institute was in possession of a piece of history. While the house had taken some severe blows through the years, it must have been a magnificent sight back then.

Very few Latinos ever owned this kind of home. As youngsters, my two brothers and I used to go with Mom to see my Tía Fita (Aunt Fita), and her husband, Tío Nacho (Uncle Nacho) Rodríguez, and our cousins. The Rodríguez family was well off. They owned a large grocery store and a small furniture company. Their home had big stairs leading up to the front porch, chandeliers in the main rooms, and a beautiful dining table elegantly covered by a hand-woven tablecloth. Mom always felt uneasy about having her three little ruffians inside Tía's house. After exchanging hellos, she'd ask us to go outside and quietly wait around the front porch until we were ready to leave.

"Déjalos, Esther, (Leave them alone,)" Tía would remark, "Están bien. (They're okay.)"

But Mom always won out, insisting that we not only go outside, but remain quiet and not disturb anyone.

The Maxwell house reminded me of those days. It was a place where Latinos like us were never invited. When it came to work, we entered by the back door. When my father finally saw the place for the first time, even in its worst condition, he said, "Necesita pierdas este lugar. (It needs a lot of work. But I want you to promise me one thing, Never lose this place.)"

I assured him it would never happen. This was going to be the permanent home where Gloria and I were going to build an institute for Latinos.

Today, the National Hispanic Institute in Maxwell is a little larger than the original thirty acres. The house is almost completely restored and the land that had formerly been sold off has been reacquired. It now has a large rock cabin for retreats and special projects.

The house also has its own unique NHI character and history. Several of the 1983 Texas LDZ class, including Joe Flóres and David García from John F. Kennedy High School in San Antonio and John Ybarbo from Austin, came over for a weekend of hard work in 1985 to help clear underbrush and mow the fields. Nearly twenty of us were scattered in almost every room inside the institute the first night, asleep after an exhausting first day of uprooting small cedar shrubs and chopping down dead trees.

This was also the famous weekend when what seemed hundreds of angry wasps, aroused from inside a dead log, stung me on the face and head. All I could feel at that instant was a hot iron exploding across my face and forehead. By the time I reached the house to throw cold water on my burning face, my swelling eyes were starting to shut. Gloria laughs to this day claiming that I looked like a Mexican Frankenstein.

Scores of other accounts have become part of NHI lore, including walks through the woods at night for frightened NHIers visiting Maxwell for the first time. There are tales of encounters with ghosts and ghost stories told by staff and visitors. No other tale, however, better describes life at NHI in Maxwell than what happened to Carlos Hernandez when he worked there.

Imagining this incident also requires understanding the daily rigors of work at the National Hispanic Institute in Maxwell. It is still common to drive by NHI and see lights burning at midnight or even three in the morning. The demands of working with several thousand Latino youth each year turns a normal work day into a ten-to eighteen-hour experience that many times includes working weekends and holidays. Staff regularly pull up with trailers filled with equipment and documents.

During one of these occasions, Carlos showed up at the front gates around 2:00 A.M. before he left by plane to another field assignment with me. Tired and exhausted from the heavy workweek, he searched for the gate keys in the dark only to realize that he had either lost or left them inside the house. Not wanting to drive back to Maxwell from Austin the next morning to drop off the equipment and records, he decided to crawl under a small drainage ditch between the bottom of the wrought-iron fence that guarded the entrance and the ground. For the next several minutes, Carlos slowly worked his six-foot, 250-pound frame, face down through the opening, literally clawing his way from one side to other. Afterwards, mud covered his entire face and clothes.

He then took the equipment and records he had placed next to the fence and carefully lifted them over the top of the locked gates to walk 300 yards up the driveway to the house.

Angry and dirty from having spent several minutes crawling through the mud, he backed his car out and went home to Austin. When the fence ended a few hundred feet later, Carlos suddenly remembered that there was a second-and open-entrance that led directly to the front steps of the institute. His only mistake was revealing his experience early the next morning to Nicole, my daughter.

The next day, on the way to the airport, she couldn't keep the secret any longer. Listening for a few moments, I casually turned to Carlos and asked why he failed to use the second opening, the one with no gate.

"I was afraid you'd ask that," he said, with a poker face look, staring forward as he drove, no visible indications of what he might have been thinking at that split second.

We weren't able to contain our laughter any longer. I imagined what Carlos must have looked like in the dead of night, crawling through an opening only big enough for a small child. This was too much for any of us to remain straight-faced and serious. It was twice as difficult for Carlos.

A few years later, Carlos left NHI and moved to Los Angeles. We first met in 1988 when he was a high school participant at the New Mexico LDZ in Albuquerque when he ran for lieutenant governor. Right before graduating from Georgetown University, he started sending us letters asking if he could work for the institute. He wanted to be part of our vision. Many young people have come through NHI over the last twenty years, including my four children. No one helped us more than Carlitos. He was my fourth son, a young person with a love for technology, a quick mind, and a caring heart carefully tucked away deep inside a tough exterior.

One late night, while working at the office, he walked into my office downstairs, plopped in a chair in front of my desk, and asked the kind of question that doesn't need answers.

"Do you know," he asked, "what kind of people survive here at NHI, Ernie?"

"Not really," I responded slowly, looking up from my work. Carlos looked off for a moment, "Only mean sons-of-bitches," he said, thoughtfully leaning back on his chair, his eyes directly fixed on mine. "Only mean sons-of-bitches."

When Carlos waved his final good-bye and drove off in his red Honda Civic, leaving behind a dusty cloud along the gravel road to NHI, I felt secure in knowing he'd survive. He came in a timid young man from Houston, having lost his father to a heart attack during his freshman year of college, not really knowing where to fit in life. But he would do well because of an important character trait in his makeup. In his stay at NHI, he'd become a mean son-of-a-bitch, a tough, young kid who well understood and accepted the price of success.

The NHI message is clear: Either you toughen up or you don't survive. Gloria and I learned these lessons when the Maxwell property was purchased. It was common to work sixteen-or seventeen-hour days, then spend evenings and weekends chopping weeds, mowing sheet rock, scraping old varnish off wood, or painting walls until sunrise.

Former employees learned these lessons the hard way. No one was going to help us, not out of charity. We first had to be examples to ourselves. Working long hours was the routine, not the exception. Like Carlos later learned, becoming tough was only one of the outcomes. Being in Maxwell, however, also went deeper. Becoming property owners meant permanency for the National Hispanic Institute. It took our vision to the next step. A different kind of attitude took hold when the organization became "landed." You don't mind the hard work, the long hours. Cultivating the investment ranks high on the priority list.

Right after purchasing the property, Merriman Morton, president of Texas Commerce Bank in Austin, paid a visit to Maxwell. He was a classmate at Southwestern University in Georgetown, Texas, and a teammate on the university basketball team. Knowing a little about our work, he brought some of his management officers with him to look at our place and get to know more about our direction.

After looking around the office for a few minutes and stepping out on the front porch, he turned and said, "This place is going to make it hard on you, Ernie. It's not worth the investment. The surroundings aren't very attractive. The community's too poor."

I stared at my college friend for a moment, carefully thought about the words he used, and nodded as though agreeing. My mind instantly raced back to my neighborhoods back in Houston in the early 1950's. None of the places where my family lived were ever that attractive to others, much less worth the investment. But they were to me. Grandma Alfaro had a downstairs apartment a block down the street from our home. Tía Felíz (Aunt Feliz) lived four blocks away in the same barrio. Tío Mike (Uncle Mke) was farther down, across the tracks, by Hennessey Park. The housed were small and inexpensive, but who lived inside was what really mattered.

I never shared my thoughts with Merriman. There was no reason. Although we were friends, we came from different worlds. NHI was my dream, not his. There was no reason to be angry or resentful, only more driven. One of these days there will be a leadership center on the very spot where Merriman said "it wasn't worth the investment." Years may be required. Only time and determination will shape the outcome. Latino youth and their families will be the principle owners of the vision, not someone else.

As the years continue marching forward, I look at NHI's house on the hill as hundreds of thoughts and memories race endlessly through my mind. The place looks much better than it first did in 1985 when Gloria looked at me and said, "buy it." Art Millicam continues in the real estate business in San Marcos and Shorty and Norvel are retired. They live in nearby Staples where they bought a new place on the San Marcos River.

Every once in a while, I catch mental glimpses of working in a house with no heating and where the temperature sometimes dipped as far down as twenty-three degrees. Other times, after a long day of office work, I spend hours moving fields at night to the lights of a rented diesel tractor. We never missed a payment, even if it meant delaying our personal salaries. Never losing the place was a personal promise to my father. It was linked to an era few members of my family ever got to experience.

Maxwell was a throwback to a past when Mexican Americans worked in the fields for pennies, picking cotton as far as their eyes could see. They lived in old, broken-down shanties on dusty backroads away from the more traveled highways. Children went to school barefoot, wearing the hand-me-downs wealthier families no longer needed. The big white house, securely nestled among the trees was where the "ámo" (the owner) once lived.

This time around there was no owner living there. Young, aggressive Latinos right out of the best colleges in the country had taken over. Their job was to dream, think, create, and attempt to carve out a new reality for Latinos. This task at times would be daunting and overwhelming. And when the thought crept into their thinking that maybe the vision was beyond their capacities to reach, they would realize how little we have actually progressed in the past one hundred years.

Despite claims by Latino leaders regarding the gains over the last several decades, all they would need to do is look around at broken-down trailer parks, young children living in small, weather-beaten houses. Maxwell is not unlike the inner cities of Houston, Los Angeles, Chicago, or New York City. In a peculiar and strangely familiar manner, the environments are alike. It is a story of struggling people coping with few resources and little hope of ever reaching larger dreams.

Acquiring the Maxwell house meant breaking from the past, but not at the expense of ever denying our culture, language or heritage. It was a statement of what happens through sustained and dedicated effort. Sheer tenacity, long hours of quiet labor, and remaining true to the vision would be the symbols of the work that remained ahead. The fact that the house on the hill had become a private hideaway from everyone else, a retreat to sit and stare off into space for hours thinking about the next step, was the reward for remaining true to the dream.

And yes, Carlitos, you do become a "mean son-of-a-bitch," but also one with a purpose.

Chapter Eleven: The House on the Hill

1. Briefly describe a situation where you made a large emotional and/or financial investment. The investment was more than you could afford at the time and required substantially more time and effort than you expected to maintain and leverage.
    a. What were you thinking before and after you made the investment?
    b. What were you feeling (before and after)?
    c. How did you cope with the situation?
2. What was the compelling purpose that pulled you in the direction of making the investment and sacrificing to protect that investment?

3. What did you have to sacrifice in order to do what was necessary to keep your investment safe? How did you justify your sacrifices and make them bearable?
4. Why was it that Ernesto concentrated so much in talking about Carlos Hernandez and his readiness for the world as an emerging young adult?

Chapter Twelve
Let the Ship Sink

"Ask not what your country can do for you. Ask what you can do for your country." When John F. Kennedy said that in 1961, a few of us understood the larger picture. We didn't pause to ask if a larger game was at stake. The philosophy and beliefs that drove the Chicano Movement in the 1960s formed the underpinning of the National Hispanic Institute between 1979 and the late 1980s.

None of us ever paused to question NHI's purpose, its work, or beliefs. We believed that our role was to encourage Latino youth to be successful, go to college, become professionals, and own their own businesses. Getting a college degree was the bottom line. Our role was to create the settings to motivate young people to think big and connect to opportunities out there somewhere in the larger, more mobile society.

It wasn't until after several of us at the National Hispanic Institute started taking a closer look at our "return on the investment," that questions were raised concerning the effectiveness of our programs. Instead of forming a new leadership base for Latinos, we began seeing nothing more than young people whose understanding of success revolved mostly around their personal and professional goals. There was little talk about the community. Their primary drive was acquiring more comforts; NHI had become a channel into the mainstream rather than a setting to gather and discuss new and different directions for Latinos.

We realized that our anxieties weren't being caused only by Latino youth enrolling in NHI programs. These attitudes were embedded in the minds of their parents. Despite claims of wanting their children to return home to become leaders in the Latino community, another more subtle agenda was also in play. There wasn't anything compelling enough in the Latino community to warrant their children wanting to stay or become involved. Their best option was to leave, find opportunity elsewhere. To them, NHI was little more than a springboard to college where the final jump could be made out of Latino culture and into the mainstream.

Initially during the 1980s, NHI paid little attention to the attitudes and views of its participants. It wasn't until 1992 that staff started challenging them to clarify their plans for the future as Latino leaders. The majority could neither articulate a role nor saw themselves as eventually going back.

Something happened to change Latino youth of the 1990s who attended NHI programs. Thirty years before, there might have been confusion in the beliefs and roles young people attempted to play in the community. However, they felt compelled to become involved. Some even believed that they could improve the quality of life of the barrio by penetrating and reforming the system at the policy level. This reasoning became the driving force for involvement. It was a good cause that was satisfying to the soul.

Years later, Latino youth coming up the ranks didn't share the same views or philosophy, at least it didn't appear that way to us. Most felt that maybe after making it in the system, they could consider giving back a little. But only after "making it."

Serious concerns over these views led to several questions directed at NHI. What was the ideology that should be adopted in carrying out NHI's mission? What were the beliefs and goals of the organization's leadership training? Were Latino youth of years past that different from those of today? Was the legacy of El Movimiento for the young to only enjoy its benefits with no other purpose?

The need for answers to these questions led the staff and board to examine NHI thinking and the validity of its work. The thought occurred that possibly the National Hispanic Institute wasn't as different as it wanted to claim. Maybe it was similar to LULAC, the American G.I. Forum, The National Council of La Raza, Aspira, the Mexican-American Legal Defense Fund, and the Hispanic Chambers of Commerce. Maybe it was the classic case of the "pot calling the kettle black" when comparing NHI's philosophy to what was being witnessed in the young.

Questions over NHI's identity and role in the Latino community were raised and consumed many hours over several years. Board and staff discussions were endless. First, a basic question had to be answered. What, in fact, was the real purpose of the 1960s? And what was the net gain for all of the involvement and sacrifice during the last thirty years?

Probably, among the most difficult challenges in life is to abandon beliefs and views that guide people and communities. The public view that guided millions of Mexicans spilling over in droves into United States in the early 1900s was the security of a better life than Mexico could possibly offer at the time under its economic, social, and political turmoil. America was also a collection of immigrants from throughout the world, similarly caught in an economic struggle to better their lives.

Despite being a young nation, fledgling American industries provided newly arrived families with instant opportunities to transform their lives. Upward mobility was there for almost anyone who didn't mind paying the price of hard work and long hours at low, but steady, wages. In the United States, people who dedicated themselves to the grueling, mostly physical requirements of long hours on the job could eventually look forward to owning a home and a car, and providing their children with health care, nutrition, and education. This was the American Dream.

The problem was that not all segments of American society were included in that dream. Latinos were discounted in much more dramatic human proportions than other groups, a development that later became a bitter core conflict in El Movimiento of the 1060s. The questions were basic: why had Mexican Americans and other Latino groups been excluded from the economic resources of American society while others enjoyed much better lives? Why had there been a consistent pattern of failure in responding to the needs of Latinos? Why had Latinos been separated from the mainstream? These were tough questions. They demanded that the country look deep into its soul before responding.

Latinos demanded a more sensitive and inclusive government that would undertake steps to make major reforms in the treatment of certain ethnic and racial groups and include them in the nation's opportunity structure.

When the National Hispanic Institute was established, the question of public purpose and direction automatically surfaced in the discussions. Was NHI established to continue the legacy of reform started by earlier civil rights groups? Was the organization's purpose to ensure that Latino youth enjoyed the benefits of the work done by past leaders? Was our mission to aid Latino youth in assimilating into the American mainstream? What were the core beliefs and vision that NHI wanted the community to adopt?

We quickly concluded that NHI was not needed to help Latino youth make the crossover to the American mainstream. An entire network of American institutions, long ago established, were far better equipped to carry out this duty on behalf of American society.

A second concern centered on El Movimiento. In the Mexican-American community, the largest Latino group in the United States, this was the work of civil rights organizations and leaders like Corky González, Cesar Chávez, Dr. Hector P. García, Dolores Huerta, José Angel Gutiérrez, and countless others like them. Were their efforts enough to make the playing field even for generations to come?

To those of us during the early years of NHI, a serious conflict existed between wanting to continue the fight for civil rights and crafting a new direction and purpose. None of us who were in our late thirties and early forties were that far removed from having picked cotton as migrants, living in the squalor of inner cities, or having witnessed the human brutalities of racial discrimination.

All of us were connected to older family members and friends who told of the human suffering they were forced to endure. It's difficult to suddenly disconnect from this history. Racial discrimination and poverty were not experiences we read about in the newspapers or watched on television. Most of us lived them and saw our family members affected by the times.

It wasn't too difficult to imagine waves of refugees fleeing Mexico into the United States in 1910. They were literally running away from a homeland ravaged by civil war. They were also fueled by the public perception that once in the United States, they would also be in the "land of the free." No better alternative could be painted for a beaten people. What they found in the United States was not a society that was accepting and inclusive of people from different cultures and backgrounds. Instead, they found a nation concerned with selfish gains at the expense of exploiting the defenseless. A nation that was best described by President Coolidge's quip: "The business of America is business."

Facing the reality must have been painful to Mexican immigrants who wanted to believe otherwise. It was the same beliefs that eventually drove Latino leaders to form organizations to protect the civil rights of those left unprotected by the law: the migrant, the poor, those left to operate outside the periphery of American opportunity. These leaders were driven by blind faith and the belief that somehow this country would respond. This is why Chicanos employed strikes, walkouts and boycotts – the same strategies that labor leaders used earlier in the twentieth century. Similar strong and vocal tactics were needed to correct the injustices Latinos faced in the United States.

Tangible benefits came from this civil rights movement. Courts intervened on behalf of Latinos to correct past wrongs. Job training programs were established to increase the skills of Latinos to compete for better jobs and higher wages. Special government agencies were established to protect the rights of Latinos and other under-represented groups against discrimination in employment, housing, health services, and education, replacing entire school boards, city councils, and county commissioners courts in communities where Chicanos had been in the majority. Special initiatives such as bilingual education programs were also established to aid in the educational development of Latino youth.

The National Hispanic Institute realized that these changes would have never taken place without the outcries of Latino civil rights organizations and the mobilization efforts of their leaders. No one ever questioned the importance of the 1960s in shaping Latino thinking in the Unites States. Activist youth and the involvement of Latino civic and political organizations left their indelible marks on the landscape of the Latino community.

Our concern was in delineating the role NHI should play in relation to those times. Was it to continue the traditions of reforms that came from El Movimiento? Was it to train youth in community activism? Should NHI become an extension of La Causa in an unfolding twenty-first century scenario?

It was difficult to confine the Chicano Movement as only a reaction to the times, a means of protecting Latinos from abuse and estrangement. It was also a bold statement clearly declaring that Chicanos not only had a place in United States society, but also weren't going to go away or lose their identity by giving way to the homogenization of the American mainstream.

Chicanos, in other words, were not European immigrants who left their countries as economic, political, or religious refugees in search of better lives. They weren't brought here against their will as slaves. Chicanos were born and raised throughout the southwest United States. They were the mixtures of European and indigenous peoples and cultures fused together centuries before in Texas, Colorado, Arizona, and throughout the southwest.

We also concluded that the injustices of the 1960s caused Mexican Americans and other Latino groups to become involved. What was lacking now was a new reason to mobilize the older Latino leaders. In the 1990s, several of them held political office while others worked in government, served on important boards and commissions, or had become well-known and respected businesspeople. Many had worked long and hard to make changes and were now being asked to defend the status quo. Making matters worse were indications that they were also tired and worn out. Progress in the Latino community had come at a tremendous price to those willing to go public with their demands. Clearly another approach had to be found.

Our conclusion was that the 1990s could not be like the 1960s. Marches, public demonstrations, and reform were no longer the compelling reasons to mobilize future Latinos. Something new was needed. La Causa had come to an end, at least as it was known before, and had to be replaced by a more compelling vision for mobilization. Abandonment of La Causa was like being at a funeral to bid your farewells to a relative you loved deeply.

"You see the body in the coffin," I'd tell the staff, "At that moment, you're overwhelmed by the emotions and the thoughts racing through your mind uncontrollably. You remember special moments that you can never erase from your mind. The Chicano Movement had to be seen in much the same way. It was extremely close to many of us. It had its reasons and served its purpose well. It did something to our soul that we could never forget or allow future generations to no longer remember. The treatment of Latinos throughout the twentieth century had been our Age of "Tristeza" (Despair) as Americans who were denied the same opportunities as others.

Could the Chicano Movement be resurrected and used as a rallying point for Latinos of the 1990s and beyond? For the National Hispanic Institute, the answer was clearly no.

In our view, there were plenty of organizations in the Latino community for these purposes, constantly attempting to widen the door of opportunity a little more to make it easier for Latinos to access the system. In frustration one day, after a long, customary discussion on assimilations versus reform at NHI, Sam Moreno, the board chairman asked. "We seem to be neutral on everything. Is there anything that's gone on before or that's going on now that we need to keep as part of our continuing mission?"

"I think a lot of good has come from Latino efforts of the past," I responded. "However, we need to measure progress on a scale of one hundred years of experiences, from the turn of the century to now, and ask ourselves questions that will lead us to the most promising answers. Have the social strategies used by out predecessors produced large-scale changes in our lives as Latinos today? I believe we can safely say that many Latinos have been well served by these changes. But have these improvements embraced most Latinos in the country? Are we better off as a people in the United States when compared to other American groups?"

I assured Sam that NHI was not pursing a separatist view, either. "Sam," I reminded him, "I love my country, the United States. I am a citizen, a sixth-generation Latino who obeys the law, pays taxes, and is a responsible, contributing person. The problem is that the mainstream only allows Latinos like us to participate under the yoke of 'minoritism,' through the practice of trickle-down opportunity. We can't continue the same reform strategy into the twenty-first century, not at the rate of a Latino growing underclass, not in relation to the illiteracy rates in our community, and certainty not in view of a changing global economy where maintaining the edge is driven by constantly having access to an educated workforce."

We discussed this subject at every opportunity. Sam was a person whose views I deeply respected. Our friendship started in Dallas in 1970. A graduate of Southern Methodist University, he had worked in South America for several years. Once back in Dallas, he established his own petroleum equipment distribution company and later worked as a deputy city manager for the City of Dallas. Through all his success in business, Sam also understood poverty. Our mothers had known each other through their church work years before.

After many discussions, Sam and I agreed that the rules for social change that were previously driven by negotiating better race relations were now being altered to a new battlefront – class conflict. The role of government also was going from protecting the rights of the disenfranchised through advocacy to a court of last resort. The private sector, especially large corporations, was being asked to play a larger social role in American civic life. And, Latinos formerly thought to be advocacy leaders for the Latino community were now changing their roles to be players in the system.

Sam was insistent. "Ernie," he asked. "You seem to be suggesting that as Latinos, the ship we've all been on for a long time through the civil rights movement has sunk. Are you saying that it should not be brought to the surface and resurrected as we knew it?"

"I'm saying that the Latino ship of this century was similar to the Titanic" I answered. "We enjoyed the glory of its promise, and those involved had a good time being on board. Let's remember it for what it was, but let's also not attempt to bring it back to life. We have to let the ship sink and everything that it stood for! It should remain what it stood for and be remembered for its lessons and legacy. But looking back or spending time correcting the past can no longer occupy our time. Moving forward to craft a new public direction for our community, a new collective understanding of what we wish to become has to be our most important priority,"

I reminded my friend that the opportunity to shape a new and different future was in our hands. Whatever we chose to become in the twenty-first century had to come from us, from our thinking as a community.

Through these long talks, we concluded that the Chicano Movement was the only way Latinos were able to stand on a number of social, political, and economic issues in the 1960s and 1970s. It gave the community a vehicle for its voice to be heard. The Chicano Movement also shaped a Latino identity that became a permanent part of American life. It provided Mexican Americans with a means of drawing public attention to their needs and hopes. And as a result, they were able to affirm their rights as citizens in the United States and seek the same protections, benefits, and opportunities enjoyed by other groups.

Sam and I also agreed that there were no easy-made, politically correct ways for these issues to have been brought before the American public. Changing society beyond the status quo was never easy or popular, especially when seeking to alter relationships between those accustomed to being in control and those like Latinos with no control. Circumstances in the 1960s required an arrogant and demanding attitude, organized action, and even civil disobedience. But as to whether NHI was established to continue this legacy, the answer again was no.

Again, I reminded Sam, "All of us need to recognize the Chicano movement as the most important event in the annals of Latino history in the United States of the twentieth century. But we should neither resurrect nor attempt to recreate what no longer should become the central focus in a new, changing world of tomorrow that is demanding other strategies, other directions. We need to let that ship sink and remain in its final resting place."

Chapter Twelve: Let the Ship Sink

    1. How can you distinguish between your beliefs that you should let go and those that you should preserve?
    2. Write a brief story about a time when you had to acknowledge that you had been dedicated to a mission, a purpose, or a goal that served a useful and meaningful purpose in the past but is no longer relevant for you?
        a. What led you to the realization that you had to let go?'
        b. What were you thinking about choosing to let go?
        c. How did you feel about letting go?
    3. Describe what you did to let you to feel okay about letting go to that mission, purpose or goal.

4. Of all the aspects of the work you did in support of the mission, purpose or goal that you let go – including the relationships you developed, the structures you built, the functions you performed, and the results you achieved – what did you preserve?

    a. Which aspects of your work did you think would still be useful? That is, which aspects did you choose to retain and preserve?

    b. How did you distinguish between what you thought you needed to let go and what you thought you needed to preserve?

    c. How did you deal with situations such as letting something go but later realized you still needed it (or if you preserved something you thought you would need but later realized it really was no longer useful)?

5. What new mission, purpose, or goal did you find or construct to replace what you let go?

    a. What new ideas, theories, philosophies, values, strategies, or plans did you construct and add on in order to support your new mission, purpose, or goal?

    b. How did you go about creating this new, compelling, meaningful mission, purpose, or goal?

Chapter Thirteen
Conflicts Within

In the late 1980s and early 1990s, the National Hispanic Institute's spiraling growth took up considerable time. We were primarily concerned with having enough money to sustain the work. Then came the challenges of taking NHI services into other states, and creating the same close working relations with students and parents that had been part of the changing formula. For several years, NHI was on autopilot. We only looked forward, rarely stopping to examine the character and thinking of new strategies.

Towards the latter 1980s, a new kind of student began to join. In those first few years, participants expressed concern for the Latino community and wanted to be involved in curbing dropouts and the rise of drug use among teenagers. In sharp contrast, many NHIers of the 1990s were interested in finding a niche for themselves in the mainstream, working on Wall Street, being employed by the Big Five national accounting firms or finding secure positions with multinational corporations. Being active in the Latino community, contributing to its development, and leading it into the next century were afterthoughts. As one of my sons bluntly put it during one of our many Sunday afternoon discussions, "Why should I feel obligated because other Latinos can't hang?"

We spent hours attempting to understand these changing perspectives by listening to parents and asking them endless questions. The youth weren't to blame. They didn't have to feel guilty for their views either. They weren't the issue. It was parents who were mainly conveying the belief that success, both social and economic, would come only if their young were encouraged to leave the Latino community. The emotional contradiction of this view was that they preferred that their children remain close to home commercial mainstream that promised better jobs and more possibilities for upward social and economic prosperity.

More importantly, parents accepted that their children would hold little equity in the American Dream. They preferred, in other words, that their young assume the risk of treading in ominous waters of racial and cultural uncertainty when faced with the alternative of "remaining behind" in the Latino community. The message was clear but incongruent: don't stay behind. The community has nothing to offer. Better that you leave … just don't forget where you came from and never be embarrassed about who you are.

Ricky Miranda, from our Lorenzo de Zavala Youth Legislative Session Class of 1983, was one of those young men caught in the flux of not knowing which way to go. He was a sophomore at Austin's Crockett High School when he first became involved with NHI. Ricky reminded me of my brother Roy because he was short, dark, with straight, jet-black hair, and built low to the ground.

There was a particular anxiety that accompanied Ricky. He was uncomfortable with the way life treated him and his two younger brothers. His parents divorced when he was an eighth grader. Ricky's mom was a custodian at his school. He didn't have a phone or a car. Ricky walked to school every day and rarely had money. In his senior year, he was cut from the baseball team because the coach wanted to rebuild with sophomores and juniors. Through all of this, Ricky always kept his composure and ready smile. There was a special toughness about this young man. Sometimes at nine or ten o'clock in the evening, the sound of our doorbell ringing signaled that our young friend wanted to talk. We lived only a few blocks apart.

"It's Ricky," my wife Gloria would say, "let him in."

Ricky had a lot on his mind. He often asked questions about our work and why Gloria and I had left secure jobs with state government to work in the community. We were success models in his view. Sometimes, as the night dragged on, Ricky would turn questions on himself. He would wonder aloud why life was being so hard on him, why his two little brothers were relegated to an existence of barely having enough, and why his parents had chosen this time in his life to divorce.

Ricky knew little about being Latino or Mexican American. Being Mexican American wasn't a proudly worn label for him and his peers. It was an identity that made him defensive and uneasy. Ricky felt that becoming an aerospace engineer would take care of all these personal challenges. With a degree in hand, he could earn enough money to buy his mother the new home she never had and send his two little brothers to college. Hours would pass during his visits to our home. At two, maybe three, in the morning, I would load Ricky's bike in my Ford Bronco and run him home.

Despite the adversity that he faced daily, his grades were solid enough for college. Gloria and I helped him enroll at The University of Texas-Pan American in Edinburg, Texas. His dream school, Texas A&M University, had earlier rejected him. At the Pan American campus, we bought him a little welcome mat and a few posters for his dorm room. Ricky didn't know what it meant to live on a college campus. Few in his family had ever finished high school, much less gone to college. By the end of his first semester, Ricky proudly earned a 3.0 grade point average. He called us regularly to let us in on his life as a student.

While on Christmas break from school his first semester, Ricky stopped by the house to say hello. Gloria had left for Christmas several days before, as was her custom, to spend time with her sisters and parents in McAllen, Texas. There stood Ricky, proudly smiling as he always did while standing on our front porch. He was wearing a brand new corduroy suit, white shirt and tie, and has nicely cropped hair with a part to one side.

Ricky was no longer the person with baggy pants and a shirt hanging down to his knees, riding his bicycle at night. He was different now. This time around, he also had a good-looking young lady standing next to him, holding his hand. Ricky's life was definitely taking a turn for the better. We visited as always making light of life's trivialities, just like we did when we first met. He was very amused by different incidents that happened his first time in college.

"The people in the Valley are weird, dude," he said, once inside the house and sitting in the living room exchanging stories.

"Hey man, everybody there speaks Spanish like they lived in Mexico, and they all think I do the same, because I look just like them. You know what I do, Ern? I look back, nod yes or no, and smile the whole time, so they think I understand. Ain't that something else?" Ricky couldn't merely laugh politely. He'd go into contortions, half curling up on the couch with laughter, his entire body shaking, and face covered with amusement.

Several weeks before leaving the first time for college, Ricky turned eighteen and voted. He joined a community semi-pro baseball team that allowed him to continue his passion for the sport. More importantly, Ricky fell in love with a young woman, a high school classmate whom he previously had been too timid to approach. Being in college and having a future made him a little more confident. To his surprise, he discovered that she had liked him since their junior year of high school and was crushed when he never asked her out.

They were together now, and no one could be happier than Ricky. He sat next to her the entire evening, holding her hand, handing her refreshments, and giving her the homemade cookies that Gloria always has around the house for guests. They acted like twins who smiled together, laughed at the same jokes, and amusingly seemed oblivious to anything else around them but each other. As was his custom, Ricky didn't leave my house until well past midnight. On his way out, after hugging both of them, I warned him, "Take care of yourself, son, particularly these days. There are a lot of crazy people out there driving."

Ricky and his girlfriend disappeared into the darkness. It was the last time I would ever see them.

Two days later, while staying with Nila, Gloria's sister, and her family in the Rio Grande Valley, we received an emergency call around four in the morning. It was from the Brackenridge Hospital emergency room in Austin. Moments after leaving his father's office late in the evening, Ricky had been broad-sided by an eighteen-wheeler that ran a red light on a foggy night at a Ben White Boulevard crossing. Tragically, both he and his girlfriend were killed.

A doctor discovered a telephone number that had been scribbled on a piece of paper in Ricky's wallet. He thought that maybe the name written on it could be his mother or some other relative. While at Pan American, Ricky used to go over to Nila's house in McAllen to wash clothes. The number the doctor found was Nila's. His home in Austin still didn't have a phone. By the time we were called, Ricky was gone. Shocked by the news, all we could do was to tell the police how to get to Ricky's house, so that they could inform his mother that her son was dead.

Sixteen years after the tragedy of this young friend, the memories that Ricky left behind are commemorated at every Lorenzo de Zavala Youth Legislative Session through the Ricky Miranda Memorial Award. At the conclusion of each program, volunteer staff select one young participant who, like Ricky, most demonstrates the spirit of never giving up, someone who overcomes personal adversity, a young boy or girl who stands tall during LDZ when faced with repeated disappointments and setbacks. Every student and parent at the awards celebration learns about Ricky and the courage that eventually took him from the point of quitting to a life of personal triumph.

Through all the years of announcing the Ricky Miranda Memorial Award recipient at the different LDZ programs around the country, sadness rushes through my mind as I remember my young friend. I find myself choking back the tears that well up in my eyes. As a high school student, Ricky brought memories back of my brother, Roy. Both of them led similar lives. Both had hearts of lions. Both were driven to succeed by an unrelenting energy to overcome severe personal odds. Both died much too early.

They never overcame feeling uncomfortable for being physically smaller than others or having dark skin. Neither one of them was to blame for his economic conditions or circumstances of life. All they knew was to angrily fight back, work extra hard, and keep dreaming for what seemed beyond their reach and what others appeared so unwilling to share.

The Ricky Miranda story is only the tip of an iceberg in the Latino community. There are literally thousands of other young people facing similar conditions. To them, the only recourse is gaining acceptance in order to attain the comforts of the mainstream. Ricky and Roy, despite being from different times, were driven by almost identical passions to excel. Both of them despised being short. Both would have preferred lighter skin. Both disliked associations with living in poor neighborhoods and not having the means to enjoy the better things in life.

At NHI, part of the work involved is uncovering answers to these perplexing challenges and constructing healthier alternatives for high-ability Latino youth who see themselves as having no other options but to disassociate by leaving. Among the many questions that we thought about, two were immediately apparent: could an attraction for Latino culture and lifestyles be instilled among Latino youth, despite the imagery conveyed in the popular media of Latinos being backwards and uneducated? And, was school the primary force in the lives of Latino youth that was influencing them to move toward life outside of Latino culture?

The answer to each was yes. A modern-day, more progressive depiction of Latinos could be devised to counter stereotypes. Strategies could include special training academies, summer research projects, and opportunities that would take NHI youth to other Latino countries to experience lifestyles much different than those largely practiced by United States Latinos. The American educational system, however, posed a greater demand. We understood that public education went beyond training children to read, write, and figure out math equations. It also indoctrinated, shaped views, and essentially laid out the pathways to an American perception of the so-called "good life." This ideological understanding led us to view the educational system as chauvinistic, close-ended, and difficult to change. An additional problem was that the culture of the educational system was also guilty of conveying the message that people who were unlike the mainstream culture had to accept a "minority" status. This was the price of membership and admission into the lager society.

Often, Gloria and I were frustrated and angry with what had happened to our parents and ourselves as youngsters; we had no other recourse but to endure the burdens of growing up in the United States. More than once, our emotions had to be tempered, letting intellect guide our thinking versus anger. Dad's advice kept popping up in my mind: *"En estos tiempos, ya no se debe pelear con coraje. Usa tu mente.* (In these times, you no longer can fight with anger. Use your mind.)"

More questions surfaced. Were our views valid or only imagined? What were the rewards of amalgamation into the American mainstream? What were the successes of Latinos who took up the challenges and left? Were there many or only a handful? Were they living in obscurity, marginalized as minorities? Were they unconditionally embraced and given the same opportunities to succeed? In the end, was it all worth the pain of changing from being one way to become something else?

Through long talks that started with hours and ended up taking months – even years – of deliberation, we eventually arrived at a few conclusions. One determination was that whoever comprised the mainstream made wholesale acceptance of Latinos a near impossibility when given the history of race relations in the United States, the previous encounters between the United States and other Latino countries, and the popular perception that Latinos were foreigners.

A second conclusion was driven by our perceptions of the American economic system. We believed that the redistribution of wealth and influence in the United States was unlikely if it meant that the majority would have to do with less. A more plausible likelihood was that mainstream culture would accept only those willing to assimilate and would keep resources unobtainable from those who were either unwilling or unable.

Analyzing our work led us to one more disturbing conclusion. Whether or not we had differences and conflicts with mainstream culture, NHI also was preaching the same philosophy it was questioning. Essentially, we were shepherds of American mainstream success. We were guiding Latino youth to adopt the same measures for success and leadership. We started to conclude that this was the wrong answer for them. Instead of pointing the finger at the larger society for our ills as a community, we now had to direct the blame inward, towards ourselves.

At the 1992 Colorado LDZ, I privately met with a few senior and junior counselors in a workroom of our dormitory at Colorado State University in Fort Collins. These were LDZ alumni who returned each summer to assist with the new participants. Junior counselors were still in high school. Senior counselors were in college. I drew a large triangle on the chalkboard to symbolize American society.

"Where," I asked, "do you feel the majority of Latinos fit in this drawing?"

"That's easy," a student immediately responded, "at the bottom."

"And where do you feel most Latinos fit in this scale?" I continued.

"The same place," another shot back, pointing his thumb downward.

"And why do you feel you go to school for an education?"

"So that we can start going up in society," another responded.

"So our perception is that Latinos are here in American society," I asked, pointing to the bottom of the triangle, "and that you as young people are getting an education to go up the ladder, right?"

They all agreed, nodding together.

"So if the conclusion is that Latinos as a community are constantly working to get up the ladder, who do you perceive as being at the top or at least near it?"

The room suddenly became silent, as though no one wanted to comment. Only their eyes spoke, daring each other to speak.

Albert Carrillo, at the time a student at the University of Notre Dame, ventured an answer.

"Okay, Ernie, I'll say it. It's Anglo society. We all know that, okay?"

An uncomfortable giggle ran among the students as though a dark hidden secret had suddenly been revealed.

"I can accept that, Albert," I answered. "But your answer is only a small part of today's discussion. Just stay with me, because I'm not only asking you these questions, but I also have to answer them for myself."

For the remainder of the evening we continued discussing the "Triangle Theory," as we came to know this classic discussion in NHI lore. The experience was similar to a group of people peering into a mirror together, searching for answers, and coming to controversial, even personally uncomfortable conclusions.

What were the requirements of gaining admission into a society dominated by a different culture, a dominant view that touched and influenced everything around and about us as Latinos?

"You have to give up everything man," a student observed. "To get to the top, you have to give everything up, your language, your customs, your way of life, everything. You gotta give it all up."

A simple, direct question only a few hours before began to turn into a nervousness that was uncomfortable to the students. These were the potentially explosive topics never discussed.

Flashbacks to my own upbringing sprang up in my mind. I remembered going with Mom as a five year old to sell Avon products in an all-Anglo neighborhood, only block away from our home in Houston's Northside.

"When we go into these people's homes," she would instruct me, "you sit in a chair and be quiet. You don't want to break their things. Maybe someday you can have a nice house like theirs."

Mom's entire personality changed whenever we walked into the homes of Anglo families. In our family, she was the person who gave orders, insisted on certain standards. There was a strictness about her. She was in command and someone you dared not speak back to. When selling her products, she completely changed. The same happened years later during my senior year in college.

During a weekend homecoming at our fraternity house, one of the members motioned me over toward the kitchen while we entertained alumni.

"Someone is in the kitchen looking for you," he said, pointing in the direction.

I couldn't imagine who it was. It turned out to be Mom, standing there, nervously looking around, not too far from the back door. Mom was an attractive woman, a leader in the church and community. People respected her work and the impact she had on entire communities, especially young people. When it came to being out of her natural surroundings, however, an anxiety seemed to take over, a discomfort that made her shy, almost withdrawn.

Forty years later, perceptions by Latinos toward Anglo society hadn't changed that much. Mom and Dad had few options when they were young. Circumstances for them during the early part of the twentieth century dictated the boundaries of their social and cultural interactions. Venturing from one world to another was restricted, often prohibited, and severely punished.

The 1990s were supposed to be different. Success was no longer defined by what you made of yourself in your own culture, the culture of your parents and grandparents, and your neighborhood. Making it was determined by how fast you moved away from family and community. Getting a college education was a proven way to achieve that end, earning the credentials for admission into the mainstream. Yet, deep inside there was recognition that this kind of change also carried a costly price tag.

Moving out also meant adhering to the requirements of another social and cultural world. It meant giving up language, and being measured by different standards like where you lived, how much money you had, what kind of clothes you wore, where you sent your children to school, where you vacationed, what you read, and how you saw life.

The Triangle Theory was a reminder of life in a societal structure where there was little chance of escaping. You either accepted living at the bottom or you redefined yourself in order to move up. There was only one way of inching closer to the top. And once you changed, there was no way back.

There were a few other problems involved: the monetary and material rewards of adapting would only take you to a certain level of life in the mainstream. The overwhelming majority of Latinos would operate only peripherally, disconnected, and alienated from the whole. The final blow would be in forever being seen as mere novelties ... and minorities.

The students invited into the discussion understood these challenges. They were the few Latinos in accelerated academic classes in high school, the few brown faces on college campuses, and the ones constantly told that they were not like the others. In their views there wasn't an option. Making it only halfway was much better than not making it by remaining in the Latino community, even if at times it meant being ridiculed, being the butt of off-color jokes, or never being considered as having the right stuff to be at the top.

My friend, the Chicano poet, Ricardo Sanchez, came to mind. I remembered one of our lengthy conversations in the early formative years for NHI: *"El problema es que estos muchachos no entienden su comunidad. Se pasan la vida cambiando de Latinos para hacerse gavachos. Es posible que pueden hacer más daño como adultos.* (The problem is that these young dudes don't understand their own community. They spend most of their lives changing from being Latino to becoming Anglos. It's possible that they may cause more harm than good once they become adults.)"

Despite our unwillingness to make this concession, Ricardo was right. Our educational system does much more than teach reading, writing, and arithmetic. The educational process also has a cultural component. For Latino youth, their identity is channeled in a different direction. Behind the veneer of education and the opportunity, they are "Romanized," taught to look at life through lenses that make Latino life in the United States appear small, insignificant, and unimportant in comparison to the host culture. Ricardo wanted me to fully grasp the dynamics of this process and the effects of cultural conversion on the mind.

"Es como vestirte con un abrigo de otra persona, (It's like wearing someone else's coat,)" he observed. *"Para sentir que tienes las mismas oportunidades como la mayoría, aceptas otro idioma como si fuera tuyo. Te vistes como ellos, oyes la misma música, aceptas otra religión, comes lo mismo que ellos, practicas las mismas costumbres, al final cambias quién eres. Chicano o Latino eres no más en nombre, una conveniencia no más para adquirir tus metas. El proceso de este cambio borra tu identidad, mata el espíritu de tu cultura. Ya no tienes dirección ni fin. No más existes. Éste fue mi conflicto y al fin mi liberación, la realización que no más de mí puede venir quién soy, no de otros, sin importar las consecuencias.* (To feel like them, you accept another language as though it were yours. You dress like them, practice the same customs, accept other religions, eat the same food as others, practice other customs, and in the end you change who you are. Being Chicano or Latino becomes only a convenience, a way of achieving your personal goals, but that's all. The process erases your identity, kills the spirit of your culture. You no longer have direction or a destination in life. You merely learn to exist. This was my life conflict and, in the end, my liberation, the realization that who I am could only come from me, not others, no matter the consequences.)"

Ricardo would have loved the town of Maxwell, where NHI is located: the old Victorian house, the Texas oaks and green pastures, the laid-back countryside of hills and winding roads.

One day, a library will be dedicated to his memory on the NHI grounds. His books will be brought back and his ideas studied. His presence at the institute, his ideas, and his writings will never be forgotten. *"¡Simón, que si, carnal!"* (Damn right, brother!).

Chapter Thirteen: Conflicts Within

1. Write a brief story about a time when you were confronted by new information that challenged some of your existing, comforting beliefs, values, vision, goals, and strategies?
    a. What did you think when new knowledge conflicted with your old beliefs?
    b. How did you feel?
    c. What did you do?
2. How did you make sure that you remained open to seeing, hearing about, taking in, and understanding a new way of looking at and understanding the world?
3. How did you reconcile and integrate new knowledge with your old, existing beliefs?
    a. Did you try to change the world so that it fits your beliefs?
    b. Did you distort your perceptions of the world so that what you see and hear fit your beliefs?
    c. Did you delete (or add) parts of the new knowledge so it fit better with your existing beliefs, values, and assumptions?
4. Did you challenge the validity of your own beliefs and assumptions and change them to accommodate your new knowledge?
5. Did you avoid or withdraw from contact with the sources of the new understanding of the way the world works?
6. How can you enlist the support of people who are close to you to meet and discuss the new information, its validity, and its implications for you, your family, and your community?
    a. How can you bring people together?
    b. How effective do you think this process could be?
    c. What might happen as a result of reflecting upon and analyzing the new perspective and knowledge?

Chapter Fourteen
Responsibility for the New

In 1957, my family owned only one car. It was used for everything: work, shopping, attending church. My brothers and I even used it for dates. More importantly, the white-and-blue 1957 Dodge hardtop was Dad's pride and joy. Dad made sure that his car was always clean and ready to drive.

One day during the summer, I gathered enough courage to ask Mom if I could borrow it. Anita Flores, a young woman from Houston's Second Ward, and I were on the verge of starting to date. Public transportation was out of the question. This was my opportunity to pull up in front of her house with the latest in look.

"Mom," I finally gathered enough courage to ask. "You think you and Dad would loan me ten bucks and the car to take Anita out for a couple of hours?"

Mom was in her bedroom ironing clothes for the week while listening to KLVL, Houston's only Mexican radio station. "I don't know, mijo," she responded. "It's okay by me, but you know how your father is about loaning out the car. Why don't you ask him?"

Taking a chance that he might say yes, I walked out back to the garage where Dad seemed to spend most of his spare time. His garage was his haven, where he cleaned his tools or repaired an old car starter. He was always busy.

Standing by the garage doorway, I gathered the courage to pop the question. "Is it all right if I borrow the car for a couple of hours?" I timidly asked.

"¿Qué dice tu mama? (What does your mother have to say about that?)" he'd ask. "She said it was okay," I shot back confidently, "but asked that you agree as well."

I finally had him trapped. Every time my two brothers or I wanted something important that required getting permission from both our parents, we became embroiled in a human Ping-Pong game. "Go ask your mother first. Go ask your father first. Did he say it was all right? Go get him so that he can tell me directly." Back and forth we would go, playing the game for "ask her first" or "ask him first."

Dad turned and stared at me for a moment while searching for his keys inside the pockets of his work pants. He tossed them in the air for me to catch. However, they hit the ceiling of the garage and fell short of my feet.

This was too embarrassing to accept. Besides, I wasn't one to beg. I was now seventeen years old, a full-grown man who stood six-four, at least I thought that to myself.

"You know what Dad," I blurted out in a challenging mock, "I don't need the car after all... not this way." Bending over to get the keys, I gave them back to him, and headed back to the house and the security of my bedroom. Dad knew that I was angry, but he did nothing to stop me. He turned and resumed working.

An hour later, I could overhear a discussion between him and Mom. Mom had her ways of defending us, making her point of view about our needs as growing teenagers.

"Ya son grandes los muchchos, Santos, (They're big kids now,)" she told him. *"Dales por su lado de vez en cuando. Ya no son chiquitos. Y también dale los diez dólares que quiere porque él no los tiene.* (Let them have their way once I a while. They're not children anymore. And, also give him the ten dollars he needs. He doesn't have any money.)"

Dad understood the message. He rarely argued with Mom. Over years of marriage, they had also become best friends.

After a few moments, Dad opened the door to my bedroom and motioned me outside. *"Ernesto,"* he said. *"Ven. Vamos para afuera.* (Come. Let's go outside.)"

Our backyard was mostly a giant concrete base that surrounded a large oak tree where we played

120

basketball almost nightly. The basketball rim was exactly ten-feet-three-inches off the ground, the official height for high school basketball. Frank Alvarez, Jr.; "Crazy Manuel," our cousin; John Mendoza; Salami; Phil Abalos; and, of course, the three Nieto boys often played there past midnight.

Dad went straight through the backyard, out to the alley that was littered with overgrown weeds, broken beer bottles, and an old junk car.

"*¿Qué miras mijo?* (What do you see?)" He asked looking back at me.

"*Pues nada papa,*" I answered. "*¿Qué quieres que vea? No más yierbas, botellas de cerveza, y ese jonque.* (I see nothing, Dad. What is it you want me to see? Just weeds, beer bottles and that junk car.)"

"*Mira Ernesto,*" Dad continued. "*Llámale a Abram y dile que se venga a la casa con su troca.* (Call Abram and tell him to bring his truck to the house.)"

Abram, my first cousin, had fought in World War II in the Pacific. After the war, he returned home and got involved in racing cars. He also opened his own car repair business.

I called Abram. After a while, he arrived and briefly visited with Dad. In less than an hour, they removed the junk car's transmission, the hood, and several other parts. Everything was put in the back of Abram's truck and off we went to Goldstein's used car parts in the Fifth Ward. Everything was sold for about $150.

When we got home, Dad walked over and asked me to sit down with him on our front porch. "Ahora, mijo," he started, "tú me pediste el carro. No solo esparabas el carro, pero también necesitabas dinero ¿verdad? (Now, son, you asked to borrow the car. You not only expected the car, but money as well?)"

I nodded.

"*Y cuándo te llevé allá al callejón, te hice un pregunta, ¿verdad?* (And when I took you to the alley, I asked you a question, right?)"

Again, I nodded.

"*Solamente viste lo peor, el jonque, la basura. Al contrario, yo vi una oportunidad y te lo demonstré con lo que hicimos. Todo en la vida, mijo, está en lo que ves y la actitud que tomas para crear oportunidades de lo que otros no le dan valor.* (You only saw the worst, the junk car and trash. In contrast, I saw opportunity and demonstrated it with what we did. Everything in life, son, is in what you want to see and what attitude you take to create opportunities from what others see as having little value.)"

Dad then reached in his pocket and handed me the car keys and a $20 bill.

As Latinos move forward in this new millennium, working towards greater self-reliance and self-direction as a community may be better than either working to assimilate into the American mainstream or pursuing social reform and justice. While these strategies worked in the past, they may not prove as useful in addressing future Latino needs. A different outlook and a new, culturally unifying social vision of community need to be crafted. This vision must also contribute to the American experience.

At the institute, this vision is defined by a concept often referred to as "community equity-building." Community equity building encourages the pursuit of principles that guide future leaders to channel their skills and talents inward to strengthen the economic, social, cultural, and intellectual capacities of the Latino community.

Equity building also involves redefining relations between Latinos and other cultures that comprise the American community. It sets into motion the redefinition of the Latino identity from that of a minority, a race, or a Third World community, to a global culture of interconnected nationalities able to work together and pursue common goals. It also encourages business development through products and services specifically designed to respond to a growing Latino consumer market. It makes Spanish the linguistic currency for exchange and communications within the U.S. Latino community and with the Latin American international community. And, it cultivates a cultural confidence with a public purpose and direction that is distinct, authentic, and enduring.

Achieving this view of community is not a simple task. Decades of work will be required. For the majority of Latinos, remaining on the same pathways will be preferable rather than venturing into an unpredictable future of outcomes where Latinos alone command the process without relying on anyone else. Skilled Latino youth of tomorrow may also be too concerned with their individual futures to risk involvement. The few bold enough to consider being part of a new Latino thinking may not be equipped with the endurance and skills to survive in community ventures that demand constant exploration and changes in direction.

Stagnation is not a viable choice. The erosion of culture continues to be the biggest impediment to a vibrant, future Latino community. Without an agenda of its own, it can neither advance its own interests nor have a rationale to train its future leaders. For the majority of Latino young people, finding a place for themselves in the larger society, and not in the Latino community, is their chief goal. Their occupations and their incomes measure success for them. Social status and material possessions become their overriding concern. Many are already in too deep to consider another option.

The early signs of these changeovers are more readily seen among Latino youth in college today, where most no longer use Spanish. They encounter difficulties when called upon to communicate in the tongue of their cultural predecessors. Their understanding of cultural relevancy is limited to membership in Latino college campus organizations. And then most of these organizations view leadership service in the Latino community as periodically extending volunteer welfare services to the disadvantaged.

For the majority, advancement is driven by a personal, not a community, agenda. Gaining an undergraduate degree remains the most expedient means of crossing over to "a better life." Identifying terms such as Hispanic or Latino are not used to signify cultural pride, but, rather, as devices to leverage entry into the larger business and professional world. For these youth, the slow and deliberate death of culture is the most obvious consequence. This erosion of identity induces distance from their community. It weakens their family ties and clouds their motivation to participate in the social, cultural, economic, and political life of Latinos.

Plainly put, cultivating a new sense of pride in U.S. Latino culture is the single most pressing need if Latinos are to learn to see each other in different way and to place more trust in each other while at the same time working together toward common endeavors. To do nothing places Latinos in an at-risk position where the costs outweigh the benefits.

In 1992, the National Hispanic Institute introduced the Triangle Theory as a social construct to depict at which levels of American life the majority of Latinos live when defined by educational attainment and income standards. Students who participated in these discussions were also asked to talk about the price that individual Latinos were being asked to pay from the standpoints of language, culture, and identity in their attempts to achieve upward social mobility.

Looking back, this approach might have been too harsh, too shocking to the nervous systems of middle-class Latino youth who recognized the changes occurring in them and their friends. Most stood in awe of this realization. They understood the impact of cultural change on their individual lives. Others remained silent, choosing instead to argue and defend the directions they were taking. None, however, could offer even a remote concept of a different reality, a new direction or beliefs to follow.

It was this inability that frustrated them the most. They knew what they didn't like and what options they were under pressure to accept. However, they couldn't articulate an alternate direction. Neither could their parents. At best, they could only defend cultural changes occurring in their livers as being the "lesser of two evils" when faced with the choices of "remaining Latino" or enjoying more affluent lifestyles. In the end, they realized and even lamented the cost of becoming converted culturally. Most, however, were too comfortable with their newfound surroundings to consider changing.

Hamah King, a long-time associate from Dallas, once referred to an old Black adage during a discussion about the lack of participation by Latino and Black professionals in the civil rights movement. "A man with a ham on his back ain't never hungry," he observed.

The same can be said for the few Latinos who are either enjoying the spoils of mainstream life or feel that they're well on the way to gaining a foothold in their perception of the American dream. Why change direction? What's the compelling reason? Attempting to gain an understanding for the community challenges facing the thirty-two million Latinos in the United States may be too ambitious an undertaking for these individuals. This is especially true when discussing the roles that culture can play in defining the identity of future Latinos. Instead, they see their roles as joining Latino organizations that break down barriers by sending role models to speak at youth conferences.

Defining a new public direction based on culture and its lessons for the U.S. Latino community of the twenty-first century will not come from those who have lived the majority of their lives in the past century. Their life experiences, positions of leadership in the Latino community, and their expertise are immaterial. The challenge of defining a new course for Latinos in the future can only come from Latino youth. It's their charge to construct the cultural teachings through which they and their children intend to live.

The topic of ownership over public direction was discussed with a close family friend, Hilario Díaz, during a two-hour flight from Austin to El Paso. Hilario, originally from the Texas Rio Grande Valley, had grown up in the barrio, fought in the Vietnam War, received his degree from St. Mary's University in San Antonio, and spent several years working with the National Council of La Raza (NCLR) in Washington, D.C. As a young man, he was heavily involved in La Causa, fighting for civil rights for Latinos. At fifty-seven years, he had mellowed a little from his early days. Both his daughters, Zoraima and Zabrina, were alumni of NHI's leadership programs and college students.

Hilario and I spent most of our time together either playing golf on Sunday afternoons or exchange tales of our younger days. This time, however, the subject was different. The older daughter – Zoraima – wanted to spend the summer before her senior year in college as an intern in Washington, D.C. She thought this would expose her to public policy. Through his old contacts at NCLR, Hilario made arrangements for her to have her wish. Instead of congratulating Hilario for his efforts, I decided to raise questions.

"Mira, Hilario," I started. "What's the deal with Zoraima in Washington? And what do you expect to have her learn by being with NCLR? You already know the answers to all of that. NCLR is not a bad organization. It really does good work and is known all over for advocating for a lot of Latinos and Latino organizations. But what is it that you expect her to gain that you already know and can't explain to her?"

Hilario looked at me for moment as though not certain of his response. "Nieto," he responded, "mira carnal, (look brother,) you know of her long-standing interest in public policy and politics. Washington is an excellent experience for her. Don't you see it? I've told you before of mija's intent to eventually get involved in politics. Being there will start her off by letting her experience how the system works. What's wrong with that?"

"Nothing's wrong with that," I responded. "Not if you expect her to spend the rest of her life in a reality that both you and I know only too well. We've lived in it all our lives. What do you want her to learn, that as a community we constantly have to suck up to others for little to nothing? That it takes years to make changes in the system? That we as Latinos are not the priorities of those who make decisions and control outcomes? What is it that you want her to learn that you don't already know and can't explain in a matter of one or two hours sitting around drinking coffee? What do you think we spent learning since the 1960s? That if we try a little harder, maybe our luck will change as a community?"

"Come on Hilario, what are you really saying to your daughter? Maybe it's that you really don't want her to explore other possibilities and directions as a Latina. Maybe you want her in the same world as you, maybe not the exact same world, but at least a similar environment, so that she can learn what and eventually come to what conclusions?"

Hilario is not the type of person who runs away from a good argument. Besides, there we were, sitting together on a two-hour flight with little else to do but talk. What words we used in arguing differences of opinion didn't matter to us. Asking each other tough questions was part of our normal routine whether discussing philosophy, politics, religion, or amusing ourselves with golf. Both of us shared a common interest in NHI as well. I was the founder and president. He was president of the institute's National Community Leadership Council, a group of parents who were involved in leadership training in local communities.

"*Mira vato*, (Look dude,)" he stated. *"¿Qué quieres que haga?* (What do you want me to do?) You talk about a new public direction for Latinos. What better place than Washington, D.C., or NCLR as a starting point? I know those guys are caught up in another reality that's completely different from NHI, but maybe that's what Zoraima needs to go see and learn about. *¿Qué no?* (Isn't that right?)"

"Chinitas, Hilario," I responded in exasperation, *"¿Qué pasó? Comó dicen los Californianos, 'parece que no tienes snap ése.'* (What's up? Like the Californians say, 'you ain't got no snap.') You don't learn to do things differently by doing the same old, same old, time and time again. You're like the slave trying to teach freedom to another slave. Freedom is not a word you imagine. You have to live and experience it. NCLR, like other Latino organizations, does great and important work for all of us, but what does that have to do with creating a new public direction for the Latino community of the future?"

"And NHI is the new public direction?" he demanded. "Is that what makes the organization different?"

"Yes," I said, "But not better than other Latino groups. The only difference is our work. The Latino community doesn't need another advocacy and reform organization to help address its needs and challenges, at least not in the conventional meaning of the word. NHI is not an extension of a college or university. It isn't a social service organization or a leadership-training project that points to corporate America as the wave of the future for college-bound Latino youth. The institute is different."

"What is it that you want NHI to pursue?" he asked, this time more curious about an answer.

"Look," I said. "We've spent twenty years attempting to delineate a public role for NHI. The next step is to find Latino youth with the intellectual capacities, skills, and motivation to do the same for the future Latino community. Your daughter may very well be one of those candidates, but she won't grow by confining her to the same old realities. We've been there and done that! What she needs is an environment that allows her the privilege of thinking, exploring new concepts, looking at Latinos through a different telescope, twenty and fifty years into the future.

"Classic American education no longer serves her interests, certainly not to address the needs of the Latino community of tomorrow," I continued. "She needs to travel to other Latin American countries to live and socialize with youth her age. That includes participating in their affairs to gauge their directions. She also needs time to talk out loud, test her theories, and jot down her perceptions about Latinos in the futures.

"Our job as a Latino community is to provide the Zoraimas of the world, my kids included, with venues for them to develop and mature. Programs like the Young Leaders Conference, the Lorenzo de Zavala Youth Legislative Session, the Collegiate World Series, and even the Collegiate Leadership Network are social toys NHI gives its students to experiment with new ideas and to test new thinking.

This kind of preparation is not possible through our high schools and colleges. That's not the reason they exist, nor should it be."

"The responsibility of creating future Latino leaders can only come from our efforts, our investments. No one else should be held responsible to participate or help. But there's also a downside to all of this, a requirement that many of us may not be willing to pay or even consider."

"What's that?" Hilario asked, by now comfortably absorbed in our discussion.

"Here's the secret, carnal," I responded. "Our part is only to help create and support the venues that cultivate new intellectual growth among Latino youth. But we cannot participate in crafting the new. That responsibility and charge must come only from their minds, their imaginations. Their ideas must be free of our historical biases and prejudices. We have to leave them alone."

Hilario found the latter part of my explanation difficult to swallow.

"What do you mean Ernesto?" he asked. "They need to know the past and all the 'chingasos' (ass-kickings) we went through, don't they? You know the old saying: 'You don't know where you're going unless you also know where you've been.' Doesn't that play a role?"

"Not in crafting a new public direction or defining a different Latino culture in the United States," I said. "Many of us will have to die off before the new is able to emerge. Maybe in the Old Testament that's what kept Moses in the desert with his people for forty years. Old ways, old thinking, and old lessons had to die first. A final break has to occur from the past in order for our young to define the new. NHI is where our young come to contemplate the future, not in terms of careers and money-making schemes, but in giving rise to the type of thinking that will take us to the next level in our evolutionary journey as a people."

Hilario and I didn't touch the subject again the remainder of the trip. We both understood our roles. We weren't there to lead or guide. One of our responsibilities in the National Hispanic Institute was to keep the learning environment from the intrusions of the old, the confining. Another responsibility was to ask penetrating questions that forced youth to think. Our most important duty, however, was the one that simultaneously gave us comfort and discomfort. The comforting part was realizing that there was much work to do in making the organization stronger and designing training experiences compelling enough to awaken youth to the need for new directions in their thinking. The disquieting realization came as we landed in El Paso.

"Want to hear the downside, Mr. H?" I asked.

"What's that?" he responded, pausing for a moment to listen.

"We have to accept that we had our day this past century," I said. "We did what we had to do. We had good times and bad times. At NHI, we can't interfere with the work youth have to perform to craft something new for themselves. It will take years, maybe generations. Our job is helping them get started, realizing the entire time that whatever they create, we won't live long enough to see."

Hilario and I stared at each other for several moments. No more words were needed.

Today, thousands of young Latinos have benefited from being involved with the institute. Some have experienced serious self-confrontations with their ideas, attitudes, and community perceptions. Others have returned home wondering what they were doing getting involved with NHI in the first place. The majority, however, have been forced to rethink who they are, what role they expect to play in society, and what they can do to participate as leaders in a Latino community.

No easy answers exist to these tough challenges. Everyone is individually left to develop his or her own conclusions. There is no right or wrong, no good or bad. As Dad used to say, "Cada cabeza es un mundo. (Every head its own mind.)" In the final analysis everyone is left to peruse life the best way they know how. For many, NHI provided an important and life-defining moment.

Since 1982, Gloria and I have received hundreds of letters every year from NHI alumni. Some write about overcoming personal obstacles at home or in the community. Others talk about having gained admission to their dream college. Almost always, they mention the way NHI influenced and encouraged them to step up, take risks, and think big.

Not too long ago, a string of wonderful experiences happened. While recruiting in South Texas, one of my visits took me to Uvalde to visits a counselor we had known for years. Her daughter, Ginger, attended the inaugural LDZ at Concordia Lutheran College in 1983. To our surprise, Ginger had recently moved back to town. She was one of only two optometrists in Uvalde. Of course, I had to go by to see her, say hello, and recall a few memories. Ginger took one look at my outdated glasses and sat me down for a quick and free eye examination.

Two weeks later, I was in Chicago with terribly sore feet. It took me almost thirty minutes to walk from the airplane to a taxicab. Immediately after returning to Austin, I made an appointment with a new podiatrist in New Braunfels, not far from NHI's offices. Once on the examination table, a young doctor poked his head around the corner and said, "Do you remember me?" It was Alex Urteaga, a 1984 participant form El Paso.

"NHI turned my life around, Ernesto," he said. "I would have never gone to college had I not gone to the LDZ."

The stories do not end there. Three weeks went by. Mom, at the time around eighty-seven years of age, was visiting with me when our board of directors at NHI was also meeting. Edward Pérez, an alumnus, was in town for the meeting. A 1983 LDZer, Edward had earned a Ph. D. from M.I.T. and an M.D. from Harvard at the same time. His parents lived only blocks from our home in South Austin. Because Mom had been having serious balance problems, I called Edward to ask his advice.

"Why don't I come over and take a close, personal look," he said. It was already late, around 10:30 P.M.

Here was Edward, a young man we got to know while at Austin's Crockett High School in 1982. I felt a rush of reassuring protection. You couldn't ask for more.

Edward was gentle with Mom, asking her occasional questions in Spanish. In turn, Mom felt comfortable with him. Nothing was seriously wrong, only a small ear infection that could easily be treated with antibiotics.

Gloria and I never take credit for the individual successes of the alumni of NHI leadership programs. We kiddingly tell parents that smartness and genius in their kids are matters they can privately steel regarding which side of the family contributed to the gene pool. We've worked hard to provide these young people with other definitions of success that don't center on material acquisition, status in the community, or level of education. Our measures have always been tied to leadership service. Leadership to us at the National Hispanic Institute also carries a moral mission that is closely tied to the spiritual training provided by parents.

We've also not lost sight of the personal ambitions that bring these youth to our doors. We provide them with the contacts and information to help steer them on their way to career goals. We introduce them to other top Latino youth who also value education and aspire to compete at the top. There is no doubt that the NHI experience has fostered a new, nationwide network of bright, young, educated Latinos.

These networks have given them a better means of making contact and staying in touch with other talented Latinos. It's also given them a point of comparison to evaluate their individual life goals and plans.

However, the NHI experience does much more than help these young men and women with career goals. The manner in which NHI leadership programs are conducted also creates a chemist that compels them to make public direction for Latinos an important part of their thinking. Participation, in other words, is not only about evolving a new class of Latino professionals. The experience fosters an awareness of themselves as a group of interconnected, highly competent individuals who possess the credentials and know-how to eventually play key leadership roles in future Latino life as shapers of thought and new community visions.

Whether or not they succeed in injecting new thoughts, new possibilities, and new directions in the cultural, political, social, and economic makeup of a future U.S. Latino community remains to be seen. It depends on the amount of time they spend as participants and leaders in the various sectors that comprise tomorrow's Latino community. The attitudes and skills they take to the table will also be factors in their success of failure in causing change to occur. Dad taught me this lesson years ago when he asked me to assess what was in the back alley behind our house. All I could see was a broken down junk car, beer bottles, and overgrown weeds. Dad, on the other hand, saw opportunity.

Latino leaders of the future need to be equipped to make the same distinctions. Depending on the perceptions they bring to the community, they will see the "peor" (worst) of Latinos, or, as my Dad did, the opportunity they represent in building a stronger tomorrow.

As Latino youth go through the NHI experience, they will at least have a basis for making these normative decisions as potential leaders. Some – probably more than we care to admit – will turn away. But many will make the right choice. They will make Latino interest their highest and most important priority and abandon "minority status" as their ticket to the top and the way out of the community. Others will sit at decision-making tables where public and private policies are made. And generations of the future will be able to read about many more Latinos playing key roles in community affairs, not only in civil rights and politics, but also in medicine, engineering, science, and finance.

We also will see more U.S. Latinos reaching out to build relationships with their counterparts in other Latin American countries, making new business opportunities possible in a modern Latino reality capable of also influencing public policy on a larger scale. Those who believed that the social movement of Latinos might have died in the 1970s will only come to find out that it underwent transformation, evolving into a new and different reality.

Through the National Hispanic Institute, students will realize the unlimited opportunities that await them, especially for those willing to re-craft Latino identity into human assets. The promise will be there for those who spend time creating Latino culture as an interconnected, international community. And new horizons will emerge for young Latinos who make their own communities an integral part of their professional studies, day-to-day life experiences, and business ventures.

The role and mission of the National Hispanic Institute will continue being to cause new thinking to occur inside the Latino community. Anger, despair, and disappointment are no longer needed to address the past. My parent's beliefs about their work with youth in the barrios are appropriate to the Latinos of tomorrow. This belief embodies NHI today:

"*Un niño con vision, ánimo, y ambición, no lo detiene los obstáculos de la vida, ni la pobreza, ni la discriminación.* (A child with vision, drive, and ambition cannot be held back by obstacles in life, not even poverty, nor discrimination.)"

Chapter Fourteen: Responsibility for the New
1. Write a brief story about a time when you recognized that you had a choice between taking a safe path to achieve a well-understood result and taking the risk of moving in an unconventional, unknown direction where there were no established pathways.
    a. What choice did you make? Why?
    b. How did you discover the risks and rewards of playing it safe versus taking a risk?
    c. How did you clarify your goal?

    d. How did you establish a pathway?
    e. What challenges did you encounter?
    f. What did you do to deal with those challenges?
    g. What did you think?
    h. What did you feel?
2. Imagine that there will come a time when you will consider committing yourself to a difficult course of action that has no clear goals and you probably will not live long enough to see the end results.
    a. What do you think?
    b. How do you feel?
    c. What will you do?
3. Imagine that young Latinos chose to prepare themselves to undertake a life journey where they will have only a vague sense of the destination and there are no roadmaps to get there.
    a. How would you establish yourself as a credible person who was competent enough to help them?
    b. What would you do to help them to learn what they do not yet realize they will need?
    c. What would they be thinking? Feeling?
4. Consider: What specific knowledge, skills, and abilities do you think young Latinos will need in order to create, assess, and recreate their own compelling vision of a desirable future and to break a new trail across uncharted territory to make that vision a reality?

Chapter Fifteen
Freeing the Mind

For Latino youth to not have a rationale for involvement in their community means promoting nothing believable, not having a community role to play, or a pathway to follow. Addressing this need for Latinos in the United States is undoubtedly an important priority in education. High unemployment rates of Latinos, delinquency, crime, illiteracy, and racial discrimination are pressing issues that haven't gone away. They are not, however, as crucial as the need to craft a new vision and belief system to guide Latino community life into the twenty-first century. Currently, there is little that galvanizes Latino youth into a cohesive union with a common goal. They have few public figures to emulate.

This was not the case thirty-five years ago. Whether there is agreement or not with El Movimiento (The Chicano Movement), an attempt was made to provide Latinos with a community cause, something to believe in that went far beyond the rigors of daily living. In today's U.S. Latino world there are not pathways to follow that the Latino community has created for itself, something uniquely its own, a set of beliefs that draws people together towards a common goal.

In the 1960s and 1970s, Latinos went to college to eventually return and become part of the community. For many, being connected and involved was their public calling. One of their beliefs was that they were needed and, as more-educated Latinos, they had leadership roles to play in bringing about long overdue community solutions.

The beliefs of many modern-day Latino youth have changed over the years. Many enter college not necessarily to return to their communities to help, but mostly to land fast-track career jobs in corporate America or government. Before, the educated and the less-educated Latinos lived among each other. There wasn't a need to read about poverty and pain. Poverty was plain enough for everyone to see and feel. The more-educated Latinos today live in suburban, affluent neighborhoods where their contact with the other Latino reality comes only as close as the freeways that take them by the barrios where their parents once lived.

"Hey, Pop," I asked my father one day several years before he died, "how do you move an entire community from believing in one particular manner to believing in something totally different?"

"No sé mijo, (I don't know son,)" he said. *"La injusticia hace a la gente ver el mundo en cierta manera y basan sus vidas en lo que creen. Muchos, por falta de educación, no ven que la injusticia afecta sus pensamientos y creencias. De por si, hablo del obrero, no del educado. Para el obrero, digo el Mexicano y otros Latinos, el sufrimiento aquí en la tierra. Es lo que ven, es la promesa, son sus creencias.* (Injustice causes people to view the world in a certain way, and they base their lives on what they learn to believe. But many, for lack of education, don't see that injustice affects what they believe and how they carry out their lives. In this case, I speak of the common worker, not those who are educated. For the common worker, I mean Mexicans and other Latinos, suffering and injustice are accepted as a mandate from God, realizing that there is a better life in the beyond. That's the reward for their suffering here on earth. That's what they see, their promise, their beliefs.)"

Dad's response wasn't enough for me. He and Mom had changed the beliefs of literally thousands of Latinos who lived in Magnolia, where they ran recreation parks for the community. There had to be a way.

"Es possible cambiar unos cuantos individuos. Eso te lo consedo. ¿Pero comunidades enteras? Esa es otra pregunta mucho más difícil. Pero sí sé esto. Tiene que haber inspiración, algo que mueva el espíritu de la persona. Si ellos no pueden ver la vision, no lo aprecian, ni le dan valor, no hay razón para seguir nuevas veredas o aceptar nuevas creencias. Tú buscas otras soluciones, no por medio de los derechos civiles, trabajos, y esas cosas. Eso es de la vida diaria. Tú buscas como cambiar el

pensamiento de la persona, en lo que ve, cree, y interpreta. Eso es mucho más profundo y permanente. Para nosotros como Mexicanos, y posiblemente otros Latinos, eso es muy importante, si es que esperamos tener más éxito en la vida como comunidad. Eso es lo que me gusta de tu trabajo, tu mission. Pero tienes que comenzar con los jóvenes, no nosotros. Ya los viejos como yo vivimos nuestras vidas, bien o mal, pero la vivimos. Tus hijos y tus nietos todavía no. Empiézalos por otras veredas para que realicen otras creencias y lleguen a otras conclusiones como humanos. (It's possible to change a few individuals. I grant you that, but entire communities? That's another question that's much more difficult. But I do know this. There has to be inspiration, something that moves the soul of the person. If they are unable to see the vision, they will not appreciate it, and they will not value it. They are left with no reasons to pursue new directions in life or accept new beliefs. You're searching for different solutions, not through civil rights, jobs, and those things. That's daily life. You're looking for ways of changing the thinking of the person, in what they see and what they interpret. That's much more profound and permanent. For us as Mexicans, and possibly other Latinos, this is very important if we expect to have more success as a community. I'm glad this is your work, your mission. But this has to start with the youth, not us. We old people already lived life, good or bad, we've lived it. Your children and grandchildren haven't yet. Start them in different pathways, so that they realize different beliefs, and, in the final analysis, draw other conclusions as human beings.)"

"¿Te acuerdas allá en la Wallisville en el bar de tu primo, Eloy, allí en el barrio de Denver Harbor?" he reminded me again, one day towards the end of his life. *"Cuando este amigo señalaba una persona que tenía sicatrices en la cara, como si fuera malo? ¿Te acuerdas qué le dije? ¿Qué el malo no era el cortado, sino el que lo cortó? ¿Y también recuerdas esa misma noche cuando me dijeron cortó? ¿Y también recuerdas esa misma noche cuando me dijeron que yo me creía muy grandote y les dije que el problema de ellos era que se creían muy chiquitos? Todo eso, mijo, estaba basado en lo que la gente ve y cree, nada más. Estas historias no tienen chiste para el que no ve, ni entiende. Pero tú sí ves y entiendes. Aprende parte de tu trabajo. Ojalá que un día la gente que se ha beneficiado del instituto comprenda lo importante de tu obra. Si no hay cambio en lo que la gente cree, no es posible avanzar. Por mi parte, aquí estaré contigo, mijo, hasta que se me acabe la vida en este mundo.* (Do you remember over there on Wallisville at your cousin's beer joint in Denver Harbor, when this friend pointed to another person who had scars all over his face, as though he was a mean person? Remember what I said, that the mean person was not the one with the scars, but the one who put them there? And do you also remember when I was told that I saw myself as being too big of a man in life, and I responded by telling them that they saw themselves as being little people in life? All of this, son, is based on what people see and believe, nothing else. These stories aren't important for those who can't see or understand. But you see and you understand. Learn well and make these life lessons a part of your work. Maybe one of these days, the people who benefit from the institute also will realize the importance of your life's mission. If there is no change in people's views and beliefs, advancement is not possible. As for me, I'll be here by your side, son, until life runs out on me in this world.)"

After all these years, Dad and Mom had helped me better understand our role and purpose as an organization. Here were two individuals, both with the bare minimum in education, no Ph. D.s, no real formal education. Yet both had a profound understanding for the work involved and the directions that had to be taken.

These discussions eventually lead to changes in our perceptions and views at the National Hispanic Institute. Before, the thrill was knowing that an NHI graduating senior had been admitted to Harvard, Stanford, M.I.T., Southwestern, or some other institution of similar standing. There was also a sense of special accomplishment that came from knowing that and NHI alumnus had landed a job with a bank, a large corporation or was living in a large metropolitan community like New York City, San Francisco, or Boston.

Today, we want to know if our former students are active in Latino community life, if they belong to Latino organizations, and if they're making themselves accessible as leaders and spokespersons. No longer do we have the expectation that Latino youth first reach success in the larger culture of the business and out to the less fortunate. In our view, the Latino community can no longer be the charity work of our alumni, their week of giving.

We also can't afford the luxury of waiting for them to grow up and mature before becoming active members in Latino community life. The new calling is to involve young Latinos now, while in junior high, high school, and college, not later or in the distant future.

The new standard at the National Hispanic Institute makes participation in the affairs of the Latino community life an everyday experience, not an occasional interest reserved for special moments, years later in their adult lives. Our leaders of tomorrow are being given a national challenge to begin now in preparation for a higher community calling in the immediate future.

When first starting the National Hispanic Institute, Gloria and I accepted the understanding that leadership training for us would be a lifetime undertaking that would require an enormous investment of time and thought to eventually see results. The first few years were spent carefully examining and analyzing each step that had to be taken along the way. The living and dining room walls in our home were often littered with pages of notes on programs under construction or thoughts we wanted to visually track during our discussions. These notes often included critiques of our own beliefs and mission, a daily confrontation with our values.

Had someone carefully tracked these talks that eventually led to the creation of NHI initiatives like the Young Leaders Conference in 1981, the Lorenzo de Zavala Youth Legislative Session in 1983, the Collegiate World Series in 1990, the Collegiate Leadership Network in 1993, or the National Community Leadership Council in 1994, the journey of changes that took place in our beliefs and thinking could be easily traced.

We didn't start NHI because leadership training was a popular theme or would give us community visibility. Our intent was to shape an organization with authenticity and substance that could satisfy the immediate needs of youth being invited to participate while also introducing them to new and motivating possibilities in a changing Latino world.

More than two decades later, the National Hispanic Institute no longer looks only at the academic credentials of talented young men and women the way we once did. NHI now searches for youth who genuinely want to have a leadership role in Latino community life. We look for critical thinkers, young people who accept the energy-draining tasks of thinking and rethinking different answers and solutions to tough and complex human challenges.

Our search is for a special caliber of Latino youth who want to make that Latino community an integral part of their daily lives. We seek individuals who are eager about becoming conversant with the events and moments that shaped its thinking and beliefs in order to understand the work and visions that drove the leadership of the past.

NHI, in other words, isn't needed as the channel through which Latino youth can enter mainstream society in larger numbers. Enough institutions from the dominant host culture already exist at the private and public levels to dutifully make social and economic mobility in the larger host society at least a plausible reality. The institute also is not needed to broaden our nation's opportunity structure through advocacy and reform, so that more room can be made for America's "minorities" and other special interest groups. The price of change is too slow and too narrow in scope to impact the masses of Latinos who invariably get left out.

And, while moving toward a multicultural society appears to be the best alternative to advance the interests of Latinos, it represents, at most, a mythical probability. One with little chance of evolving under the force of dominating influences that see a growing Latino community not as a valued partner for the future, but a threat to the power they currently control.

The challenge facing the National Hispanic Institute is to give rise to a community belief system capable of leading Latino youth in a different direction, one compelling enough to attract them to develop a sense of exploration. The challenge must motivate them enough for them to work toward constructing strategies that will advance the cultural, economic, and social interests of the U.S. Latino community without having to abandon their basic belief in democracy and the American free enterprise system.

They must be helped to find alternative ways of channeling their skills and capacities to participate and contribute to U.S. society without having to surrender their cultural identities, language, or relationships with the larger Latino world. And, their minds have to be freed to explore the uncharted, to recognize the implications of an exploding twenty-first century Latino world, and to identify the strategic roles they must learn to play as future leaders.

Constructing a third reality used to stump my father the most when sitting in the backyard of his Houston home, sipping coffee, peering into the future. Those early thoughts remain part of NHI thinking today. What moves young people to want to make major changes in the way they live life, in their interactions with others, and in their views can come only from a vision that compels them to act. According to my father, this was the way to work with future Latino leaders. They first need to recognize the advantages of having ownership over what happens to them and eventually their own children.

My friend Sam Moreno again played a role in helping to unfold a better understanding of NHI's work. It started with one of our many discussions on Latinos in Dallas back in 1973. I was working with the federal government and lived close to Sam's home. Once in a while during the week or on Saturday afternoons, we'd get together on issues in the Latino community, at times arguing for hours over differences in our views. This time around, however, the subject shifted to religion.

As a young, thirty-year-old man with a growing family, my curiosity dealt with the amount of time spent by the church on sin, forgiveness, and especially the need to declare our human frailties and shortcomings in front of everyone else to hear. I shared several episodes as a boy attending El Mesías Methodist Church in Houston when the minister would issue a challenge for members of the congregation to publicly kneel before the altar and ask God for forgiveness.

"As a young, seven-year-old, I hated this part of the service," I explained to my friend. "I'd turn to Mom hoping for some clue about what to do. Her look, her cold stare, said everything. To a mom who grew up in the church as a child under two Methodist missionaries and a highly strict grandmother, it was 'her way or the highway.' Up from the seat I'd go, walking sheepishly to the front to make my amends with the Man upstairs.

"Why?" I used to ask Sam. "Why was this Sunday ritual so darn important? And why in front of everyone to see? I hated it. It was an eerie, intimidating feeling that made me wants to run and hide."

Sam found my questions humorous. "You don't understand, Nieto," he would say laughingly. "You really don't understand, do you?"

"Look," he explained in a more serious and instructive tone, staring directly into my eyes. "Can you imagine what it took to convert Mexican Catholics to become Mexican Protestants? Somewhere back in time maybe not through your mother or father, or maybe not through your grandparents or even farther back. But someone in your family was probably Catholic or even 'indios' (Indian). To get people to abandon their religion, their way of dealing with their spiritual needs, is a pretty big step. Maybe one of the more important things people ever did back then with their lives was going from being Catholic to becoming a Protestant. And then, it took at least the same intensity, if not more, to keep them from going back once they changed faiths. Conversion goes to the very roots of the person's essence, the person's identity, and existence. It's everything one believes in, especially when it comes to life here on earth and the hereafter."

"Can't you see it? *¿No entiendes?* (You don't understand?)" he continued. "The whole Methodist movement back then for Mexicans was evangelical. Conversion became institutionalized into the everyday practices of the Mexican American Methodist Church. "Shouting from the pulpits, constantly demanding that the congregation members affirm their faith, requesting that they declare their sins in public, these practices became part of the ritual, the way people were kept tied to the new faith. And while this may have been needed for recent converts, it was no longer applicable to a fourth generation Methodist like you. But again, this is what religious conversion is all about."

From that initial discussion, Sam and I spent many more hours together, captured in a long and extensive exchange of views. We no longer, however, stayed on religion. Instead we started analyzing how conversion worked culturally in the Latino community. Was it possible that Latinos were being converted culturally, similar to the way in which earlier members in my family were once moved from being Catholics to becoming Protestants? Was the term cultural conversion more descriptive of the process rather than acculturation or assimilation?

Both of us agreed that the term conversion was the more appropriate of the three options. Conversion, not assimilation or acculturation, was the final destination, the ultimate aim. Integration, acculturation, and assimilation, all the popular terminology of the day, were merely channels that eventually led Latinos to conversion. Conversion was designed to be permanent in their lives. It was the goal of our public school systems and institutions of higher education in the name of democracy and freedom.

We also agreed that conversion for Latino youth had other underlying implications. It meant a conscious and unconscious devaluing of their former selves. In essence, a "disconnect" from their past to adopt new thinking. It connoted the giving up of language, food, music, former relations, and lifestyles as part of the ritual, the process to evolve their new identities. Young people were daily getting caught in this human web of change and challenged to make the commitment, at whatever the costs, to craft their new identities in accordance with stipulations of another world.

These exchanges with Sam and also my parents gave us much to examine in the work ahead for NHI. The evidence of a changing Latino youth community clarified what we were seeing before our very eyes, especially for socially mobile, academically adept, college-bound young men and women, eager to carve out a promising and secure future for themselves. It didn't take too much more to understand the reasons why a growing number of Latino youth were growing up no longer speaking Spanish, why so many of them know so little about Latino history in the United States and other Latin American countries.

These youngsters were not merely assimilating or acculturating. They were undergoing wholesale conversion, similar to the religious experience Sam had described earlier. Their belief systems and outlooks were undergoing enormous and permanent changes. In the process, the prospects of making participation in Latino community life an important priority were becoming less of a reality, no longer an important life goal.

Being Latino was no longer an identity to be proud of from an ethnic and cultural point of view. It was now a strategy, a social means to an end, a special rite of passage into mainstream, the way to get a foot in the doorway. More disturbing was that these young men and women were not "rank and file Latinos." They didn't come from the working class, blue-collar sectors of Latino life. They were the better educated, more socially acceptable, and better equipped to participate and fit into mainstream culture. NHI's challenge was to find ways of attracting their interest. The goal was to make a case sufficiently compelling for them to become involved in advancing Latino community life by recognizing the advantages of a growing Latino consumer market.

If Dad were still around, I'd still want him to answer the same question: "Hey, Pop! How do you change entire communities?" I would ask again. After thinking for a moment, his response would probably be different this time.

"Dales oportunidades para que ellos tengan éxito entre la comunidad Latina," he would say. *"Y también reconoce sus esfuerzos y capacidades. Pero no trates de cambiar quiénes son. Dales maneras en que ellos puedan recibir reconocimiento dentro del pueblo de ellos, por medio de sus amigos y familiares. El cambio, eso tiene que venir de ellos mismos. Tú tienes que tener fé que ellos quieran y deseen mejores vidas. Por medio de pláticas, hallarán sus veredas. Pero hazlo con respeto y mucho cariño.* (Give them opportunities to succeed in the Latino community. And also, recognize their efforts and capacities. But don't try to change who they are. Give them ways of receiving recognition from within the Latino community, through their friends and their families. Change has to come from inside of them. You have to have faith in them, for them to want better lives for themselves. Through discussions, they will find their way. But do it with respect and a lot of love.)"

Both Gloria and I readily admit that we've gained the most from NHI for more than two decades, and we'll continue to learn as we journey on into the future. Early on, we dismissed the notion of becoming politically involved and of having other personal motives for our work. We stopped considering ourselves as being liberals or conservatives, Democrats, Republicans, or members of another party. Changing or reforming the system were also dropped as being important goals in our lives. Our search instead became one of defining something much larger to capture the imagination of young people and move them to heights beyond the mere need for personal gain, careers, and material rewards.

My parents were right the entire time. Their work of forty years before in Houston, Magnolia, the Fifth Ward, Denver Harbor, and Northside wasn't to prove anything to anyone outside of the communities they served. Their search was for meaning inside the community, inside the minds of the people who lived there. A little more light was beginning to appear for us. The journey had taken a long time. Now, however, it was starting to make sense. Change is difficult, almost impossible, when trying to convert people into something they're not. NHI spent years in the role of gatekeeper for Latino youth who were attempting to make the jump from one culture to another. This time it was better for us to step in and participate inside the Latino community, instead of standing outside, pointing elsewhere for our young to follow.

Today, there is a certain comfort level at the institute regarding our developing beliefs and new directions. While some Latino parents may continue encouraging assimilation as a social strategy for their children to achieve their individual economic and social dreams, pursing this option has stopped being part of NHI thinking. Supporting the goals of El Movimiento as a concept and model to train future leaders is also out. The Raza Unida movement was no doubt a crucial life-defining experience for Latinos throughout the nation at one time. Today, it's more urgent that this model of advocacy and reform be transformed from the politics of dissent and reformation of the 1960s into an experience that results in community rediscovery and reinvestment.

What is needed with this legacy of rediscovery and reinvestment is to define a more modern and motivating strategy for a twenty-first century Latino community which will ultimately rest in the hands of Latino leaders who are currently being shaped and those yet to come.

The realization of this challenge will also become more apparent as Latinos change the demographics of the United States and as the rest of Latin America becomes increasingly important to our nation's future. Latino leaders of the future will quickly conclude that Latinos are not just the 32 million who live in the United States, but also include the 565 million who reside in twenty-four Spanish-speaking countries, and are within easy reach of one another.

At NHI, the challenge of molding new pathways for future Latinos is beginning to unfold. The new, emerging Latino mainstream on this side of the planet is becoming ever present; an explosion is occurring before our very eyes. Cities and schools, once places where Latinos comprised a distinct minority population, are new essentially brown, no longer white or black. Technology is also tying Latinos together into one huge village of people who enjoy a shared language and history. But caution must also be observed to prevent the same problems from occurring in the twenty-first century world that characterized the past one hundred years. This time one culture cannot hold another hostage.

For younger, more educated future Latino leaders on the rise, much more training is needed to prepare them for leadership roles not only in their own communities, but also for the world stage of Latinos. In their haste to acquire the conveniences and comforts of modern, contemporary life, they must avoid ending up being transformed beyond cultural recovery. New strategies are needed to help them acquire similar career comforts and purchasing power to buy better cars and live in larger, prettier homes. NHI has never been against the four-letter word known as "rich." Pursuit of the good life, on the other hand, shouldn't result in isolation from Latino community life through loss of cultural identity, cultural cohesion, and language, all of which make them unable to move about, interact, and participate within a collective whole that is beginning to comprise a new Latino reality of tomorrow.

Several years ago, my son, Chris, and I were in Monterrey, Mexico, to help my daughter Nicole move her belongings to an apartment located not too far from a university she planned to attend, El Instituto Tecnológico de Estudios Superiores de Monterrey. Nicole was there to complete the final requirements for a dual M.B.A. after having completed similar work at The University of Texas in Austin. While parked outside a McDonald's, waiting for my daughter's friend, Maru, to bring us the apartment keys, I asked Chris to go inside and buy us a couple of hamburgers. He paused for a second or two, turned, and said, "Dad, you know I can't speak Spanish. How do you expect me to talk to them or know how to order food?"

His response was strikingly similar to barriers being faced by most top Latino youth in the United States today. They go beyond language. In his response, Chris was revealing much more than his inability to communicate; his concerns also described his outlooks, sentiments, attitudes, and perspectives. As a young person with leadership potential in the Latino community, he was already starting out with more strikes against him than advantages.

This incident is mentioned only to raise the question of responsibility, not to criticize my son. Whose responsibility is it to ensure that Latino youth receive the proper training and instruction to be the type of leaders needed in the Latino community of tomorrow? Is this the role of our public schools and universities?

Currently, neither the public school system nor our colleges and universities recognize this need as pertinent to who they are or their mission. Nor should Latinos expect these institutions to change in the near future, even if the majority of policy makers, administrators, and teachers are all Latinos.

America's educational system continues to be guided by one set of views, principles, and beliefs that date back years and generations. As Latinos, we all know what those are and what drumbeat everyone is expected to follow, irrespective of our culture, language needs, mental and emotional anguish caused to ourselves and our children, or the views and beliefs we are forced to adopt as a community.

The question, however, no longer centers on whether or not we should continue fighting the system to be more responsive to our needs. The more appropriate question is to determine whether or not the channels provided by our nation's educational system represent the only choice for the Latino community to educate and train its leaders of tomorrow to accomplish its own agenda and serve its future needs. The answer to that question is clearly no. Our nation's current education and training system is not the only choice.

My father used to remind me of the reason that DeZavala Park was built in the Houston Latino community in 1951. "No era porque querían a los Mexicanos; era porque no los querían. (It wasn't because they liked Mexicans; it was because they didn't like them.)" In those days, there weren't many parks in the Latino community at all. Most were located in more affluent, middle-class Anglo communities where the Latino youth population started going and causing "trouble."

Building DeZavala Park was a way of keeping Latino youth within their own community. Today we see similar practices in the creation of alternative schools, charter schools, school voucher programs, magnet programs, and high school graduation plans. College and universities often practice the same by using college entrance examinations and talent search programs as ways of finding the few Latinos who are college eligible while signaling the majority of others to find other ways of preparing for the future.

I can almost hear my father reminding me with that smirk on his face, *"No es porque quieren a los Mexicanos mijo. ¡Acuérdate! Es porque no los quieren, nomás a los pocos mejorcitos. Lo que ellos hacen para nosotros solamente es para la conveniencia de ellos, no para nosotros. Ya es tiempo que hagamos para el bienestar de nuestra comunidad para adquirir nuestras metas y así compartir con otros.* (It's not because they like Mexicans, son. Remember that! It's because they don't like them, only the few, the better ones. What's being done is for the convenience of others, not us. It's time that we work toward our own well-being as a community today so that we can reach our goals and share with others.)"

This view is used neither to cause further displeasure nor alienation from our nation's educational system. As Darrell Royal, legendary football coach at The University of Texas, once responded to public concern over a faltering offensive system, "We're not going to change dance partners in the middle of the ballgame. Instead we're going to continue dancing with who we brung." The same reality holds true for Latinos. We should neither abandon the present system nor attempt to sabotage its direction. In the same respect, we should also not believe that major changes are just around the corner.

As a community we have the capacity to create different pathways that add much needed value in training future Latino leaders. First, however, Latino youth need the encouragement and support that make studying possible in other Latino countries, so that they can acquire a familiarity with the people and their thinking. They need to conduct independent research to acquaint them with growing business and economic opportunities in the larger Latino marketplace. They need to participate in transnational youth think tanks to build friendships with their counterparts from other Latin American countries.

Other ideas include the creation of private language and cultural academic think tanks throughout the United States to give Latino children a different and much more exciting view of Latino life. Thought also has been given to raising consumer awareness among Latinos to circulate their hard earned dollars in the Latino marketplace rather than buying from businesses who give back little in return to the Latino community.

Crafting a set of beliefs to guide the training of future Latino leaders started with the first class of students in Austin in 1981. The mission continues with the understanding that nothing is set in stone, at least not yet. Each year, new ideas and concepts are discussed, always with the intent of arriving at a more precise purpose and direction. Knowledge is gained from taking risks and making mistakes, never allowing the journey to lose site of its mission.

At the National Hispanic Institute, no one has preconceived ideas about which fork in the road to take whenever confronted with difficult challenges. Neither do formulas exist that spell success, nor are there guidelines for each decision that has to be made along the way. Instead, faith provides the courage to create solutions as obstacles appear. This spirit of adventure and a dauntless belief in the Latino community have been the ingredients for the majority of NHI's successes, both past and present.

In the early 1980s, there were two NHI programs that conducted leadership training for less than 300 high school students a year. Today, more than twenty years later, new opportunities have taken NHI nationwide, into Mexico, and, more recently, Puerto Rico. More than 3,500 participate in formal NHI programs. In fact, the institute grew at a much faster pace after deciding to no longer look to government, corporations, or foundations for help – instead looking to other Latinos for guidance, ideas, and support.

Pursuing a direction that relied mainly on the Latino community forced Gloria and me to let go of former beliefs in order to see another kind of Latino world and future. It was our time to get "out of the box" and change the paradigm confining the ways in which we had learned to see and interpret who we were as a community.

Re-crafting our beliefs and views was anything but easy. It became a personally painful and draining experience, similar to a divorce that demands letting go of the old in order to start out fresh again. Being Latino in the United States in a white world over the past 100 years had been abusive and unchanging, much like the battered spouse who goes to court for having been beaten time and time again. The social sores had long been obvious, plain for everyone to notice. They spanned generations, dating back to the previous century, even before. No promises of reform could ever undo the harm inflicted on our community. The injuries were permanent, woven into our collective memory as Latinos.

It wouldn't be easy to forget a César Chávez who only wanted fifty cents an hour more for the sun-scorching labor of migrant farmworkers. It would also be difficult to overlook a Corky Gonzáles in Denver, Colorado, who worked tirelessly for decent housing and opportunities for Latino youth to get a better education. The same could be said for a Reyes López Tijerina in New Mexico, who reacted to the government's reign of supreme power over people's property right to feed their herds without due process. In Texas, we could never dismiss a José Angel Gutierrez whose struggle was for Latinos to enjoy the right to vote without being scared away from the polls by control-conscious, uncaring local officials.

For standing up for the Latino community, for demanding inclusion in the American Dream, for wanting the same basic protections and opportunities of citizenship that others enjoyed, these former leaders were called radicals, un-American, separatists, and racists.

Almost forty years later, history is repeating itself in front of our eyes as the English-only movement gains momentum; as crime, drug abuse, and violence run rampant in Latino inner-city communities; as divorce rates and single head-of-household families increase to unprecedented levels; and as dropout and low educational attainment by Latino youth remain alarmingly high. Poverty for Latinos is no longer temporary. It's become part of a growing underclass where opportunity no longer makes a difference.

More Latino youth than ever are relegated each day to human warehouses, separated out, permanently sealed off from society, left to their own coping skills to survive, so long as they are not threats to others. Containment is the new social buzzword for intervention. However viewed, mainstreaming people has been little more than a pathway to success mainly for those entitled by their birthrights.

No matter the promise of institutions, government, or corporations, the rank-and-file Latinos on the street realize that the promise of new opportunities is not all embracing, at least not for them. Hard as these realities are to accept for anyone with a conscience, they can no longer represent the main challenge of the future.

This time around, the goal has to be shaping a different leader with a different thinking, a different set of values, and different beliefs and outlooks. The new, emerging Latino leadership has to be much larger in numbers, better educated and trained, and more capable of constructing answers to complex human problems.

Distinct from their predecessors, their mission must no longer be to arouse anger or point fingers at conditions, either past or present. Their public calling has to be altogether different.

Today, one of NHI's most urgent needs is the construction of a rationale for civic, social, and economic advancement that exhorts Latino youth to recognize and appreciate the advantages of building equity in the Latino community, to invest their intellectual resources towards its development.

Another NHI imperative is to broaden the institute's capacity to train more Latino leaders through different community venues conducted in partnership with Latino-owned businesses, political, civic, and cultural organizations, and the religious sectors of the community. NHI also has to expand its work beyond the borders of the United States to provide its youth with direct ties to peers in other Latino countries, so that they can begin developing a global perspective.

NHI's most challenging task, however, remains in re-crafting a Latino community view that stands on its own feet without outside assistance, and as a result, is in a stronger position to contribute to the overall quality of American life. This mission can be realized, however, only as new-age Latino leaders are trained and equipped with the abilities to imagine the new and the confidence to shape an emerging Latino identity.

Something has to be done to make the American Dream an invigorating force in the lives of Latino youth. The version of the new dream, however, cannot be the same one promulgated during the past century, the view that anyone can make it if they pick themselves up by the bootstraps. The American Dream for Latinos has to be based on a vision that's reachable and motivating for them, in which they are the principal players, and accept important and visible leadership roles in the process. It has to be crafted in keeping with Latino family values, traditions, and customs. It must also be porous enough for innovation and creativity to surface and allow beliefs and views that are no longer useful to be cast aside. It must be attractive and captivating to cause new heights in personal and community achievement to be reached while healing the scars of past eras.

Most of all, the Latino American Dream must be based on a belief system that places no limits on how high, far, or wide Latinos can go in pursuing their dreams. They need only the quiet confidence of knowing that they possess the intellectual capacities, values of culture, and dedication to find new ways of taking the Latino community to a higher playing field while also making their own unique contributions as Americans to the rest of society.

As time has passed since the founding of the National Hispanic Institute, Gloria and I continue talking to each other, as we have for so long, discussing NHI and comparing, remembering what our parents taught us. Her father and mother are no longer with us. My father died in 1993 at almost ninety years of age. All three of them would be proud that we never abandoned our roots, never failed to respect our family and community.

As young people, we might have run away for a moment, the two of us searching for our own truths and beliefs. Both of us, however, always came back to the comforts of a culture that's understanding, embracing, and supportive. Enough thanks can never be expressed to the thousands of parents, young people, and other friends who have allowed us to share a moment in their lives, for giving us the opportunity to see tomorrow through their eyes. Throughout this journey, however, neither Gloria nor I can overlook the roles our parents played in shaping our lives.

Juan de León, Gloria's father, would still refer to her as "la coyote," for being the youngest of five sisters. Herlinda, Gloria's mother, would continue being proud of her "consentida" (the one who favors you most), sleeping in the same bed with her daughter, talking endless hours into the night in her "casita" (little house) on Erie Street in South McAllen.

And Dad would look at me with his penetrating stare and endless questions to ask, remembering Mom's constant admonition when as their child she would say, "Déjalo, Santos. Un día de estos vas a ver, vas a ver. (Leave him alone, Santos. One of these days, you'll see, you'll see.)"

Chapter Fifteen: Freeing the Mind
1. How do you define a successful life?
   a. What would it look like if you were living a successful life?
   b. How would you feel if you were living a successful life?
2. Where do you believe you are most likely to be successful?
   a. Within the Latino community? Explain.
   b. In mainstream society and its institutions? Explain.
   c. Moving back and forth between the Latino community and mainstream society? Explain.
3. In what ways do you believe Latino communities should change?
   a. How might Latino communities transform themselves?
   b. What should Latino communities let go?
   c. What should Latino communities preserve?
   d. What should Latino communities add on?
4. Briefly describe a time when you were confronted by obstacles that denied you access to what you wanted.
   a. How did you make sense out of these obstacles?
   b. What did you feel?
   c. What did you do to successfully overcome these barriers to entry?
   d. What did you do that was unsuccessful?
   e. What did you learn about yourself?

Epilogue

It's unimaginable to me that more than twenty years have passed since the founding of the National Hispanic Institute. I was thirty-nine years old in 1979, eager to completely turn myself over to the Latino community. I wanted a more cultural life. I no longer could withstand the drudgery of following the same old tired, dull, and anonymous schedule of working eight to five, going home, watching television, piddling around, sleeping, waking up, and going back to work. The world for me had been reduced to only serving my material needs. It no longer meant having purpose and direction. It became an insulated existence where knowing the neighbors next door was not important, much less sharing anything in common with them. Something had to give.

Dramatic changes took hold of my life. A failing marriage came to an end. A fifteen-year career in government dissolved. In a relatively short period of time, I went from being an executive to unemployment. In one sweeping motion I was fired, asked to remove my personal belongings from my desk in a matter of minutes. Suddenly, there was no money, no means to pay bills, to provide child support, or to have a roof over my head.

Difficult as these circumstances were at the time, my decision was to get out altogether and do something totally different. I was no longer willing to perform the same menial tasks. The most painful price of change was no longer being with my children on a daily basis. I had always been there for them.

The National Hispanic Institute was officially born on July 20, 1979. This was nothing magical. We received notice from the Texas Secretary of State's Office. The friends that helped put the organization together were excited about having an official identity.

More than two decades later, an idea that started out as a casual conversation at a well-known Austin beer garden became an organization known for its work with thousands of top Latino youth from high schools and colleges across the nation.

These are young men and women who today enroll in college and universities at a ninety-eight percent rate. They receive their undergraduate degrees in four to five years and bring a new and potentially invigorating vision of leadership to an evolving twenty-first century Latino community.

Despite its success, the National Hispanic Institute is not without its stories of despair and setbacks. There are a number of accounts of individuals who will long be remembered for their contributions. The story is collages of countless youths and adults who believed in a vision and were willing to risk venturing into uncharted waters to derive new meaning from becoming involved.

This push for a new direction continues today with increasing recognitions for the good that can be achieved. There is a quiet, almost invisible urge among Latin youth who participate with NHI to connect to something bigger, more refreshing, more invigorating. The urge comes at a time that finds Latinos exploding as a population and recognizing a connection to a world community comprised of over half a billion in twenty-four Spanish-speaking countries.

The need exists to critically examine the truths and beliefs that have led Latinos to this point in their development in the United Sates. They must look back at the history and the environment that shaped and influenced their thinking. What has caused them to pursue particular pathways in their attempts to overcome personal obstacles and achieve important community goals? The assessment also should include looking at what Latinos must take with them into the future, what they want their children to have as part of their legacy, and what caliber of leadership training they need to not only survive in the new millennium, but also to thrive.

This account documents a process of transformation that involves two distinct, but integrally tied, entities. One story is about NHI the organization and its evolving public mission. The other is about Gloria and me, the principal organizers from the start.

The tale of NHI is like the experiences of Latino organizations and their leaders throughout the United States. Leadership comes from doing, from having daily interactions with the people being served, and addressing issues and obstacles along the way. Experiences are evaluated, thoughts are questioned, different alternatives are proposed, and adjustments are made to better manage the process.

The people who head these organizations learn and transform. They soon find out that life is never static. It is dynamic, constantly taking different directions. These experiences are highlights in this book. It reveals the insides of a national Latino organization that has completed an important milestone in its journey. It describes special moments and events that shaped the thinking of its leaders and caused them to change at different times and at different intervals in the organization's evolution. The story mentions encounters that forced self-initiated confrontations with old ideas and concepts in order to adopt new ones - new beliefs, new truths - that today give authenticity, purpose, and direction to the Institute.

In the 1980s, NHI might have seen the Latino community as a segment of American population that lagged behind other groups. That is not so today. The prevailing view is that Latinos have fared well despite the impositions of racial discrimination and a history of exclusion from opportunity. NHI views Latinos as an enduring people who have a strong work ethic and a remarkable allegiance to their responsibilities as American citizens, a collection of individuals with talent and skill, deep in religious beliefs and an unyielding commitment to family. These changes in perception have brought the Institute to abandon the view of Latino as "minorities" or "people of color" who should unite with other so-called oppressed classes in a continuing quest for human justice. A new recognition has emerged in NHI thinking.

Latinos are undeniably American. They are also historically tied to a larger global culture that spans two continents and numerous countries. Another important realization also has emerged. Human and social justice is still considered important, but not the top priority in the new century. For NHI, equity and wealth-guiding in the Latino community are the most important endeavors that it must shoulder.

These views are neither accidental nor planned. Ten years ago, there was little to distinguish the work of that National Hispanic Institute from that of other contemporary Latino organizations. Back then, NHI's mission was to widen the base of opportunity for Latino youth to access higher education in their professional and career development. Leadership training for young upstarts was designed to help them cope with the workplace, strengthening their chances for better jobs and higher incomes.

NHI saw its principal duty as breaking down barriers standing in the way of Latino progress. The goal was to increase significantly the number of Latinos in decision-making positions across all levels of employment. Leadership meant upward mobility into the larger system. A key Institute role was to guide these young men and women to recognize the relationship between having solid academic credentials and attaining economic and social success in the workplace. The goal was for them to understand leadership from the standpoint of climbing to the top. Once there, they were supposed to help those who were less fortunate.

The Institute's work was clear: identify the most qualified Latino youth in the nation and steer them towards the best colleges and universities. Once there, the next step was placement in the professional marketplace. Only scant consideration was given to their civic roles and duties as leaders in the community.

Years passed before the Institute's thinking and leadership programs came under scrutiny. An upstart organization attempting to survive financially had little time to spend on an in-depth, self-review of direction, philosophy, and work. It was soon apparent that its work in the 1980s varied little from the majority of Latino thinking. Audiences might have varied somewhat. Styles might have also been different. The training and the outcomes were similar, no matter how much NHI might have wanted to perceive itself as offering the Latino community something refreshingly new.

In the end, the Institute was nothing more than a reformist-oriented organization born out of the civil rights era. It saw its primary role as exhorting Latinos to make the crossover into the American mainstream with as much ease as possible. The goal was for them to gain access in greater frequency and larger numbers. NHI's job was to champion this cause. There was little reason offered to look at life from any other perspective.

Change for the National Hispanic Institute was difficult and challenging. At times the experience of change became painful, especially for those who held themselves accountable for the beliefs driving their life's work. Questioning of the beliefs that guided NHI started in 1992. The transformation that took place was crucial in the life of NHI. It became the price of growth, a test of the Institute's very core.

Before, it was exhilarating whenever NHI leadership participants wrote announcing their official acceptance to highly regarded institutions like Harvard, Rice, or Stanford. There were similar moments whenever their letters described certain events in their leadership experience with the Institute that motivated them to excel in school and seek admission to name brand colleges. Rarely was there an occasion to evaluate whether their experiences with NHI had any bearing on eventually improving the quality of life for Latinos.

All that mattered was that these young people were preparing themselves to enjoy better and more secure incomes, more expensive homes, better cars, and greater career opportunities, whether or not they, in turn, valued participating in Latino life as integral to their personal growth. This realization became especially problematic knowing that NHI was the culprit in saying one thing without ever considering the consequences. NHI wished success for these young people, but was unable to translate their accomplishments in the context of a Latino vision. The only measurements that mattered were material gain, career mobility, social status, and economic success.

It took years to reshape these views, to retool the use of the word "success" when applied to involvement in community life. Eventually, success no longer became interchangeable with the social or career accomplishment of former students. They started hearing questions challenging them to explain the value of their college majors in terms of the quality of life for the community. What impact did they intend to have on the lives of others? What did they intend their legacy to be as a result of their chosen professions? What vision did they have for the community that was compelling enough to pursue particular studies or life directions? What was their leadership agenda in the Latino community?

Today, the premise of the National Hispanic Institute is different from years past. The concept of community equity-building has become the goal and cornerstone of Institute leadership training programs. This approach is altogether different from the training that before centered primarily on civil rights, reform, or breaking into the system. Increasing participation by Latinos in public policy is no longer considered paramount in addressing community concerns.

Conducting training that heightens public awareness towards Latino community issues has ceased to be the practice. And, influencing future leaders to look to government or corporate America as resources for community intervention and change is no longer part of the curriculum.

In addition, conventional American education is criticized. Today, NHI views institutions of higher learning as no longer the sole sources of educating future Latino leaders, especially for those who choose to live and participate mainly in a Latino playing field. New skills and expertise are being required of the merging leadership in response to a burgeoning Latino population whose unique needs have little to do with mainstream America.

In its evolution, NHI has learned to look inside the Latino community for answers. The success of this shift has given special confidence to the Institute in its understanding of the Latino community. It has also meant encouraging Latino youth to seek new and larger roles for themselves as valued community members. The pace in which these changes in behaviors and perceptions occur may remain unanswered in the immediate years ahead. Exhorting tomorrow's leaders to develop an owner's mentality as individuals with community purpose, rather than society's minorities, is NHI's most important work and goal.

The experiences that shaped Latino development in the twentieth century no longer serve as the basis to pursue different solutions in the twenty-first century. Civil rights and advocacy leadership are being replaced by a thinking of self-direction that fosters equity and wealth among Latinos in economics, culture, language, and human purpose. Rather than remaining separated by customs and nationality, NHI leadership training encourages youth to redefine themselves as part of a global culture. A new sense of optimism and positive public direction is replacing the age-old expectation of despair and tragic outcome that has permeated Latino life over the past one hundred years.

As the twenty-first century unfolds, NHI takes the position that Latino advancement can no longer hinge on asking the larger dominant society to become more inclusive. Change is seen as coming only as Latino reinvent themselves as a people, as they alter their views of who they are as a community and how they relate to each other as individuals, groups, and nationalities.

An important first step is to let go of old attitudes and truths in order to embrace new beliefs. Crafting these beliefs is a challenging task, perhaps harder than letting go of the old ones.

Achieving these ends has not been easy or without a price to pay. Old habits and old views are hard to replace. Latino youth are being asked to abandon the "bottom up view" as the way of attaining the good life. They are being influenced to let go of the social yokes and labels that have long defined their roles in American society. Permitting themselves to continue being seen as minorities, persons of color, or as Third World citizens is dangerous and destructive in their search for a healthier and more productive identity.

NHI assumes the view that Latinos who expect to be full participants in the American Dream can no longer believe in the American promise as it has been defined for them over the last century. Youths realize that Latinos cannot succeed in environments that limit them to background roles. They cannot succeed so long as they see themselves as being a drain on the resources of others, or as a potential threat to the well-being and stability of the dominant culture. They are challenged to consider the prospects for failure of a community unable to grow and move forward. They discuss the difficulties that Latinos encounter when driven to believe that it is they who are at fault for failing to participate more fully in the American experience rather than the imposition of social, institutional, and legal barriers over the years.

And they are asked to think about the reasons Latinos find it difficult to hasten their advancement when the vast majority of their time is spent defending themselves or attempting to change society rather than building their capacities to contribute as bone fide American citizens.

NHI contends that the new century offers Latinos vast opportunities to take different pathways in the drive for personal and community success. The first few steps are in the time Latinos are willing to invest in finding ways of divorcing themselves from the beliefs and truths that have guided their collective thinking through the years. NHI training takes the position that Latinos tomorrow cannot be extracted from concentrating on the issues that separate them from individual nationalities.

Instead, we provide them with the means that take the best of different Latino cultures to weld together a vision of who they intend to become as a global society of tomorrow. The Institute encourages Latino youth to confront the disillusionment and anger that come from the realization of not having been justly served by the American Dream. The realization is that the search for a new public direction is most difficult when distilled through the suffering and outrage of parents, grandparents, and those before. The Institute identifies these sources of anger and disappointment with the intent of transforming them into a constructive, creative, problem-solving energy and resolve for Latino youth to become leaders responsible for crating a thriving and modern Latino reality.

Finally, NHI training challenges young Latinos to take a critical look at the truths and beliefs that have been the beacons of guidance and hope throughout the last century for most Latinos in the United States. They are advised to no longer see all beliefs and truths as serving the best interests of tomorrow's community. Students learn to distinguish between those beliefs that, in their opinions, should be discarded and those that must become building blocks for the future.

Painful as this process of critical evaluation may appear to some, students gain the courage to let go of the old to make room for the new. Not all changes contemplated or proposed are popular or able to generate support.

Students conclude that it is they who will live the future. This responsibility and challenge rightly belong to them: future leaders being challenged to define a course of action for themselves and their children yet to come. They also realize that time is on their side, allowing for dialogue, discussion, and debate to take place. They know that the year 2000 boldly marked a new age for Latinos. The twenty-first century is their opportunity to dream and experiment with bold new ventures.

The story of the National Hispanic Institute unveils an organization moving toward a new direction in the life of the Latino community. It is also documents the pains, the disappointments, and the personal victories of two individuals who eventually were forced to confront themselves in their search for a new experience. No answers are offered. Only questions are raised. The story depicts a journey through which different conclusions and points of view regarding Latinos in the past and future emerged. The composite of these experiences and events is most important in understanding the National Hispanic Institute and its message to the young.

Change and progress occur only through dedicated youths who willingly assume ownership and control over their preparation as future leaders of the Latino community.

It is up to the Latino leaders of tomorrow to ask themselves difficult and penetrating questions to form a different set of beliefs.

It is up to these Latino leaders, who possess courage and imagination, to craft new human pathways where no one has traveled before.

It is up to them to leave a legacy for others to follow.

Epilogue

1. Briefly describe your vision for Latinos in the future as a distinguishable population in the U.S. What role would you play in this vision?

2. Briefly describe your vision of how U.S. Latinos will relate to and interact with the many Spanish-speaking nations across the globe. What role would you play in this vision?

3. What are the implications of Ernesto's story about his Dad's comment that, while Ernesto saw trash and other people's discards in the alley, Santos saw opportunities?

    d. For you? For your family? For your community?
    e. For NHI?
    f. For Latino populations in the U.S.?
    g. For the global community of Spanish-speaking nations?

7. Briefly describe what you see as the potential advantages and disadvantages for the National Hispanic Institute to focus Latino youth's attention on building equity and wealth within the various U.S. and global Latino communities.

    a. How do you feel about each of these alternatives?
    b. What are you able and willing to do to support either of these alternatives
    c. What have you learned about yourself and your: Beliefs? Values? Hopes? Fears? Aspirations? Assumptions?

Made in the USA
Middletown, DE
04 July 2021